LEGAL STRATEGIES FOR THE DEVELOPMENT AND PROTECTION OF COMMUNAL PROPERTY

PROCEEDINGS OF THE BRITISH ACADEMY • 216

LEGAL STRATEGIES FOR THE DEVELOPMENT AND PROTECTION OF COMMUNAL PROPERTY

Edited by
TING XU AND ALISON CLARKE

Published for THE BRITISH ACADEMY
by OXFORD UNIVERSITY PRESS

Oxford University Press, Great Clarendon Street, Oxford OX2 6DP

First edition published in 2018

British Library Cataloguing in Publication Data
Data available

Library of Congress Cataloging in Publication Data
Data available

Typeset by
Keystroke, Neville Lodge, Tettenhall, Wolverhampton

Printed in Great Britain by
TJ International Ltd, Padstow, Cornwall

ISBN 978-0-19-726638-0

ISSN 0068-1202

Contents

Tables

Notes on Contributors

Simone Abram is Reader at Durham University in the Department of Anthropology. She has published on planning, tourism, urban regeneration and related fields. Her current research addresses questions of ownership and property in Norwegian families, and the ethics of energy. Her books include *Media, Engagement and Anthropological Practice* (with Sarah Pink, 2015), *Elusive Promises: Planning in the Contemporary World* (with Gisa Weszkalnys, 2013), and *Culture and Planning* (2011).

Abraham Bell is a professor of law at the University of San Diego School of Law in the US and at Bar Ilan University Faculty of Law in Israel. He teaches and writes in the areas of property, copyright, international law, and economic analysis of law. Bell clerked for Justice Mishael Cheshin of the Supreme Court of Israel and for the Justice Department. He was a visiting professor at the University of Connecticut Law School and Fordham University Law School.

Sarah Blandy is Professor of Law at the University of Sheffield. Her research is interdisciplinary and empirical, currently focusing on the law and practice of collectively owning, managing and sharing space. She has published widely on the socio-legal aspects of property law. Relevant publications include *Researching Property Law* (with Susan Bright, 2015), 'Collective Property: Owning and Sharing Residential Space' (*Modern Studies in Property Law*, 2013), *Multi-Owned Housing: Law, Power and Practice* (with Ann Dupuis and Jennifer Dixon, 2010) and *Domestic Fortress: Fear and the New Home Front* (with Rowland Atkinson, 2016).

Alison Clarke is Emeritus Professor of Law in the School of Law at the University of Surrey. She is a property lawyer with a particular interest in the integration of communal and customary rights into property rights regimes regulating land and other natural resources, and in comparative analysis of property principles. Recent publications include 'Creating New Commons' (in *Current Legal Problems*, Oxford University Press, 2006); 'Integrating Private and Collective Land Rights: Lessons from China' (*JCL*, 2013); 'Property, Human Rights and Communities' (in T. Xu and J. Allain (eds), *Property and Human Rights in a Global Context*, Hart Publishing, 2015); and 'Land Titling and Communal Property' (in W. Barr (ed.), *Modern Studies in Property Law*, vol. 8, Hart Publishing, 2015).

Malcolm Combe is a lecturer at the School of Law at the University of Aberdeen with interests in property law (particularly land reform), commercial law and clinical legal education. He is the Faculty Director of the Aberdeen Law Project, putting him in a supervisory role of the student-run pro bono legal initiative. In 2016 he became Chair of the Scottish University Law Clinic Network, a body that seeks to coordinate pro bono student legal activity across Scotland. He is a Council member of The Stair Society (a Scottish legal history society) and was an adviser to the Scottish Government-appointed Land Reform Review Group from June 2013 to May 2014.

Wei Gong is a visiting fellow at the School of Law, University of Sheffield. He holds a PhD in Law from Renmin University, China. He had practised law for more than 12 years in China before coming to the UK. His recent publications include 'Taking as Giving, Appropriation as Access: Transfers of Land Development Rights and China's Recent Experiments' (with T. Xu, *Northern Ireland Legal Quarterly*, 2013); 'Communal Property Rights in International Human Rights Instruments: Implications for De Facto Expropriation' (with T. Xu, in T. Xu and J. Allain (eds), *Property and Human Rights in a Global Context*, Hart Publishing, 2015).

Rosalind Malcolm is Professor of Law and Director of the Environmental Regulatory Research Group in the School of Law, University of Surrey. Currently co-investigator of two FP7 EU multidisciplinary research projects, she is part of the research community at the University of Surrey which was awarded the Queen's Anniversary Prize for Water and Sanitation in 2012 for its collection of research work in these fields. Publications include 'Small Independent Water Providers: Their Position in the Regulatory Framework for the Supply of Water in Kenya and Ethiopia' (with Ayalew, Chenoweth, Okotto and Pedley, *Journal of Environmental Law*, 2014), joint winner of the Richard Macrory Prize for the best article in the *Journal of Environmental Law* (2014).

Walters Nsoh is a lecturer in law at Birmingham Law School, University of Birmingham. He holds a PhD in Law (Surrey) and an LLM (Dist) (Kent). His recent relevant publications include *The Privatisation of Biodiversity? New Approaches to Conservation Law* (with Reid, Edward Elgar, 2016); 'Customary Land Rights, Indigenous Rights and Land Expropriation in Cameroon' (in T. Xu and J. Allain (eds), *Property and Human Rights in a Global Context*, Hart Publishing, 2015); and 'Whose Ecosystem Is It Anyway? Private and Public Rights under New Approaches to Biodiversity Conservation' (with Reid, *JHRE*, 2014).

Gideon Parchomovsky is the Robert Fuller Jr. Professor of Law at the University of Pennsylvania School of Law in the US and a professor at the Bar Ilan University Faculty of Law in Israel. He teaches and writes in the areas of property, intellectual property, contracts, and corporate and commercial law. He clerked for Justice Eliyahu Mazza of the Supreme Court of Israel and has served as the President of the Israeli Private Law Association.

Juanita Pienaar is a professor in Private Law at Stellenbosch University. With a research focus on property law and land reform she has co-authored some of the standard property law publications, including *Silberberg and Schoeman's Law of Property*, *Principles of the Law of Property*, the 'Land' chapter in *Constitutional Law of South Africa*, and the Land Reform section of the 'Land' title in *LAWSA*. She was an acting judge in the Land Claims Court and is currently departmental chair. Her monograph, *Land Reform*, was published in 2014. In 2016 she received the Chancellor's Award for Research Excellence.

Margherita Pieraccini is a senior lecturer in law at the University of Bristol Law School. Her research is interdisciplinary and focuses on nature conservation law, marine policy, commons, legal pluralism and social-ecological resilience.

Christopher Rodgers FAcSS, FRSA is Professor of Law at Newcastle University. He has written widely on common property and environmental governance, and has been Principal Investigator of several UK Research Council projects on commons governance. Recent publications include *Contested Common Land: Environmental Governance Past and Present* (with A. Winchester, E. Straughton, M. Pieraccini, Earthscan Publishing, 2011) and *The Law of Nature Conservation: Property, Environment and the Limits of Law* (Oxford University Press, 2013). Chris is Editor in Chief of the *Environmental Law Review* (Sage Publishing).

Benjamin Weitz is a JD candidate at the University of Pennsylvania Law School where he serves as the Online Executive Editor for the *University of Pennsylvania Law Review*. He holds a BA in English and American Literature from Middlebury College.

Ting Xu is a senior lecturer at the School of Law, University of Sheffield, and 'Changbai shan Scholar' visiting professor at the School of Law, Jilin University. She is the author and editor of two books: *The Revival of Private Property and Its Limits in Post-Mao China* (Wildy, Simmonds and Hill Publishing, 2014) and *Property and Human Rights in a Global Context* (edited with Jean Allain, Hart Publishing, 2015). She is Principal Investigator of a project, 'Diversifying Ownership of Land? Communal Property in the UK and China', funded by the British Academy International Mobility and Partnership Scheme 2014–17.

Preface

This volume is one of the outputs of the research project funded by the British Academy International Partnership and Mobility Scheme 2014–17, 'Diversifying Ownership of Land? Communal Property in the UK and China'. We wish to thank the British Academy for providing funding for this project.

Following a series of successful workshops and seminars which have explored various aspects of communal property in the UK and China, the scope of the research network has been extended from a UK/China comparison to research into communal property from a global perspective. As the output of the expanded research, a workshop on 'Legal Strategies for the Development and Protection of Communal Property' was held at the School of Law, University of Sheffield, on 23–24 May 2016. This workshop brought together scholars experienced in practices, projects and experiments involving the development of communal property, along with property theorists who look at property beyond the traditional, individualist and exclusive ownership model. This volume includes papers submitted to this workshop. We wish to thank all participants in the communal property research network and this workshop and contributors to this volume for their intellectual engagement and support for this project.

Communal property is a concept which, we argue, encompasses at least three important aspects: the resource which is used communally or collectively; the institution governing the resource; and the rights held by the community. Communal property constitutes an important form within the full spectrum of property. Whilst private property has traditionally been posited as a prerequisite for economic development, the importance of communal property, transcending the public/private divide in property rights, is now increasingly apparent globally. Different forms of communal property, and related patterns of property holdings, are being explored in a revival of interest in projects constructed as cooperatives, community benefit societies, co-housing and related social enterprises.

We have now come to a crucial stage of broadening the legal parameters of studying communal property, by turning our attention to other regions of the world. Indeed whilst historically communal property has had very different meanings and functions in the UK, China and other regions of the world, parallel developments are emerging, and modern perceptions are converging even as each region faces its own unique challenges in the management of land and natural resources. These developments have raised an important question: what legal strategies are most likely to promote the development and protection of communal property? Answers to this question will not only guide domestic debates on resource governance and community development, but also provoke global discussions and help to formulate global guidelines to address pressing challenges.

Contributions to this volume focus on legal strategies for the development and protection of communal property as it relates to land and other natural resources. We consider how these strategies 'map' over different jurisdictions (England and Wales, Italy, Israel, Scotland, Cameroon, South Africa and China) and through different jurisprudential approaches. Some strategies we look at are based in ownership, some in use, some in co-operative enterprise, and some in regulation through public agencies. Some are formal and others informal, and the 'communal' ranges from private collective groups, through public or private holdings for public or community purposes, to holdings on the basis of stewardship or trust.

Contributions to this volume look at property from a variety of different perspectives. They place the focus on communal property from their different standpoints and link the empirical with the theoretical. In so doing, they challenge the theory of communal property through empirical case studies; at the same time, they encourage scholars who engage with communal property 'practices' in different jurisdictions to explore the theoretical grounding of communal property. In this way, they not only link theory with practice but also link the local with the global.

We would like to express special thanks to the British Academy publication committee, Professor Kevin Gray, Brigid Hamilton-Jones, the anonymous reviewer of the book proposal, the anonymous reviewer of the volume, and all anonymous reviewers of chapters for their kind help and support with this book project.

TX and AC
April 2017

1

Introduction

TING XU AND ALISON CLARKE

Context, significance and themes

The importance of communal property, transcending the public/private divide in property rights, is increasingly apparent globally. In England and Wales, for example, a wide range of developments over the last half-century has revived interest in communal land and resource rights amongst academics, policy makers and social commentators, and concern over how they are to develop within existing legal and economic frameworks. On the one hand, the enactment of the Commons Registration Act in 1965 re-awoke interest in, and guaranteed the continued survival of, traditional agricultural and recreational commons which have long existed in England and Wales, as they have throughout much of Europe and the rest of the world. The 1965 Act however also – and perhaps inadvertently – opened up the potential for recognition of newly emerging commons, a potential which was rapidly realised as local activists moved to legalise their informal recreational spaces by registering them as greens under the 1965 Act. This movement has brought increasing tension with developers, as pressure has grown to prioritise the development of land for housing, and meanwhile austerity has started to threaten the future of traditional parks and communal open spaces and facilities, forcing reappraisals of institutional arrangements for governance of these kinds of communal resource. All these changes have led to, or at least been accompanied by, a revival of interest in projects constructed as co-operatives, community benefit societies, co-housing and related social enterprises, prompting fundamental re-examinations of the different forms which communal property institutions and associated patterns of property holdings can take.

As we see in this volume, parallel developments can be traced in other parts of the world, with similar growing awareness of both the need to recognise and de-marginalise traditional patterns of communal resource use, and the potential for harnessing communal property institutions as a vehicle for reasserting local and community identity, and community participation in resource governance.

The term 'communal property', and its related concepts, carry various connotations and they are used in different ways and in a variety of contexts, as we see below. We may use 'community of property' to describe a matrimonial regime.[1] We may vaguely define communal property as a property regime juxtaposed with private property.[2] We may simply equate communal property with the term 'commons', defined by Dietz et al. as 'a diversity of resources or facilities as well as property institutions that involve some aspects of joint ownership or access'.[3] There is, however, no consensus concerning the definition of commons or communal property or any of the related concepts. Commentators often confuse communal property with resources owned by the government or by no one,[4] and there is a tendency to use interchangeably linked concepts such as 'the commons', 'common-pool resources', 'common property', 'communal property' and 'public goods'.

The concept 'communal property', in whatever sense the term is used, characteristically entails sharing and the right to access. When juxtaposed with private property, however, the notion of communal property can also carry negative connotations, suggesting curtailment of individual autonomy in pursuit of extreme communitarianism. The creation of artificial conceptual boundaries, such as communal versus private, collectivity versus autonomy and access versus exclusion, is in part due to the dominance of a 'standard liberal model' in theorising about property.[5] This theoretical model can be traced back to the 'possessive individualism' embedded in Locke's work, revived by Hardin and Demsetz,[6] and perhaps now best represented by Henry Smith and others.[7] Under the influence of this model,

[1] E. Cooke, A. Barlow and T. Callus, 'Community of Property: A Regime for England and Wales?', The Nuffield Foundation, November 2006, p. 1: www.reading.ac.uk/web/files/law/CommunityofProperty_Version021106.pdf (arguing that 'community of property is one example of a matrimonial regime: that is, the systematic organisation by the law of property rights that result as an automatic consequence of certain relationships – traditionally marriage and more recently registered partnerships', while 'all forms of community of property provide for a rule-based sharing of property . . .').

[2] F. I. Michelman, 'Ethics, Economics and Law of Property', *Tulsa Law Review*, 39(3) (2003), 663–690 at 668.

[3] T. Dietz, N. Dolšak, E. Ostrom and P. C. Stern, 'The Drama of the Commons', in E. Ostrom, T. Dietz, N. Dolšak, P. C. Stern, S. Stonich and E. U. Weber (eds), *The Drama of the Commons* (Washington, DC, National Academy Press, 2002), p. 17.

[4] E. Schlager and E. Ostrom, 'Property-Rights Regimes and Natural Resources: A Conceptual Analysis', *Land Economics*, 68(3) (1992), 249–262 at 249; M. A. McKean, 'Success on the Commons – A Comparative Examination of Institutions for Common Property Resource Management', *Journal of Theoretical Politics*, 4 (1992), 274–281 at 280.

[5] C. Hann, 'A New Double Movement? Anthropological Perspectives on Property in the Age of Neoliberalism', *Socio-Economic Review*, 5(2) (2007), 287–318 at 290. For the work of Hardin and Demsetz, see for example G. Hardin, 'The Tragedy of the Commons', *Science*, 162 (1968), 1243–1248; H. Demsetz, 'Toward a Theory of Property Rights', *American Economic Review*, 57(2) (1967), 347–359.

[6] Hann, 'A New Double Movement?', p. 290.

[7] See for example T. W. Merrill and H. E. Smith, 'Optimal Standardisation in the Law of Property: The *Numerus Clausus* Principle', *Yale Law Journal*, 110 (2000), 1–70; H. E. Smith, 'Mind the Gap: The Indirect Relation between Ends and Means in American Property Law', *Cornell Law Review*, 94 (2009),

economic analysis for a long time dominated the intellectual ground in the study of communal property, but, as this volume demonstrates, a wider range of theoretical and analytic approaches is now moving us into more sophisticated intellectual territory. To give this concept 'communal property' substance, we need to unpack the complexity embedded in the notion by tackling many artificial dichotomies and transcending disciplinary boundaries. It is becoming clear that a dynamic, multidimensional framework is required for analysing communal property. In order to duly broaden the legal parameters of studying communal property, we need to draw on the work done by scholars working in other disciplines. Seeking legal strategies for the development and protection of communal property does not mean we should give state law primacy.

Our discussions in this volume focus on the challenges arising from studying communal property, addressing these four areas:

1. Conceptual clarification: what kinds of resource rights and claims can be usefully categorised as communal property in different jurisdictions.
2. The boundaries of communal property: for example, its relationship with private property and how private property interests and communal property interests coexist in a communal property regime; its spatial and temporal dimensions; how to ascertain the interplay of state law and community norms in regimes of communal property, especially in complex plural legal systems.
3. The role of communal property in resource management and community development.
4. The legal recognition and protection that should be afforded to communal property.

We see how legal strategies for the development and protection of communal property 'map' over different jurisdictions (England and Wales, Italy, Israel, Scotland, Cameroon, South Africa and China) and jurisprudential approaches. As we see in the following chapters, some strategies are based in use, and some in regulation through public or privatised agencies. Sometimes 'communal' means a private group, and at other times a 'public' body holding on behalf of, or for the good of, the public or the community. It may even mean a group of institutions or individuals with diverse interests in a resource co-operating over its regulation and governance. In yet other cases it involves reliance on nominally private property moderated by principles of stewardship and trust. Nevertheless, within this diversity we identify a converging trend across various jurisdictions, that is, acknowledging the 'hybridity' of communal property and adopting mixed legal strategies in sustaining and protecting it.

959–989; and the works cited and discussed by J. B. Baron, 'The Contested Commitments of Property Law', *Hastings Law Journal*, 61 (2010), 917–968 at 918–921 and 924–927.

Contributors to this volume approach the key questions raised above through a series of case studies, enabled by drawing on a number of perspectives and methods from anthropology, environmental studies, human rights, sociology and geography. In this Introduction, after this section, which sets out the context, significance and themes of this volume, the next section reviews the spread and potential reach of communal property. The third section emphasises the importance of examining the nature of communities and highlights the possibilities and challenges of vesting the power of governing communal resources in communities.

The spread and potential reach of communal property

Broadening the legal parameters for studying communal property necessarily involves giving some attention to what people mean by 'communal property'. This is an area notorious for confusions in terminology and in concept, as Franz and Keebet von Benda-Beckmann point out,[8] and we have already noted. However, as an essential first step we need to acknowledge the sometimes bewildering variety in the kinds of movements, institutions and resources which are currently described by reference to commons/communal property vocabulary. This is not so as to arrive at a definitive 'meaning' of communal property, but rather to identify the current spread and potential reach of the ideas it seems to encapsulate.

When modern scholars and activists use the term 'commons' or 'communal property', they are likely to have in mind one or more of (at least) six different things. They might be referring to *community resource use*, where a resource is used communally by a group of people; to *community management of resources*, where a community has overall control or management of an area of land (or some other resource system), with some of the resources within it being used individually by members, and others being used communally by the group as a whole, or by sub-groups within the community; to *public open space*; to *protest commons*, meaning local or public movements claiming back resources for public or community use or benefit; to *common heritage resources*, meaning resources which are regarded as part of the common heritage of humankind, such as land, water, knowledge, or the internet; or to *cultural resources*, meaning tangible or intangible resources of cultural importance to a particular community.

Since 'communal property' appears in nearly all of these identities in the following chapters, it is worth saying more about each, and about how they relate to traditional classifications of commons property and commons institutions.

[8] '"Communal" or "communal property" is perhaps the most general and misleading concept pervading interpretations of property systems, academic theories and policies': F. von Benda-Beckmann and K. von Benda-Beckmann, 'How Communal Is Communal and Whose Communal Is It? Lessons from Minangkabau', in F. von Benda-Beckmann, K. von Benda-Beckmann and M. G. Wiber (eds), *Changing Properties of Property* (New York, Berghahn Books, 2009), pp. 194–217 at p. 194.

Community resource use

For many, this is archetypal communal property. It involves a community of people, sharing a common interest or locality, and managing and utilising a resource in its own self-interest, usually in accordance with rules which the community itself evolves and polices. Traditional agricultural and recreational commons of the kinds identified by Rodgers in England and Wales and Pieraccini in Italy, and the traditional collective kibbutzim in Israel described by Bell, Parchomovsky and Weitz, all come within this category, and so too do, for example, communal areas in residential developments.[9] These are all examples of classic limited-access communal property: the community has a right to exclude outsiders from the resource (or at least to prevent interference by outsiders with their communal resource use), and members of the community have a right not to be excluded from it. Some of these commons are, as a matter of law or fact, also open to the public, but in practice the community is usually not much concerned with keeping 'the public' out, and the resource is used predominantly by the community, regarded as 'belonging' to the community, and managed in the community's interests. As a matter of terminology, in this kind of resource use, 'communal property' will usually refer to the resource itself, but sometimes it may refer to the communal property rights that the community has in the resource.

Community management of resources

A community may, on the other hand, have overall control or management of an area of land or of some other resource system such as a forest, but organise its resource use so that some of the resources on the land or within the system are allocated for individual use by members of the community (perhaps houses, or personal goods, or areas for individual cultivation) and others are allocated for communal use (perhaps communal living areas, or areas for communal agricultural activity). The 'individual' rights of the members may amount to private property rights legally recognised outside as well as within the community, or they may be recognised only within the community. Probably the most important examples are found in the kinds of customary land tenure described by Nsoh in Cameroon and Pienaar in South Africa, in Bell, Parchomovsky and Weitz's traditional collective kibbutzim in Israel, and in rural collectives in China as described by Xu and Gong. In many of these examples, there are family, household, lineage or gender groups nested within the overarching community, each with its own communal rights over some of the resources. Again, there is a degree of exclusion here: individuals and

[9] S. Blandy, 'Collective Property: Owning and Sharing Residential Space', in N. Hopkins (ed.), *Modern Studies in Property Law*, vol. 7 (Oxford and Portland, OR, Hart Publishing, 2013), pp. 152–172.

groups within the community can exclude the rest of the community from 'their' resources, and the community itself can exclude outsiders, but again exclusion may be elastic and/or a matter of degree. Here 'communal property' is usually used to mean the resources which are allocated for communal use by the community as a whole or by sub-groups within the community, or their respective communal property rights in relation to those resources. Sometimes, though, it refers to the whole of the area or resource system controlled by the community, or to the aggregate of all the property holdings of the community and its members in their area or resource system. This can be of immense importance to culturally or ethnically distinct communities, as a reflection of their 'ownership' of, or identification with, 'their' area.

Public open space

These are classic open-access commons, consisting of spaces like public parks, public squares, beaches and perhaps coastline, which members of the public have a right to use, or are free to use, usually recreationally or for public assembly. The nature of the public 'right' varies considerably, especially between different jurisdictions: it may be anything from a formal public property right or public law right, to established de facto usage. Further, as Abram and Blandy demonstrate in their case study of public parks in Sheffield in this volume, public open spaces may be provided under a variety of different institutional arrangements. An important point is that although they may be legally open to the public, they are often regarded as local community assets, managed in the interests of the local community, and in practice used only by the local community. Here again, then, exclusion is an ambiguous concept and there is a blurring of the distinction between public and community. And also again, 'communal property' can refer to the space itself, or to the public rights in respect of the space.

Protest commons

More recently, as noted by both Pieraccini and Malcolm and Clarke, the term 'commons' has come to be associated with protest movements claiming resources back for the community or the public. Malcolm and Clarke trace these movements back to Gerard Winstanley and the seventeenth-century Levellers and Diggers in England, but more recent manifestations include the Occupy movement as well as the Italian protest groups identified by Pieraccini. Protest movement activists often organise themselves collectively, and they tend to see themselves (and to be seen) as pursuing public and/or community objectives and to be concerned with resources of community value or which they regard as forming part of our common heritage (i.e. within our next category). Their activities often involve occupation of publicly or privately owned land or buildings, sometimes in order to put them to some public or community use, but always at least to some extent in order to make a political point about resource control and use. This is 'communal property' in its loosest, but by no means least important, sense.

Common heritage resources

'Commons' and 'communal property' have also come to be associated with a growing environmental and political interest across most of the world in viewing some resources as part of our common human heritage. The resources most often considered are 'natural' resources such as land, water, forests and landscape, as well as products of human ingenuity such as the 'knowledge commons' and the internet. These resources are regarded as 'commons' because of the perceived common interest in their preservation for present and future generations, and also because of a sense that this common interest requires, in appropriate cases, guarantees of free public or community access, or public or community participation in their regulation and governance, or public or community participation in the benefits they generate. Malcolm and Clarke consider how this plays out in relation to water, in general terms and in terms of its regulation and governance in England and Wales, pointing out the historical and normative importance of communal property in its various forms in enabling water to function effectively as what they call a 'common treasury'. They also point to the link we have already noted, between resources such as these and the protest commons. As far as terminology goes, 'communal property' can be used in this context loosely as a normative description of these common heritage resources, and more precisely to refer to the collective management and regulatory institutions that Malcolm and Clarke argue necessarily evolve to reflect their common heritage status.

Cultural resources

This arena of commons discourse is not covered directly in this volume. It is concerned with tangible and intangible resources regarded as the cultural heritage of a particular cultural or ethnic community, and part of the current debate is as to whether the notion of property is of any use at all in identifying (let alone resolving) any of the complex issues involved in its recognition and preservation. In other words, these resources are certainly 'communal' resources, in the limited-access sense noted above, but it has to be left for another occasion to consider whether they can helpfully also be regarded as 'property'.

Bringing in communities

As we have seen in the previous section, the concept of communal property is multidimensional, consisting of combinations of various different elements including the resource itself; communities governing the resources; activities of commoning; shared values and interests; a set of norms and rules; and rights and claims in relation to the resource. Each element is worth a close examination: the nature of communities, as well as their connections with other elements, is the key to understanding communal property.

Distinguishing resources from property governance institutions

Confusions often arise when we do not distinguish the attributes of common-pool resources and the characteristics of communal property regimes. Ostrom and Hess, for example, have given a detailed analysis of the distinctions between common-property and open-access property regimes, between common-pool resources and common-property regimes, and between a resource system and the flow of resource units.[10] A 'common-pool resource' refers to 'a natural or man-made resource system that is sufficiently large as to make it costly (but not impossible) to exclude potential beneficiaries from obtaining benefits from its use'.[11] The term 'common-pool resource' is purely descriptive, telling us the physical nature of the resource (Malcolm and Clarke in this volume). Common-pool resources are not just associated with communal property, as communities are not the only possible holders of ownership or other property interests in common-pool resources. Rather, property interests in common-pool resources (whether ownership or other property interests) can be vested in the government, individuals or other public, quasi-public or private institutions.[12]

In a review of 'the commons', Helfrish elaborates on what she sees as a process of transition from a common-pool resource to a commons, which may well be applied to explain the difference between a common-pool resource and its property governance institutions and to highlight the importance of bringing communities into the discussion of communal property:

> [. . .] it is clear, that a common pool resource is not yet a commons. Instead, it has to be turned into a commons by its users. One cannot talk about the commons without talking about the communities that use and sustain it.

[10] E. Ostrom and C. Hess, 'Private and Common Property Rights' (Northampton, MA, Edward Elgar, 2007), https://papers.ssrn.com/sol3/papers.cfm?abstract_id=1304699.
[11] E. Ostrom, *Governing the Commons: The Evolution of Institutions for Collective Action* (Cambridge, Cambridge University Press, 1990), p. 30.
[12] Ostrom and Hess, 'Private and Common Property Rights', 7.

> Something becomes a commons because a certain community shares a common understanding of how it wishes to use a shared resource. In other words: The commons is not about the resources. It's about us![13]

As Abram and Blandy point out in this volume, Linebaugh also suggests that it may be helpful to talk of 'commons' as a verb:

> To speak of the commons as if it were a natural resource is misleading at best and dangerous at worst – the commons is an activity and, if anything, it expresses relationships in society that are inseparable from relations to nature. It might be better to keep the word as a verb, an activity, rather than as a noun, a substantive.[14]

Understanding communities

However, the concept of 'community' is fluid. Xu and Gong in this volume have outlined several efforts made to seek the identifiers or common characteristics of community. Locality is certainly important, as in some kinds of community people are likely to be bound together and share a sense of belonging (see Abram and Blandy in this volume) through an experience of living in the same place. Community is, however, not merely a territorial concept. Customs, shared interests and common values may constitute various bonds that hold communities together. For example, the resource use of some groups, such as fishing, herding or pastoralist groups, is often bound by common culture or their communal use of the same resources, and the resource use of other groups, such as indigenous peoples, may be integral to their cultural identity. Moreover, we can see community as networks of social relations, comprising different types of 'collective involvement' formed by different values and interests.[15] Actual group life may consist of different ideal types of community.[16] Therefore, as Xu and Gong in this volume discuss in the Chinese context and Pienaar discusses in the South African context, actual community life may comprise communities nested together at different scales.

[13] S. Helfrish, 'The Commons: Year One of the Global Commons Movement', *CommonsBlog*, 29 January 2011: https://commonsblog.wordpress.com/2011/01/29/the-commons-year-one-of-the-global-commons-movement/.

[14] P. Linebaugh, *The Magna Carta Manifesto: Liberties and Commons for All* (Berkeley, University of California Press, 2008), p. 279.

[15] R. Cotterrell, 'A Legal Concept of Community', *Canadian Journal of Law and Society*, 12 (1997), 75–91 at 81.

[16] R. Cotterrell, *Law's Community: Legal Theory in Sociological Perspective* (Oxford, Oxford University Press, 1995); R. Cotterrell, *Law, Culture and Society: Legal Ideas in the Mirror of Social Theory* (Aldershot, Ashgate, 2006); R. Cotterrell, 'Community as a Legal Concept? Some Uses of a Law-and-Community Approach in Legal Theory', in R. Cotterrell, *Living Law: Studies in Legal and Social Theory* (Farnham, Ashgate, 2008), pp. 17–28; R. Cotterell, 'Rethinking "Embeddedness": Law, Economy, Community', *Journal of Law and Society*, 40 (2013), 49–67.

The absolute homogeneity of community is only 'imagined'.[17] In addition to the increasing mobility of people (for example, migration) and the deconstruction of spatial boundaries (for example, by urbanisation), values, ideologies and interests that used to hold communities together may change, leading to the grouping, regrouping, or even the dissolution of communities (see Xu and Gong, Pieraccini, and Bell, Parchomovsky and Weitz in this volume).

Questions often arise as to how to sustain communities and communal property. For example, McKean argues that 'individual co-owners of [communal property] may be unable to sell their shares, or may forfeit their shares upon change in residence . . .'.[18] Ostrom and Hess later observe that 'well-defined and secured property rights may not involve the right to alienation'.[19] In the present Chinese system, as Xu and Gong discuss in this volume, members can leave the community, but if evidence shows that they no longer rely on the community to make a living and obtain provision of social welfare after their departure, both their membership and the land rights allocated to them will be revoked by the community. Within the contractual period (30 years), members can alienate the land rights allocated to them to outsiders, but such transfers need to get the consent of the community. This mechanism makes sure that the community holds ownership interests in rural land, while allowing the transfer of other property interests in rural land subject to certain conditions. However, as Bell, Parchomovsky and Weitz demonstrate in relation to property rights of individual members of kibbutzim in Israel, other jurisdictions have had more difficulties in devising systems which might allow members to realise the value of their individual interests without threatening the cohesion of the community.

Emphasising the importance of communities does not mean we should romanticise them. Whilst communities are often closely associated with 'a sense of belonging, warmth and companionship',[20] communities may embody hierarchy, inequality, patriarchy and privilege. For example, women's property rights are often ignored, or even suppressed, in a communal context. We could find such examples in the Chinese (Xu and Gong in this volume), Italian (Pieraccini in this volume) and South African contexts (Pienaar in this volume). Pieraccini calls for the development of deliberative participatory decision-making practices and shared governance in the development of communal property regimes. Moreover, we can question if communities should endorse total equality. For example, Xu and Gong argue that the endorsement of extreme egalitarianism in China led to the free rider problem and the eventual collapse of the commune system. Similarly,

[17] J. Clarke, 'Community', in D. M. Nonini (ed.), *A Companion to Urban Anthropology* (London, Wiley-Blackwell, 2014), pp. 46–64 at p. 54.
[18] McKean, 'Success on the Commons', 252.
[19] Ostrom and Hess, 'Private and Common Property Rights', 17.
[20] T. Blackshaw, *Key Concepts in Community Studies* (London, Sage, 2010), p. 1.

in the Israeli context, Bell, Parchomovsky and Weitz point out that some renewed kibbutzim have adopted a different basis for allocating the kibbutz's assets and profits, with distribution closely linked to labour, marking a contrast to approaches adopted in traditional kibbutzim.

The 'who and how' question on communal property

Uncertainties arise when we pursue a deeper analysis of the 'who and how' question on communal property. For example, who decides the membership of the community? How ought communal property rights to be exercised? What mechanisms for decision-making should there be within the community? And how does it alter the picture if a community forms itself into a legal entity – whether by using a trust-type mechanism or a standard form of company, or using a vehicle specifically designed for communal property holding – to sue or be sued in disputes over their communal property and to hold their communal assets?[21]

The form and structure of legal entities which communities may or must form in order to hold property interests in their resources, is a recurring theme throughout the chapters in this volume, together with broader questions of institutional structure and governance. In his chapter on the recent and still-evolving land reforms in Scotland which are giving communities increasingly extensive rights to acquire communal ownership of land, Combe gives detailed consideration to the form and structure of the legal entities which communities may or must assume in order to take advantage of these new rights. The very much more complex questions of different forms of institutional communal property governance in South Africa are highlighted by Pienaar in her chapter, in particular the different implications of governance by traditional authorities and by statutory forms of communal property association. In their chapter and in a very different context, Abram and Blandy trace the development of the organisational forms which have been involved in the urban parks in Sheffield they study, concluding that there is a mismatch between these legal arrangements and experiences of belonging and ownership, and that a consequent difficulty in articulating a discourse of communal property in this context undermines efforts to secure the funding needed to protect and maintain these important community resources. This mismatch between legal form and experiences of belonging and ownership is echoed in Nsoh's chapter on the lack of proper recognition of customary land tenure law in Cameroon, where he concludes that 'a majority of citizens' live and use their resources 'on an individual and communal customary law basis as if the written laws do not exist'. For Cameroon, moreover, this mismatch has implications for the wider rule of law, as Nsoh points out. Xu and Gong also look at the very particular forms of the institutions involved in the

[21] Ostrom and Hess, 'Private and Common Property Rights', 17.

organisation and regulation of collective property in China, including the collective economic organisation in China which may manage collectively-owned land formally albeit without being accorded status as a legal entity. On a broader level, both Rodgers and Pieraccini in their respective chapters provide detailed analyses of Elinor Ostrom's design principles for successfully managed common-pool resources, discussing their applicability for the governance of common land in England and Wales (Rodgers) and traditional commons in Italy (Pieraccini). For Malcolm and Clarke, on the other hand, the important question is not so much the institutional form of governance and regulation of what they see as a 'common treasury' resource (specifically water, the subject of their chapter), but rather that it should facilitate collaboration and co-operation at all levels, which, they argue, necessitates a key role for communal property in the diverse forms they elaborate.

In many of the institutional arrangements discussed in the chapters in this volume, there are complex and often developing tensions between the individual, the community and the state. In the case of water, the critical point for Malcolm and Clarke is the role of communities in the governance of a common treasury resource which is both a common resource and a human right, in a political context dominated by privatised state-regulated industry and international regulation. For Bell, Parchomovsky and Weitz in their chapter on the evolution of what they describe as unique property norms in the Israeli kibbutz, the issue is the emergence of private property within the kibbutz, traditionally committed to socialism, as Israeli society has moved towards a free market economy, and the intricate legal challenges this has presented to the Israeli courts. China faces similar challenges. Gong and Xu in their chapter discuss the creation of the right to farm within the collective ownership system, which has created a hybrid property regime where private land rights have been selectively readmitted and integrated into collective land rights.

A related common theme through many of the chapters in the volume is the link between communal property, custom and legal pluralism. This is a central issue for Pienaar in her chapter where she explores the complex interconnections between customary law and communal property in land in South Africa. She shows how customary law and communal property are integral strands interwoven into what she describes as South Africa's 'tapestry of diversity' and considers how they are implicated in the challenges and opportunities South Africa faces in maintaining the 'unique, rich fabric' of this tapestry. Nsoh points out the equal although different complexity in Cameroon, which he sees as demonstrating the 'continuous difficulty in reconciling Western land law principles on the ownership and use of communal property with customary land tenure systems in post-colonial sub-Saharan African societies'. At a more abstract level Rodgers argues for a legal pluralist analysis of traditional forms of communal property in England and Wales now regulated by the Commons Registration Act 1965 and the Commons Act 2002, focusing on 'the functionality of differing customary and legal norms' but also 'sensitive to the *sources* from which rules derive normativity'.

Exploring the links between communal property and legal pluralism reinforces the argument that the notion of communal property is deeply embedded in dynamic social relations. This argument chimes with the distinction drawn by legal anthropologists between 'categorical' and 'concretised' property relations.[22] 'Categorical' property relationships specify 'property-holders, property objects, and the rights and obligations attached to these'.[23] 'Concretised property relations' manifest themselves in actual social relationships 'between actual property-holders with respect to concreted valuables'.[24] 'Categorical and concretised property relations may change with different speed'.[25] In some instances, categorical property rights may remain unchanged but be sufficiently flexible to accommodate socio-economic transformations and the resulting changes in concretised property relations. In other instances, however, categorical property rights do not catch up with these changes, or may even reject them, leading to a gap between these two kinds of property rights.

Conclusion

The following chapters demonstrate that communal property is multidimensional. These dimensions concern not only relations between people and resources but also relations between the individual and groups of people with respect to resources. Communal property includes rights and claims to access, use and control of resources; its legitimacy comes from various sources including social recognition and practices; it encompasses diverse interests and values – human, social, and environmental – beyond narrow commercial interests and market values; it may entail activities of commoning. The diversity embedded in communal property poses challenges to seeking legal strategies for the development and protection of communal property. It is difficult to subsume different kinds of communal property in one unified normative framework, and perhaps this is something that should not even be attempted. Each communal property regime has to operate within its own legal and normative frameworks, and we should not expect them all to be the same. Certainly, this is the conclusion reached by Pieraccini in her chapter where she contrasts the parallel developments in Italy of a revival of interest in traditional Italian commons and the emergence of what we have characterised as protest commons. Her conclusion is that, despite the similarities she draws out, the differences between what might be seen as two extremes of 'communal property' are just too great, 'rendering impossible the transfer of legal concepts from one category to the other'.

[22] Von Benda-Beckmann et al., *Changing Properties of Property*, 27.
[23] Von Benda-Beckmann et al., *Changing Properties of Property*, 16.
[24] Von Benda-Beckmann et al., *Changing Properties of Property*, 19.
[25] Von Benda-Beckmann et al., *Changing Properties of Property*, 28.

Communities are not static. When the boundaries of communities shift, the composition of communal property changes. Moreover, communal property is constantly being defined and redefined through law-making, customary practices and social movements. A particular difficulty lies in accepting the moral autonomy of the community. For example, a community does not necessarily aspire towards equality among members: many choose to adopt instead hierarchical structures. What seems to be important for community cohesion is that governance structures within a community are perceived as fair by its members, but this may bring us into conflict with notions of social and gender equality. There are real difficulties when a state's conceptions of fairness are not the same as those of the community. This is why the 'who and how' question on communal property is extremely important. What are the decision-making processes within communities? What mechanisms are likely to encourage participation by members in the governance of community resources? Should we recognise the autonomy of community norms, but at the same time, subject them to controls of constitutional legitimacy? The contributors to this volume explore these questions from various perspectives; their work needs to be developed by others, continuing to look beyond traditional conceptual and disciplinary boundaries.

Indeed whilst historically communal property has had very different meanings and functions in various regions of the world, parallel developments are emerging, and modern perceptions are converging even as each region faces its own unique challenges in the management of land and natural resources. These developments have raised an important question: what legal strategies are most likely to promote the development and protection of communal property? Answers to this question are going to be jurisdiction-specific. But these answers will not only guide domestic debates on resource governance and community development, but also provoke global discussions and help to formulate global guidelines to address pressing challenges.

2

Commons Governance, Normative Pluralism and the Enduring Role of Custom

CHRISTOPHER RODGERS[1]

Introduction

The governance of the commons is shaped by a mixture of customary and legal norms that can shift and change over time and space. The role that different norms play in commons governance may vary from time to time and from common to common. The common lands of England and Wales are illustrative of this, in that their governance is structured around a complex mix of formal legal norms, customary rules, and social practices that lack normative effect. This chapter will focus on the governance of common land in England and Wales. It will consider the role of custom alongside other normative rules used to structure its governance, and argue that a legal pluralist perspective is essential if we are to understand and recognise their respective roles, and especially how these have changed over time and space.

The successful management of all common resources relies upon interactions between networks of private actors (typically appropriators – those with rights to use the resource –and landowners), motivated by the need to protect shared resources and to negotiate shared purposes and solutions.[2] This will produce customary practices and norms that play an important part in securing the effective management of the common resource. This is especially apparent in the management of common land, where custom and more formal legal rules have subsisted side by side for centuries and have always played complementary roles in its governance. This raises interesting questions as to the respective roles of 'law' and

[1]This chapter draws in part on research funded by the Arts and Humanities Research Council. I am grateful to Julia Aglionby, Ole Pedersen and Angus Winchester for comments on earlier drafts. The views expressed in the chapter are solely those of the author, as are any errors that have eluded scrutiny.
[2]Cf. R. A. W. Rhodes, 'The New Governance: Governing without Government?', *Political Studies*, 44 (1996), 652–667, esp. at 660.

'custom', how customary practices are captured and given normative effect in the governance of common land, and how changes in customary practice are formally recognised and captured in legal norms. Notwithstanding the introduction of legislation governing the registration of common land and common rights, this chapter will argue that custom retains an important role in the governance of common land – a role that the courts have recognised in several recent cases.

Common land: context past and present

The contemporary common lands of England and Wales extend to approximately 550,000 hectares.[3] The common land that survives today falls into three legal categories. The Commons Registration Act 1965 defined 'common land' to mean either land that was subject to rights of common, or the waste land of a manor.[4] To these can be added those areas of open public space that were expressly excluded from the 1965 Act, but are protected by statute – for example the New Forest and Epping Forest.[5] Common land is a valuable public resource and subject to open public access.[6] Many of the surviving commons were formerly 'wastes' of a manor on which the local population were permitted to graze livestock and take vegetation for animal food, bedding and other purposes. Many commons are within protected wildlife or landscape areas – for example Sites of Special Scientific Interest,[7] National Parks and Areas of Outstanding Natural Beauty.[8] Much of this land is of high nature value, concentrated in the upland areas of the North and West of England, and of Wales,[9] but some commons can also be found in the sandy heaths and wetlands of lowland England and in the open spaces around the margins of urban settlements.[10]

[3] Currently 546,357 ha in total. There are 372,991 ha of registered common land in England (3 per cent of the land area) and 173,366 ha in Wales (approximately 8 per cent of the land area). These figures exclude Epping Forest and the New Forest, which between them provide another 24,453 ha of common land. See generally: www.foundationforcommonland.org.uk/the-commons-lands-of-great-britain.

[4] Commons Registration Act 1965, section 22. The waste of a manor was registrable as common land even if there were no rights of common exercisable over it.

[5] These are separately protected by statute, for example the Epping Forest Act 1878, and the New Forest Act 1964.

[6] Countryside and Rights of Way Act 2000, section 1 and schedule 1.

[7] Notified under section 28(1), Wildlife and Countryside Act 1981, as amended.

[8] See Natural England, *Trends in Pastoral Commoning in England: A Study for Natural England* (The Pastoral Commoning Partnership with HH Bowes Ltd, 2008), pp. 18–21 and tables 3.1 and 3.2.

[9] Nearly 40 per cent of common land in Wales is concentrated in upland areas of the county of Powys, and 35 per cent of that in England is concentrated in the North-West region, with a large proportion of this in the Lake District National Park. See further: www.foundationforcommonland.org.uk/the-commons-lands-of-great-britain.

[10] See W. G. Hoskins and D. Stamp, *The Common Lands of England and Wales* (London, Collins, 1963), pp. 104–110.

Common land has an unusual legal status, coloured by its origins in medieval forms of customary land use, and by the impact of the enclosure movement in the eighteenth and nineteenth centuries. As such, it occupies an ambiguous middle ground between private and communal property. Unlike many commons found elsewhere in Europe, common land in England and Wales is not communally owned. It is privately owned land over which others possess use rights that give them legal access to some of the land's resources. Its origins and subsequent history are closely bound up with the manorial system of land tenure. The manorial system was, from the thirteenth century, underpinned by a system of property rights in which the ownership of the manorial 'waste' lands was vested in the lord of the manor, but members of the local community ('commoners') enjoyed use rights over it that were legally recognised and protected.[11] These rights are today recognised in English law as *profits a prendre*, i.e. a property right in the form of an incorporeal hereditament that confers a right to take from the land of another some part of the soil or minerals, or some of its natural produce.[12]

English law developed a complex classification of commoners' land use rights, which described both the basis of each right and its nature and purpose.[13] Most common rights were 'appurtenant' – that is, attached to a land holding (the 'dominant tenement') as a subsidiary right and exercisable over a 'servient tenement' (the common land). It was also possible to hold common rights 'in gross' independently of a holding of land – and this type of common right could be transferred by the right holder to anyone, without transferring land.[14] This was an anomalous category of right, although it was (and is) common in some parts of the country.[15]

In principle, any product of the soil, natural product found on common land or wild animal could be the subject of a right of common. The most economically significant common right is the *common of pasture*, which gives a right to graze livestock on common land. The management of collective grazing was, before the Commons Registration Act 1965, organised on each common by one of two customary principles – either by the principle of levancy and couchancy, or by the imposition of 'stints' as a measurement of permitted grazing. The rule of levancy and couchancy determined the number of grazing livestock allowed on the

[11] The legal framework for manorial property rights was laid down in the statutes of Merton (1235) and Westminster II (1285) (sec. 46) and was confirmed by the Act for the Improvement of Commons, 1549 (Statutes, 3 & 4 Edw. VI, c. 3).

[12] See *Alfred F Beckett Ltd. v Lyons* [1967] Ch 449.

[13] See, for example, E. F. Cousins, *Gadsden on Commons and Greens*, 2nd edn (London, Sweet & Maxwell, 2012), 2-34 to 2-61; A. Sydenham, *Commons and Greens: The Modern Law*, 2nd edn (Corsham, Lime Legal Ltd, 2016), at 3.2.1–3.2.7.

[14] See Cousins, *Gadsden on Commons and Greens*, 2-26.

[15] Cousins, *Gadsden on Commons and Greens*, p. 72 refers to rights in gross as 'most unusual'. But for examples of their widespread existence and registration in Norfolk, see C. P. Rodgers, E. A. Straughton, A. J. L. Winchester and M. Pieraccini, *Contested Common Land: Environmental Governance Past and Present* (London and Washington, DC, Earthscan, 2010), ch. 9.

common by reference to the capacity of the dominant land (that to which the rights attached) to feed livestock over the winter months, i.e. by the amount of fodder that could be produced by the dominant holding to which the rights attached. The number of animals that could be grazed on the common in the summer months was not expressed in a numerical form. Stints, on the other hand, permitted a fixed number of livestock to graze the common land.[16]

The other principal common rights are the common of turbary and common of estovers. *Common of turbary* gives the right to take peat or turf for fuel, and in principle must always be attached (appurtenant) to a building or house. The right is limited to taking what is necessary for heating the dominant tenement, and cannot be divided or apportioned, e.g. if the house to which it is attached is divided and sold in separate lots. *Common of estovers* is similar and gives the right to take wood or other vegetation for purposes necessary for the use of the dominant tenement. It fell into three sub-categories. 'House bote' was the right to take timber for repairing houses, or for fuel; 'plough bote' to take timber for making or repairing agricultural implements; and 'hay bote' to take timber, shrubs or brush to make or repair hedges and fences. The right also extends to taking animal bedding (bracken or rushes, for example), gorse, heather and reeds. A common right of estovers should in principle be limited by reference to what is necessary for the maintenance of the dominant tenement to which it is attached, and which it is intended to benefit – or alternatively be defined by reference to the quantity of produce to be taken from the common. It is generally accepted that, like turbary, a right of estovers cannot be severed from the land it benefits, even if the right is quantified.[17]

English law also recognises several other rights of common. *Pannage* gives the right to graze pigs in woodland or forests. The *common of piscary* gives the right to take fish from a lake, river or stream belonging to another. Any land covered with water may be registered as common land, and therefore subject to a right of piscary, provided it is not foreshore vested in the Crown. Rights to take minerals or constituent parts of the soil itself can also be the subject matter of a right of common. Most rights to take soil will be subject to the same restrictions as turbary and estovers. Finally, the right to take wild animals (*ferae naturae*) from the land of another can subsist as a *profit a prendre* in English law, and can therefore also exist as a right of common over common land.[18] In practice it may be difficult to distinguish this category of common right from sporting rights that have been

[16] For a detailed analysis, see A. J. L. Winchester and E. A. Straughton, 'Stints and Sustainability: Managing Stock Levels on Common Land in England c 1600–2006', *Agricultural History Review*, 58 (2010), 29–47.

[17] Cousins, *Gadsden on Commons and Greens*, 2-39; A. Sydenham, *Commons and Greens*, at 3.2.4. The severance of a right of estovers is, in any event, now prevented by Commons Act 2006, section 9 and schedule 1.

[18] Cousins, *Gadsden on Commons and Greens*, 2-48.

granted by the landowner, e.g. by a contractual grant of a right to shoot, hunt or wildfowl over another's land.[19]

The customary origins of many common rights meant that they were reflexive and could change over time to meet new conditions, including improvements in agricultural production methods. However, it also meant that there was no standardisation of property rights in common land: custom would naturally vary from one locality to another, and from time to time. It is also important to appreciate that some customs were captured and elevated into *customary law* through, for example, their adoption by the courts as the basis for adjudicating on land use rights or ownership, while other customary practices were not, and retained their normative effect through social practice rather than by becoming 'formal' law. The assimilation of customary practice into formal legal rules was (and indeed still is) dependent on whether it satisfied the 'rules of recognition'[20] applied by the legal system to confer formal legal normativity on social practice, e.g. in this case whether the practice is 'reasonable' and has been elevated into the status of a legal rule by long practice that comes within the legal doctrine of prescription.[21] A customary land use right could be elevated into a legal right by prescription if a court found: that it had been practised from 'time immemorial' (i.e. since 1189); or if it had been practised for 20 years or more under the doctrine of 'lost modern grant'; or (in the case of a *profit a prendre*) if it had been exercised for 60 years or more without interruption 'as of right'.[22] Two important consequences flow from this distinction, both of which will be explored in more detail below. The first is that 'customary law' does not necessarily correspond with actual social custom as practised by commons appropriators in their management of common land. The second is that, once recognised as customary *law* a social practice can only develop and change in accordance with the internal rules of the legal system – whereas social customs and norms are produced and changed through a variety of processes separate from the legal system.[23]

From the late nineteenth century onwards, there was increased pressure to protect the remaining common land that had survived the enclosure movement. This ultimately resulted in the establishment of the Royal Commission on Common Land

[19] But see Rodgers et al., *Contested Common Land*, at pp. 178–179 for a discussion of the registration of wildfowling rights as common rights in the commons registers for the Brancaster and Thornham Commons in Norfolk (CL 41, CL 65, CL 124 and CL 161, Norfolk County Council).

[20] See H. L. A. Hart, *The Concept of Law*, 3rd edn (Oxford, Oxford University Press, 2007), pp. 46–49, 94–96. And further below at note 52.

[21] See further Cousins, *Gadsden on Commons and Greens*, 3-76 to 3-82.

[22] Prescription Act 1832, sections 1, 2. Use of a right 'as of right' and without interruption for 30 years cannot be defeated by proof that it commenced after 1189, and becomes absolute and indefeasible after 60 years unless enjoyed with written consent. The relevant qualifying periods are 20 years and 40 years for rights classified in law as easements rather than profits. Most common rights are profits.

[23] See B. Tamanaha, 'Understanding Legal Pluralism', *Sydney Law Review*, 30 (2008), 375–411 at 380.

in 1955 to make recommendations for the protection and future use of common land. The Royal Commission's report was published in 1958 and recommended the establishment of statutory registers of all common land and of common rights.[24] The Royal Commission's recommendations were partially implemented by the Commons Registration Act 1965. The 1965 Act required the separate registration of all common land, and of the common rights exercisable over it, and of the persons claiming to be owners (both of land and rights), in registers kept by commons registration authorities at local government level, principally county councils.[25] The commons registers capture and define the property entitlements and land use rights of both landowners and commoners, but they do not provide evidence of title in the sense that the national Land Register does. The Act provided two registration periods within which land and rights had to be provisionally registered: the first ran from 2 January 1967 to 30 June 1968, and the second from 1 July 1968 to 2 January 1970. The authorities were required to register all applications by 31 July 1970.[26] Land that was not registered within this period was deemed not to be common land, and rights that went unregistered ceased to be legally exercisable.[27] Objections to the registration of land and/or common rights were referable to specially appointed commons commissioners for decision.[28] If no objection was made then the registration became final at the end of the period for objections[29] – this was typically two years from the initial registration of the land and/or common rights.[30]

Commons registration was intended by the Royal Commission to be the first stage in a plan to preserve the commons. They also recommended the introduction of statutory rights of access for the public to all common lands, and the establishment of statutory management associations to oversee schemes for their improvement and management. Public rights of access to registered common land were not granted until the passage of further legislation in 2000,[31] and legislative

[24] Royal Commission (1958) *Royal Commission on Common Land 1955–1958: Report*, Cmnd 462, 1958, esp. at para. 404ff. The registers were intended to be a 'modern Domesday Book' of common land and common rights: see M. Shoard, *This Land Is Our Land* (London, Gaia Books Ltd, 1997), p. 341.

[25] Commons Act 2006, section 4. Commons registration authorities are (in England) county councils, district councils for an area without a county council, a London borough council or (in Wales) a county or county borough council.

[26] Commons Registration (Time Limits) Order 1966, SI 1966/1470.

[27] 1965 Act, section 1(2). Because they were not exercisable, they were extinguished: *Central Electricity Generating Board v Clwyd County Council* [1976] 1 WLR 151; *Oxfordshire County Council v Oxford CC* [2006] 2 AC 674 at [18] (Lord Hoffman).

[28] 1965 Act, sections 6, 18.

[29] Commons Registration (General) Regulations 1966, SI 1966/1471, reg. 5; and Commons Registration (Objections and Maps) Regulations 1968 (SI 1968/989). Two periods for objections were specified: 1 October 1968 to 30 September 1970 in the case of provisional registrations made during the first registration period, and 1 May 1970 to 31 July 1972 for those made in the second registration period.

[30] 1965 Act, sections 5(2), 7(1).

[31] The Countryside and Rights of Way Act 2000, section 1.

provision was not made for the establishment of statutory commons councils to manage common land until 2006.[32]

The 1965 Act was seriously deficient in several respects. The registration of common land and common rights was based on a single exercise carried out between 1965 and 1970. There was no obligation to update or amend the registers if land or rights were subsequently transferred. When provisionally registering common rights, there was no process for assessing the sustainability, or historical accuracy, of the rights claimed. The registration could be challenged before the commons commissioners, but the time limits for initiating objections were short.[33] Consequently many allegedly incorrect registrations of common rights became final without prior scrutiny. Similar problems arose with the registration of common land, as no provision was made for the correction of the registers to remove land that was incorrectly registered as common land, or to register land that had been inadvertently omitted. There was also no standardisation in the way in which commons registration authorities recorded entries in the commons registers.

These problems will eventually be addressed by reforms introduced by the Commons Act 2006. The registration provisions in Part 1 of the 2006 Act provide for the amendment and correction of the existing commons registers. The 2006 Act requires the commons registration authorities to maintain the registers established under the 1965 Act, which will be 'rolled over' and become commons registers held under the 2006 Act.[34] The 2006 Act makes provision for the correction of incorrect entries or omissions from the register of common land, for the registration of new common land, for changes to registered common rights and for the registration of new rights of common created after it comes into force.[35] It is intended to introduce much greater clarity and certainty into the commons registers, and to provide a more secure basis for the registration of both common land and common rights. It will also, when fully in force, provide for the amendment and updating of the commons registers so that they more accurately capture the claimed ownership and extent of common rights.

The 2006 Act does not, however, reopen the registrations of either common land or common rights undertaken under the 1965 Act. The property rights established by registration under the 1965 Act therefore remain unaffected, and are an important constituent of the governance arrangements for common land. The Commons Act 2006 is, moreover, being introduced in stages across England and Wales. It currently only applies in nine registration authorities: Cumbria, North Yorkshire, Devon, Kent, Cornwall, Hertfordshire, Herefordshire, Lancashire (excluding

[32] Commons Act 2006, sections 26–37.
[33] See note 29 above.
[34] Commons Act 2006, sections 1, 2.
[35] Commons Act 2006, sections 3(1), 3(3).

metropolitan districts), and Blackburn with Darwen.[36] Until it has been fully implemented across the whole of England and Wales, the registration of common land and common rights will be subject to a dual registration system, one under which the 1965 Act will continue to apply in many areas pending the full extension of Part 1 of the 2006 Act.

Law and custom: pluralism in commons governance

The governance of common land is underpinned by statutory, customary and contractual normative orders, and conditioned by the complex interactions between them. Notwithstanding the introduction of extensive 'formal' law by the registration provisions in the 1965 and 2006 Acts, the normative order for the governance of common land still leaves considerable legal 'space' for custom to play an important role. The way in which registration was introduced by the 1965 Act is important in determining and shaping this role. And where agriculture is an important land use on common land, public funding will often be available to support environmental land management.[37] This means that environmental land management agreements concluded by public bodies with commoners and landowners are often now important in the governance of common land. The principal land management scheme for England was, until the end of 2014, the *Environmental Stewardship* scheme,[38] which contained specific strands allowing the entry of common land into management agreements.[39] The *Countryside Stewardship* scheme replaced Environmental Stewardship in England from the beginning of 2015. Common land can be entered into the higher tier of Countryside Stewardship, which is targeted at protecting

[36] Commons Registration (England) Regulations 2014 (SI 2014/3038). It has also been implemented in all other registration authorities in England for certain 'corrective' applications to amend the registers (under section 19(2) and schedule 2 paras 6–9 of the 2006 Act). The transitional period for correction of the registers in these areas runs to 14 December 2018.

[37] Funding can be provided by the EU member states within their Rural Development Plans. These are governed by the 2013 Rural Development Regulation, which governs rural development planning for the period 2014–2020: see Regulation (EU) 1305/2013 of the European Parliament and of the Council of 17 December 2013 on the support for rural development by the European Fund for Rural Development (EAFRD OJ L347/487 (20.12.2013)).

[38] See *Environmental Stewardship Handbook*, 4th edn (2013) (NE349), available at: http://webarchive.nationalarchives.gov.uk/20140523111208/http://publications.naturalengland.org.uk/publication/30034?category=45001. And the *Higher Level Stewardship Handbook*, 4th edn (2013) (NE350), available at: http://webarchive.nationalarchives.gov.uk/20140523111208/http://publications.naturalengland.org.uk/publication/2827091.

[39] *Common Land and Shared Grazing: Supplement to the Environmental Stewardship Handbook* (October 2011) (NE316), available at: http://webarchive.nationalarchives.gov.uk/20140523111208/http://publications.naturalengland.org.uk/publication/30034?category=45001.

vulnerable and priority natural habitats. If more than five commoners will benefit from payments under a management agreement, however, a formal commoners' association must be formed to oversee performance of the agreement.[40]

It follows that custom will contribute but one strand, or element, of the multiple normative orders that will be in play at any one time. Common land is therefore illustrative of the *reality* of legal pluralism, and of the way in which different customary and legal rules can combine to deliver the effective management of common land.[41] It can also illustrate their interactions and interpenetrations, and their respective *functions* in commons governance. Their functionality is best examined against the wider institutional setting for the successful governance of common-pool resources. Elinor Ostrom's scholarship on 'successful' common resource management[42] identified several 'design principles' that provide 'an essential element or condition that helps to account for the success of [. . .] institutions in sustaining the common pool resource and gaining the compliance of generation after generation of appropriators to the rules in use'.[43] How the compliance of appropriators is captured – whether in legal or customary rules – was not something with which Ostrom was concerned. It is, however, important to an understanding of the respective functions of customary and legal norms in the governance of common land.

Ostrom's design principles were broadly conceived.[44] She observed that a successfully managed common-pool resource will have clearly defined boundaries and a clearly defined membership of use-rights holders, it will have collective choice arrangements so that individuals affected by operational rules can participate in modifying them, and compliance must be monitored, with graduated sanctions that are available and applied for the infringement of operational rules. There should also be access to low-cost conflict-resolution mechanisms and external recognition of the appropriators' self-organisation, in that the right of appropriators to devise their own institutions will not be challenged by external authorities.

Ostrom's work has inspired a growing literature on commons governance, much of it developing new and sophisticated reinterpretations of governance arrangements, and recognising the institutional diversity that is invariably present in

[40] *Countryside Stewardship: Higher Tier Manual* (DEFRA, March 2016), at para. 3.2.6, and Annex 5 (Common Land and Shared Grazing: additional information), available at: www.gov.uk/government/uploads/system/uploads/attachment_data/file/509675/cs-higher-tier-manual.pdf. There must also be an internal agreement between the commoners as to division of payment, and allocating responsibilities for obligations in the land management agreement.

[41] Editors' note: For further discussion of legal pluralism, see also Nsoh, Pienaar, and Pieraccini in this volume.

[42] E. Ostrom, *Governing the Commons: The Evolution of Institutions for Collective Action* (Cambridge, Cambridge University Press, 1990).

[43] Ostrom, *Governing the Commons*, p. 90.

[44] Editors' note: For further discussion of Ostrom's design principles, see also Pieraccini in this volume.

commons governance.[45] 'New' institutionalist scholars have developed Ostrom's ideas, and she came to recognise that the institutional complexity of the modern commons required a fine tuning and reshaping of her governance criteria. Her later work stressed the need to recognise institutional diversity, the dynamism and reflexivity of common-pool institutions and their openness to change and evolution over time. This scholarship recognised that the complexity of commons governance makes it necessary to identify, and to provide for, the nesting of different institutional arrangements within an overall governance framework that is not always 'tidy'.[46] Implicit within this approach is the recognition that there will be multiple normative orders in play at any one time to implement these institutional arrangements – and that the interplay between these, also, may not always be 'tidy'. The common lands of England and Wales are an example of a common-pool resource with specific characteristics, and their governance exemplifies and illustrates many of these insights.

The central importance of Ostrom's work for lawyers lies in establishing *whether and how* the design principles may be given 'normative' effect – are they regarded as creating a binding rule to guide behaviour, or as permissive in the sense that they confer power on commoners to make binding rules governing the future behaviour of appropriators or others?[47] Normativity may be conferred in different ways, and it is not *necessary* that Ostrom's design principles always be given normative effect in a particular manner – through legal rules or through non-legally binding social norms – if they are to be successful in delivering effective governance. Some of Ostrom's governance principles will normally be mediated by law – others will not. In practice, many of the key principles for effective commons governance will be mediated by custom and customary rules, sometimes with normative legal effect.

The legal ordering applied in the governance of common land may take several forms. The definition of use-right holders (Ostrom's first principle) is implemented in English law through the identification and allocation of property rights by the registers of common rights in land.[48] The application of graduated sanctions may be applied through organisational rules recognised as having normative effect by commoners without the force of 'law', e.g. through the management rules adopted

[45] For example: T. Dietz, E. Ostrom and P. C. Stern, 'The Struggle to Govern the Commons', *Science*, 302 (2003), 1907–1912; T. Dietz, N. Dolsak, E. Ostrom, P. C. Stern, S. Stonich and E. U. Weber (eds), *The Drama of the Commons* (Washington, DC, National Academy Press, 2002).

[46] See especially E. Ostrom, *Understanding Institutional Diversity* (Princeton, NJ, Princeton University Press, 2005), pp. 286ff.

[47] For a general review see W. Twining and D. Miers, *How to Do Things with Rules*, 5th edn (Cambridge, Cambridge University Press, 2010), pp. 94–97. And see J. Raz, *Practical Reason and Norms* (Princeton, NJ, Princeton University Press, 1990); W. Twining, 'Normative and Legal Pluralism – A Global Perspective', *Duke Journal of Comparative and International Law*, 20 (2010), 473–517.

[48] For a wider discussion of this issue, see E. Scotford and R. Walsh, 'The Symbiosis of Property and English Environmental Law – Property Rights in a Public Law Context', *Modern Law Review*, 76 (2013), 1010–1045.

by an unincorporated commons association formed by commoners to manage a specific common(s).[49] The latter may be a highly formalised association with a written constitution and rules, or it may be a more informal group that has developed informal rules of practice which might, nevertheless, be regarded as contractually binding (and as such create legally binding management norms). And dispute resolution may be provided informally by customary practice without the involvement of state-sanctioned legal norms.[50] In practice the 'mix' of normative rules applied to secure the effective governance of common land can shift and change, often subtly, over time and in different circumstances, and from one common to another. But customary rules will in most cases be a key ingredient in the overall institutional governance arrangements.

The governance of common land can, then, provide important insights into the issues raised in the institutional scholarship on wider common-pool resource governance. Common land is subject to a multi-faceted legal regime that brings together a blend of legal and customary rules and practices to deliver effective commons governance. At least six different systems of normative ordering can be detected in the governance arrangements for common land in England and Wales:[51] 'official' or positive law; 'customary law' (in the sense of customary practices that have been recognised by the secondary rules of the legal order and thereby given formal normative effect);[52] custom in the looser sense (in the sense of shared social rules or customs that have not been accorded formal legal recognition);[53] notions of 'good neighbourliness' (as distinct from practices recognised by appropriators as having the binding force of custom, whether legally sanctioned or not);[54] economic norms;[55] and, finally, social practices embedded in community practice.

[49] For a discussion in the context of common land, see C. Short, 'The Traditional Commons of England and Wales in the Twenty First Century', *International Journal of the Commons*, 2 (2008), 192–221.
[50] See Rodgers et al., *Contested Common Land*, ch. 2, esp. pp. 22–31.
[51] Cf. Tamanaha's categorisation of normative orders in his legal pluralist analysis discussed further below (which is somewhat different); B. Tamanaha, 'Understanding Legal Pluralism', *Sydney Law Review*, 30 (2008), 375–411 at 397–399.
[52] See H. L. A. Hart, *The Concept of Law*, 3rd edn (Oxford, Oxford University Press, 2007), pp. 46–49, 94–96; and above, note 20. Hart characterises the secondary rules as 'rules of recognition', e.g. in English law that a custom must be reasonable. And for a discussion of the role of 'collective intentionality' in creating institutional facts such as custom, see J. R. Searle, *The Construction of Social Reality* (London, Allen Lane/Penguin Press, 1995), esp. pp. 37–43.
[53] This may be the case, of course, because an occasion when such recognition can be conferred has not arisen, e.g. because a customary practice has not been the source of litigation before the courts leading to a judicial decision that may have conferred (under the rule of recognition applicable in English law to case law as precedent) formal legal status on the custom in question.
[54] As to which see Rodgers et al., *Contested Common Land*, pp. 36–37 and pp. 172–173; K. Wrightson, 'The Decline of Neighborliness Revisited', in N. L. Jones and D. R. Woolf (eds), *Local Identities in Late Medieval and Early Modern England* (New York, Palgrave Macmillan, 2007), pp. 19–49.
[55] For example, in the case of a common on which agriculture is the predominant land use, changes in the economic subsidies paid through the EU common agricultural policy will be an important

These different normative orders often exist side by side and may in some situations complement each other, while in others some may be dominant – and in some contexts, they may compete for dominance.

Law and custom: continuing interactions

Despite the introduction of commons registration by the Commons Registration Act 1965, and its reform in the Commons Act 2006, there remains considerable scope for customary practice to supplement and interact with the normative rules established by the legal order for the governance of common land. The ability of custom and practice to develop and change over time has made them valuable tools for the governance of the commons. Custom and practice will, however, interact with 'formal' legal norms in different ways on different commons and in different contexts.

The space for a continuing role for custom in the contemporary governance of common land is shaped largely by the deficiencies of the registration process undertaken under the Commons Registration Act 1965. The registers reflect the rights claimed by commoners, and rights of common were often registered generically without clear quantification or a detailed description of the common resource to which they gave access. For example, registrations of the ancient customary right of 'estovers' are widespread in the commons register*s* in England and Wales, but the customary rights were typically registered generically and without further elaboration – whereas this right encompasses a wide range of different and specific resource uses that apply on different commons, e.g. the right to take timber for 'house bote' or 'plough bote', the right to take vegetation, 'samphire rights' (in Norfolk)[56] and other local permutations.[57] The nature and quantity of produce to be taken is rarely, if ever, specified in the registers. And in the case of grazing rights over common land, the number of animals for which rights were registered is sometimes excessive, and bears no relation to the capacity of the common land over which the rights are registered to provide fodder and nourishment for the number of grazing animals for which rights are registered. In these cases, custom has a role in defining the nature and parameters of the commoners' property rights, by filling out

determinant influencing land use decisions, e.g. the number of grazing animals to stock on the common.

[56] There are, for example, 292 entries of estovers that include 'samphire rights' in the rights section of the common register for Brancaster common in Norfolk (CL65, Norfolk County Council). These are expressed as giving the holder a right to take from the common 'herbage, estovers, samphire, soil, fish, shell fish, bait and wild fowl'. Rock samphire is an edible succulent halophyte that grows in the salt marshes fringing the North Sea coast of Norfolk.

[57] For further examples from the commons registers for Thornham and Brancaster, Norfolk, see Rodgers et al., *Contested Common Land*, pp. 177–178. And see Cousins, *Gadsden on Commons and Greens*, 2-38.

detail missing from the registers – a role that has been confirmed by the courts[58] and is wholly attributable to the flaws in the registers established under the 1965 Act.

This situation arose because the 1965 Act made no provision for the checking of claims against sustainability criteria, or indeed against historical and customary practice prevalent in the locality prior to the provisional registration of common rights. This will be corrected by the Commons Act 2006 which, once fully in force, will require that all new registrations or amendments to the commons registers must be checked against sustainability criteria. An application to register a right can be refused 'if in the opinion of the commons registration authority the land over which it is to be created would be unable to sustain the exercise of (a) that right and (b) . . . any other rights of common registered as exercisable over the land'.[59] Where rights are registered in future, the use of the formal legal rules in the 2006 Act will capture sustainability issues in the property rights of the commoner at the point of registration. This will not, however, provide the flexibility needed to deal with fluctuating circumstances that may arise in the future, e.g. reductions in the available common grazing due to climate change and a greater incidence of drought.

Custom will, therefore, continue to provide flexibility to adapt commons management, and can modify or sidestep formal legal rules where this is rendered necessary by changing circumstances. This raises interesting questions about the way in which inherently flexible customary rules are captured in the legal norms for property rights and commons governance. Where the courts have applied a customary rule in arriving at a judicial decision on common property rights, this will have the effect of assimilating the practice into the common law. This is a rule of recognition, and will elevate customary practice into customary 'law' in the sense described above.[60] One important consequence of recognising custom as having created a formal legal norm in this way will, however, be that future changes will not necessarily be reflected in the normative legal order within which the law has captured that custom. Clothing social practice with normative (legal) force will capture key aspects of a custom at a specific point in time. Where land use practice has continued to develop, and adapt, this may lead to a mismatch between the local custom practised by commoners and the legal rules that apply, in theory, to adjust property rights in the commons.

The enduring importance of customary norms in the governance of common land becomes clearer if we consider in more detail (i) the role of customary rules in quantifying the resource 'take' permitted by common rights and, (ii) the problems in ascertaining the number of grazing animals permitted by registered rights of pasturage.

[58] See *Dance v Savery* [2011] EWCA Civ 1250, discussed further below.
[59] Commons Act 2006, section 6(6).
[60] See Hart, *The Concept of Law*, pp. 94–95.

It was noted above that in the case of estovers and turbary, the precise nature of the right is rarely specified in the registers, which will record simply a 'right of estovers' or 'turbary' as belonging to the commoner.[61] To ascertain not only the precise *nature* of the right granted, but also the *quantity* of the resource to which it gives access, it will always be necessary to look behind the registers at the customary practice on which the right is based – it may, for example, confer a right to take bracken for animal bedding, wood or shrubs for fuel, or rushes for matting or bedding. These rights are often registered as attached to a cottage or dwelling, in which case the quantity that can be taken is customarily limited to what is necessary for the use or sustenance of the occupants of the dwelling.[62] And in cases where the registered right is unquantified, the right is also limited by custom to the needs of the dominant tenement. For example, a right of estover may be limited to the quantity of bracken or rushes needed to provide animal bedding for the number of livestock to be grazed on the common. In the case of turbary it will be limited to the number of hearths in which the peat or turf can be burnt.[63] The produce taken cannot be sold for commercial gain or used for other purposes.[64]

Custom is also important in the quantification of registered grazing rights. The 1965 Act provided that 'where a right consists of or includes a right, not limited by number, to graze animals of any class, it shall . . . be treated as exercisable in relation to no more animals . . . than a definite number'.[65] Once the registration became final, the right became exercisable 'in relation to animals not exceeding the number registered' and was conclusive proof of the matters registered.[66] The legal effect of this provision on the property rights reflected in the registers has been discussed by commentators,[67] the commons commissioners,[68] and by the judiciary[69] on several occasions, but clarity remains elusive. In *Bettinson v Langton*[70] it was held that the customary rule of levancy and couchancy had no future role to play in quantifying grazing rights, having been replaced by the registration of fixed numbers of grazing rights under the 1965 Act. The custom's primary role was, however, not to provide a numerical measure of grazing entitlement, but rather to ascertain the *relative* entitlements *inter se* of different commoners over the common by reference to the relative

[61] See notes 56 and 57 above. And see Cousins, *Gadsden on Commons and Greens*, 2-38.

[62] See, for example, Cousins, *Gadsden on Commons and Greens*, 2-40.

[63] See *Lord Chesterfield v Harris* [1908] 2 Ch 397.

[64] See *The Earl of Pembroke's Case* (1636) Clayton 47.

[65] Commons Registration Act 1965, section 15.

[66] 1965 Act, section 15(3) and section 10.

[67] See G. D. Gadsden, *The Law of Commons* (London, Sweet & Maxwell, 1988), at 4.23; Cousins, *Gadsden on Commons and Greens*, 3-94, 3-95; Rodgers et al., *Contested Common Land*, pp. 56–57.

[68] See *Re the Black Mountain, Dinefwr, Dyfed* [1985] 272/D/441, 16 DCC 219.

[69] For example, in *Bettinson v Langton* [2001] 3 All.ER 417 (House of Lords); *Dance v Savery* [2011] EWHC 16 (Ch); [2011] EWCA Civ 1250 (court of appeal); *Littlejohns v Devon County Council and Duchy of Cornwall* [2016] EWCA Civ 446 (court of appeal).

[70] [2001] 3 All.ER 417. And see *Hall v Moore and Harris* [2009] EWCA Civ 201.

size of the dominant tenements, and their ability to produce fodder to overwinter livestock that was grazed on the common in the summer months.

Given the excessive registration of levant and couchant rights under the 1965 Act, the number of registered grazing rights will frequently exceed the capacity of the common over which they are registered. Consequently, the principal function of the custom – that of ascertaining the relative rights of access to the common resource by those with common rights – remains very important. This cannot be determined by reference solely to the numbers of grazing rights registered in the commons registers.[71] Furthermore, in *Re the Black Mountain, Dinefwr, Dyfed*[72] it was held that the registered number of pasturage rights[73] provides only an upper limit on the number of grazing stock permissible, and that if the number of animals grazing the common was considered to be excessive then legal redress can be sought.[74] This should in principle be the case even though the number of animals put to the common by the grazier (and alleged to be causing the damage) was less than his full registered entitlement. Where a prescriptive right of common pasture is claimed to have arisen by long usage, moreover, the customary principle of levancy and couchancy will always be applicable to quantify the right.[75]

The ability to 'look behind' the registers at customary usage in order to fill out necessary detail and context is now expressly recognised in the Commons Act 2006, which provides that registration does not 'affect any constraint on the exercise of a right of common *where the constraint does not appear in the register*'.[76] This recognises the relevance of customary restrictions on the exercise of common rights – including, for instance, customary constraints stipulating that the rights may be exercised only at certain times of the year, or that livestock should be acclimatised and settled on the common in accordance with local custom, or that

[71] A limited view of the impact of *Bettinson v Langton* was also taken by the court of appeal in *Dance v Savery* [2011] EWCA Civ 1250; 'That case had nothing to do with the question, with which the present case is concerned, namely whether the effect of section 15 of the 1965 Act combined with section 10, was conclusive that a registered right to graze the specified number and type of animals was not a split right in the absence of reference to another register unit or was . . . merely to state conclusively a maximum number of animals that could be depastured at any time on the register unit' (judgment para. 64, Etherton LJ.).

[72] [1985] 272/D/441, 16 DCC 219 (Commissioner Baden Fuller QC).

[73] I.e. the specific legal issue here was the meaning of section 15(1), Commons Registration Act 1965: rights should 'be treated as exercisable in relation to no more animals . . . than a definite number'.

[74] For example, by the owner of the soil over which the common rights are exercised, who retains the right to surplus grazing after the common rights have been exercised. Clearly, if the exercise of registered common rights can be restricted as suggested here, this will amplify the 'surplus' grazing available to the owner of the soil. And see Co.Litt.122a.

[75] See *Chesterfield (Lord) v Harris* [1908] 2 Ch 397, 421 (Buckley LJ.). Although note that it is not possible since the passage of the Commons Act 2006 to create a *new* right of common by prescription: Commons Act 2006, section 6. And see *Littlejohns v Devon County Council and Duchy of Cornwall* [2016] EWCA Civ 446.

[76] Section 18(5), Commons Act 2006 (emphasis added).

the times at which stock may be turned onto the common are to be determined by reference to manorial court records, or other ancient custom, even if these are not mentioned on the register.

In *Dance v Savery*[77] the court of appeal adopted an expansive interpretation of this provision, as allowing wide reference to customary practices as to the use and historical exercise of common rights when filling in detail omitted from the commons registers. In *Dance* itself the court recognised that a right of pasture separately registered against two different but contiguous units of common land on Dartmoor had by customary practice in the past been split across the two, and did not give separate rights to the full registered quantity of rights in each case.[78] Similarly, in *Hall v Moore*[79] it was held that the exercise of grazing rights on a common could be limited to one year in three, even though this restriction was omitted from the commons register. It resulted from a change of local customary practice that had not been recorded in the register. The application of custom to restrict the number of registered grazing rights that can be exercised in this way – either by reference to quantum relative to the land over which they are exercisable,[80] or in temporal terms[81] – will considerably reduce the potential grazing pressure, and degradation of the natural environment, that might otherwise result from a literal reading of the commons registers.

A continuing role for custom can also be found in other aspects of the governance of common land. So, for example, a right of common *pur cause de vicinage* (because of neighbourhood) is an ancillary right to a right of common grazing that permits a commoner to graze straying animals on a contiguous common. This is an ancient right entirely conditioned by the custom in each neighbourhood, usually referred to as 'intercommoning'. In legal terms this was a permissive right that applied where two or more neighbouring commons usually intercommoned with each other. It was a customary right, and so was implicit in any individual common right held over either common. The right did not give the holder the right to place his livestock on a neighbouring common: rather, it recognised that animals may stray, and protected the commoner from an action for trespass where his stock strayed onto the waste of a neighbouring manor. To use Blackstone's phrase, if livestock were to escape and stray onto the neighbouring common then 'the law

[77] [2011] EWCA Civ 1250. See especially para. 68 *et seq.* of the judgment (Etherton LJ.).

[78] The court refused to limit its enquiry of custom and practice by reference to the *travaux preparatoires* of the Commons Act 2006: 'The wording of section 18(5) [of the 2006 Act] is clear and is not restricted to customary constraints such as those mentioned in the Explanatory Notes. As the introduction to the explanatory notes makes clear, they do not form part of the 2006 Act and were not endorsed by Parliament. They were prepared by DEFRA and cannot confine the meaning of the legislation' (Etherton LJ. at para. 68).

[79] [2009] EWCA Civ 201.

[80] As in *Dance v Savery* [2011] EWCA Civ 1250.

[81] As in *Hall v Moore* [2009] EWCA Civ 201.

winks at the trespass'.[82] It is a permissive right, and can be terminated at any time by the landowner.

Vicinage is arguably a separate right, distinct from the substantive common rights of pasture to which it is ancillary.[83] If this is the case,[84] then it will always be necessary to go behind the commons registers to ascertain the extent and nature of the vicinage rights ancillary to each registered right of pasture.

Positioning custom in commons management

Although custom retains considerable importance, it must be remembered that it is only one of several types of normative rule relevant to commons governance. It is, moreover, important to adopt a legal pluralist perspective if we are to identify how different normative rules sometimes compete with customary rules for dominance, and how they intersect and complement each other in commons governance.[85]

Some exponents of legal pluralism have argued that different types of normative rule should be viewed simply as social facts, and that we should talk instead in terms of 'normative pluralism'.[86] One consequence of this approach would be to render the distinction between legal and non-legal norms redundant.[87] This approach has merit, especially in its focus on the normative nature of the rules themselves (not their source) as the key to a pluralist analysis. Nevertheless, the source from which different rules derive 'normativity' and create binding and prescriptive obligations – through the legal system or as non-legally recognised social fact – is important to an understanding of the governance of common land, and cannot be ignored.

Rules of recognition and normative ordering

The source by which rules assume binding obligatory effect is important to an understanding of the hierarchical interrelationship between competing normative

[82] W. Blackstone, *Commentaries on the Laws of England*, Book 11 'Of the Rights of Things' (Oxford, Oxford University Press, 2016 [1765–1769], ed. S. Stern), p. 33.
[83] See for example *Jones v Robin* [1845] 10 QB 581; [1847] 10 QB 620 ('it is not properly a right of common or *profit a prendre*, but rather an excuse for a trespass', at 632).
[84] This is generally recognised to be the case by commentators: see for example Cousins, *Gadsden on Commons and Greens*, 2-33.
[85] See M. Pieraccini, 'Sustainability and the English Commons: A Legal Pluralist Analysis', *Environmental Law Review*, 12 (2010), pp. 94–114, esp. pp. 105–110.
[86] See for example the categorisation of normative orders offered by Tamanaha, 'Understanding Legal Pluralism' above, note 51. B. de Souza Santos adopts a different system: see *Towards a New Common Sense: Law, Science and Politics in the Paradigmatic Transition* (London, Routledge, 1995), esp. pp. 429ff.
[87] See Twining, 'Normative and Legal Pluralism – A Global Perspective', esp. 496–498.

rules. Where there are competing normative rules in play, as in the governance of common land, which is to be given primacy in a dispute? Although a legal pluralist approach requires us to recognise the relevance and application of both formal law and custom, it is important to pay attention to the hierarchy of legitimacy and enforceability conferred by the legal system on different formal and customary rules. In the context of common land, however, we should not assume that 'formal' legal rules created by statute or by judicial decision will always have primacy – an assumption that has been referred to as the 'ideology of legal centralism'.[88] There is also a growing recognition among legal scholars of the importance of recognising both the pluralities of the sources of law and custom, and the pluralities of legal interpretation of individual norms.[89]

Attempts to categorise normative rules for the governance of common land – and, indeed, of common-pool resources more generally – into categories of 'positive' law as opposed to 'unofficial' or customary rules ignore a key point. A normative rule may be represented in positive 'law'[90] but make virtually no contribution to the governance of common land. Many legal norms are 'hollow' in the sense that, although they have the normative force usually accorded to positive 'legal' rules, they are redundant in one of two senses: either (i) the rule itself has no meaningful application at all, or (ii) it is in some social contexts ignored by commoners and *performs* no meaningful function. In these cases, 'hollow' legal rules are often displaced by customary practice, which provides a working set of rules for those using the common resource that are more appropriate for their needs and for the circumstances of the common in question.

A classic example of the first phenomenon is presented by the legislation providing for the definition of property rights in the statutory commons registers established by the Commons Registration Act 1965. It was noted above that the registers state the maximum number of animals that a commoner can graze over a common,[91] or the type of produce they may take – as estovers or turbary, for example. The number of registered pasturage rights often bears no relation to the capacity of the land over which the rights are nominally exercisable to sustain the numbers of livestock for which rights were claimed on registration. In practice, commons management in such cases is often conditioned by environmental land management agreements agreed between commoners and the statutory conservation bodies[92] – for example under the Countryside Stewardship scheme or under

[88] J. Griffith, 'What Is Legal Pluralism?', *Journal of Legal Pluralism*, 24 (1986), 1–55 at 3.

[89] See for example R. Cotterrell, *Law, Culture and Society: Legal Ideas in the Mirror of Social Theory* (London, Routledge, 2006).

[90] See for example Tamanaha's categorisation of norms, including positive law, in Tamanaha, 'Understanding Legal Pluralism' above, note 51.

[91] Commons Registration Act 1965, section 13.

[92] Natural England or Natural Resources Wales: Natural Environment and Rural Communities Act 2006, section 32.

statutory powers applicable in protected areas such as Sites of Special Scientific Interest (SSSIs), many of which include common land.[93] The registers reflect property entitlements, but they play little role in commons management.

An example of the second kind of 'hollow' legal norm is to be found in the formal limitations on the property rights granted by a right of common grazing. The common right of pasturage confers a right to take grass from the land by the mouth of sheep, cattle or other livestock.[94] It does not confer a right to bring additional animal feed onto the common land to feed livestock. This limitation is often ignored. The statutory conservation bodies will usually expressly prohibit the supplementary feeding of livestock on common land that is within a protected area such as an SSSI, by including it in the list of operations likely to damage the conservation interest served on common graziers when the SSSI is notified.[95] Although the right of common pasturage gives no right to carry out the supplementary feeding of livestock, the inclusion in an SSSI notification of a prohibition in this form makes it a criminal offence to do so without the permission of the conservation body.[96] Even when clothed with 'formal' legal normative effect in this way, however, the prohibition on supplementary feeding may be ignored on some commons, while on others the rule is observed. Customary practice has more prescriptive impact ('normativity') in this context than the relevant legal rules, and can in some cases supplant legal rules in commons governance.

Custom: flexibility and adaptation

The way in which a rule is granted obligatory (normative) effect is important in that it determines *how that rule may subsequently change and adapt*. A rule clothed with formal legal normativity will henceforth be governed by the internal normative architecture of the legal system that has conferred normativity upon it. It can only be changed in accordance with the internal rules of the legal order of which it is now part. In the case of a customary rule that has been assimilated into

[93] For example, under section 15, Countryside Act 1968 (as amended by Countryside and Rights of Way Act 2000, section 75(3)) in Sites of Special Scientific Interest; or under section 7, Natural Environment and Rural Communities Act 2006 (general power conferred on Natural England to conclude an agreement with any person having an interest in land).

[94] See *Besley v John* [2003] EWCA Civ 1737. The registered rights in the rights section of the commons register will specify which type of livestock (for example sheep or cattle) the right of pasture applies to. In some cases the right will be expressed as applying to sheep with a numerical conversion into a smaller number of cattle to be grazed – the quantum of which will depend on local custom and practice, as reflected in the 1965 registrations.

[95] For examples see Rodgers et al., *Contested Common Land*, p. 104 (Eskdale, Cumbria), p. 155 (Elan Valley, Powys).

[96] Under Wildlife and Countryside Act 1981, section 28E.

the common law through case law, for example, the rule of *stare decisis* (binding precedent) will apply – the rule established in case law must be followed by a court in later cases, and is only capable of modification or change if overruled by a higher court in the judicial hierarchy, if distinguished on its facts in a later case, or if overruled by a legislative act (for example a statute or statutory instrument).[97]

This is what makes the modification of customary rules that have been assimilated into the common law so difficult. It also explains why some rules of customary practice are still regarded as 'good law' if they have been recognised in earlier judicial decisions, often many years previously, even though the practice in question is now entirely redundant. They have never been raised and argued in a subsequent case, and because the practice in question is now redundant it is unlikely that they ever will be. This is a limitation of the common-law approach to precedent and case law that is observable in many areas of judge-made law, and not just in relation to commons governance.[98]

It is important that the rules of recognition used to determine the normative effect of different rules adequately reflect the flexible and iterative nature of customary practice in commons management. The relationship between case law and custom illustrates the difficulty this poses, and emphasises the importance of adapting property rights to reflect the constantly changing requirements for the effective management of common land. Part 2 of the Commons Act 2006 offers a new approach to this problem by facilitating the establishment of commons councils to oversee the governance of common land in England and Wales. A statutory commons council can be established by the secretary of state where sufficient local support can be demonstrated, e.g. by commoners and local communities. Establishment is by a formal establishment order with the approval of the secretary of state.[99] Once established, the commons council will have statutory power to make management rules for the governance of the common(s) for which it has been established.[100]

[97] As to which see Twining and Miers, *How to Do Things with Rules*, pp. 289ff.

[98] See for example some of the leading cases in the law of nuisance, where decisions made by Victorian judges are still the source of key legal rules: for example *Salvin v. North Brancepeth Coal Co.* [1874] 9 Ch App 705, in which the need for physical observable damage was established as necessary for an action of private nuisance – a rule still cited, for example, in *Clerk and Lindsell on Torts*, 21st edn (London, Sweet & Maxwell, 2014), at 20-07 and 20-26. This rule was established in an age when limited scientific means were available for detecting the environmental hazard of industrial processes, and when juries were used for assessing damages in nuisance cases. The courts have been trying to move to a more sophisticated approach to identifying damage in more recent cases: see for example *Blue Circle Industries v Ministry of Defence* [1998] 3 All.ER 385.

[99] 2006 Act, sections 26, 27. There is a standard constitution applicable to determine the membership and proceedings of a commons council, once established. This can be varied by the terms of the establishment order for a specific commons council: The Commons Councils (Standard Constitution) Regulations 2010, SI 2010/1204.

[100] 2006 Act, sections 31, 32.

The establishment of a commons council will enable those with an interest in the common to create flexible management rules. A commons council will have the functions and powers that are conferred on it by its establishment order.[101] These are wide, but not unlimited: it can confer the power to introduce binding rules to regulate agricultural activities on the common, governing the management of vegetation, and the exercise of common rights.[102] The primary function of a commons council will therefore be to focus on introducing rules that address the objectives identified in its establishment order. This will enable it to adopt rules that are customary in origin, reflect local practice, and which will inevitably vary from common to common. They will also be flexible, in that they can be varied from time to time.[103]

The first commons council was established in 2014 for Brendon Common in the Exmoor National Park.[104] A second was established for Bodmin Moor (Cornwall) in September 2016,[105] and at the time of writing a consultation is taking place with a view to establishing a commons council for the commons in Cumbria. The establishment orders for both the Brendon and Bodmin commons councils confer the power to make management rules for: regulating agricultural activities on the common, the management of its vegetation, managing the rights of common and their exercise (including the leasing or licensing of rights), maintaining boundaries and removing unlawful boundaries, and removing encroachments on the common. They also permit both councils to maintain a 'living' commons register, recording the actual grazing of animals on the common.[106] This will give a more transparent and accurate record of the use of common rights than is available through the statutory registers – which solely record entitlements, and not the use of common rights.

[101] 2006 Act, sections 26, 31(1).

[102] 2006 Act, section 31(3)(a), (4). Model establishment orders have been published by the Department for Environment, Food and Rural Affairs for a commons council applicable to a single common, and one for umbrella application to several commons collectively: see the West Barsetshire Commons Council Establishment Order 2010, and the Barset National Park Commons Council Establishment Order 2010, available at: www.gov.uk/government/uploads/system/uploads/attachment_data/file/501138/Barset_model_order_-_umbrella_commons_councils.pdf; www.gov.uk/government/uploads/system/uploads/attachment_data/file/501142/West_Barsetshire_model_order_-_single_commons_council.pdf.

[103] See for example the model West Barsetshire Commons Council Establishment Order 2010, reg. 7, which provides for the publication of proposed changes to the management rules at least one month before they come into force, and provides for the consent of the secretary of state to any proposed changes: www.gov.uk/government/uploads/system/uploads/attachment_data/file/501142/West_Barsetshire_model_order_-_single_commons_council.pdf.

[104] Brendon Commons Council Establishment Order 2013, SI 2013/2959.

[105] See the Bodmin Moor Commons Council Establishment Order 2015, SI 2015/1515.

[106] See the Bodmin Moor Commons Council Establishment Order 2015, SI 2015/1515, regs. 5, 8; and the Brendon Commons Council Establishment Order 2013, SI 2013/2959, regs. 5, 8.

Conclusion

This chapter has emphasised the enduring role of custom in the governance of common land. Positioning customary norms against those of a 'formal' legal character requires a *functional* interpretation of the roles played by differing categories of normative rule. Legal norms are primarily concerned with issues of entitlement and the allocation of property rights, for example through the registration process for common land and common rights under the 1965 and 2006 Acts. Customary rules are, by contrast, mainly concerned with establishing normative rules for the *management* of common land. The primary role of custom is seen in establishing normative rules for *how and when* the common resource is to be used by commoners, and how it is to be shared by them *inter se*. Nevertheless, the role of customary rules can also involve imposing restrictions on legal entitlements, and to this extent custom still has a role to play in defining property entitlements.[107] Decisions such as those in *Dance v Savery*[108] and *Hall v Moore*[109] are illustrative of the elevation of custom to a position superior to that of 'formal' legal rules of entitlement if these are at variance with the customary historical practice applied in the management of individual commons. The court of appeal in both cases gave effect to customary practice in a way that overrode the written ('legal') expression of property entitlements in the commons registers established under the 1965 Act.

Adopting a legal pluralist approach that is also sensitive to the *sources* from which rules derive normativity enables us to position custom in the hierarchy of norms applicable to the governance of common land, and facilitates an appraisal of its effectiveness. Prior to its reform by the Commons Act 2006, it fell short of Ostrom's design principles for effective commons governance in several respects. The commons registers do not identify the current ownership of common land and rights with sufficient accuracy: the registers often offer only a snapshot of the ownership of common land and common rights at the point of registration, more than 40 years ago. These problems will be largely resolved when Part 1 of the 2006 Act has been fully implemented. Similarly, current governance arrangements fail to identify and impose clear and graduated sanctions for breaches of management rules on many commons. Where there is damage to the common by (for example) over-grazing, who is to take legal action to restrain the inappropriate use of common rights?[110]

The establishment of a commons council under Part 2 of the 2006 Act will address many of these issues. It will provide for clear and graduated sanctions for

[107] *Dance v Savery* [2011] EWCA Civ is itself a good example of a customary rule restricting the extent of legal entitlements and their potential exercise.
[108] [2011] EWCA Civ 1250.
[109] [2009] EWCA Civ 201.
[110] See *Re the Black Mountain, Dinefwr, Dyfed* [1985] 272/D/441, 16 DCC 219. Above, note 72.

inappropriate resource use, and enable commoners to participate in modifying land management rules. It will also provide external recognition of the commoners' self-organisation and of the management rules they adopt. The latter can clothe customary practice with binding legal effect in a form that is flexible, and provide robust arrangements for the imposition of sanctions for inappropriate resource use. The continuing relevance of legal pluralism in commons governance must, however, be acknowledged. The 2006 Act itself recognises a hierarchy of rules for the establishment and functioning of commons councils. A commons council requires an establishment order (formal law) which will set out its objectives and powers; the management rules it adopts will be given formal ('legal') normative effect by the 2006 Act, but be based in some cases on customary practice; but the council will require the consent of persons with an interest in the land if that person's consent would otherwise be required.[111] The legal rights of the owner of the soil will therefore be largely unaffected.[112] Finally, the 2006 Act requires commons councils to have regard to the 'public interest' when carrying out their functions.[113] The 'public interest' is expressly defined to include nature conservation and public access, and reflects the importance of legislation (formal law)[114] in shaping the institutional structure and functions of otherwise self-regulating commons councils.[115] Where a commons council has been established and adopts management rules based on local custom and practice, therefore, there will still be important – and multiple – interpenetrations between customary local practice and 'formal' law.

[111] 2006 Act, section 33.
[112] Although management rules adopted under the 2006 Act can restrain or regulate the exercise of the owner's right to use the surplus grazing on the common.
[113] 2006 Act, section 31(6)(b).
[114] For example, Part 1 of the Countryside and Rights of Way Act 2000 in relation to public access on common land.
[115] 2006 Act, section 31(7).

3

Taking Stock of Italian Commons: Un-Common Grounds?

MARGHERITA PIERACCINI

Introduction: what are Italian commons?

Drawing on the commons literature, a distinction can be made between traditional and new commons.[1] Traditional commons are associated with rural landscapes and are concerned with access to, distribution and management of common-pool natural resources, such as land or fisheries, in a given locality among a limited set of users. New commons refer to various shared (or shareable) resources such as the internet, biodiversity, knowledge, public urban areas, not-for-profit organisations, etc., aimed at the promotion of social justice and sustainability.[2]

This chapter focuses on Italian commons, exploring the different articulations of property and property relations in both traditional and new commons. Traditional and new commons in Italy have seldom been studied together by lawyers. Traditional commons have been the subject of study of a large number of agricultural lawyers and legal historians for a long time,[3] while new commons have been the focus of a sub-set of radical private law scholars.[4] Recently,

[1] G. Bravo and T. de Moor, 'The Commons in Europe: from Past to Future', *International Journal of the Commons*, 2 (2008), 155–161.

[2] C. Hess, 'Mapping New Commons', presented at the Twelfth Biennial Conference of the International Association for the Study of the Commons, Cheltenham, UK, 14–18 July 2008: http://surface.syr.edu/cgi/viewcontent.cgi?article=1023&context=sul.

[3] See, for example, E. Romagnoli and C. Trebeschi, *Comunioni Familiari Montane* (Flero, Padeia, 1975); P. Grossi, *Un altro modo di possedere: l'emersione di forme alternative di proprietà alla coscienza giuridica postunitaria* (Milano, Giuffrè, 1977); F. Marinelli, *Gli usi civici* (Milano, Giuffrè, 2003).

[4] See, for example, the work of Ugo Mattei, *Beni comuni: un manifesto* (Roma-Bari, Laterza, 2011). M. R. Marella, 'Il diritto dei beni comuni. Un invito alla discussione', *Rivista critica del diritto privato*, 1 (2011), 103–118; M. R. Marella, 'Il diritto dei beni comuni. Oltre il pubblico e il privato', in G. Allegri, M. R. Allegri, A. Guerra and P. Marsocci (eds), *Democrazia e Controllo Pubblico dalla prima modernità al web* (Napoli, Editoriale Scientifica, 2012), pp. 75–88.

Proceedings of the British Academy, **216**, 38–57. © The British Academy 2018.

a few attempts have been made in the Italian commons literature to map out both traditional and new commons, pointing to the possibility of applying the legal principles of traditional commons to new commons.[5]

This chapter contributes to this mapping exercise by providing a critical overview of traditional and new commons in Italy to understand if there are similarities between the two categories or if they inhabit an un-common ground. Contrary to those scholars who have proposed an application of the legal principles of traditional commons to the new ones, this chapter argues that traditional and new commons understand property too differently to be subsumed under a unified normative framework. Although both challenge the private/public dichotomy in property law and are permeated by a sustainability ethos, it is only with the new commons that the social function of property becomes centre stage and with it a procedural understanding of property aimed at deliberative democracy. In a sense, new commons in Italy are an example of open-access commons, defined by Benkler as:

> institutional arrangements that cover much larger ranges of resources in modern society, and these resources are generally open to the entire public or at least to some very large, and largely undefined, set of users, both individual and corporate. Their defining feature is not finely designed allocation of well-behaved and predictable (with known uncertainties) resource sets and needs, but high flexibility and an absence of power of exclusion by early users and uses of the resource against later users or uses.[6]

The traditional Italian commons fit squarely within the agrarian domain and are primarily concerned with the question of rights to land (whether private, state or in common ownership) of particular communities, representing a type of limited-access commons 'where members of a clearly defined group have a bundle of legal rights including the right to exclude non-members from using that resource'.[7]

Therefore, while the law on traditional commons, both in its different customary manifestations and in statutes, has been concerned with land-based claims, in the new commons debate, the law is employed for discussing constitutional questions about procedural and substantive rights in relation to the public good. Property is however still centre stage: while, in traditional commons, property is about claiming, acknowledging and sometimes silencing rights of commons depending on the relationship between statutory law and customary law, in new commons

[5] A. Dani, 'Il concetto giuridico di "beni comuni" tra passato e presente', *Historia et Ius*, 6 (2014), 1–48; F. Marinelli, 'Usi civici e beni comuni, Rassegna diritto civile', 2 (2013), 406–422; V. Cerulli-Irelli and L. De Lucia, 'Beni comuni e dirittti collettivi', *Politica del Diritto*, 1 (2014), 3–36.

[6] Y. Benkler, 'Between Spanish Huertas and the Open Road: A Tale of Two Commons?', in B. M. Frischmann, M. J. Madison and K. J. Strandburg (eds), *Governing Knowledge Commons* (Oxford, Oxford University Press, 2014), pp. 69–98 at p. 92.

[7] C. Hess and E. Ostrom, 'Ideas, Artifacts and Facilities: Information as a Common Pool Resource', *Law and Contemporary Problems*, 66 (2003), 111–145 at 121.

the Italian Civil Code's categorisation of property is deconstructed in an attempt to fight against neoliberal laws and policies. Interestingly, the tools used for such deconstruction often include references to key constitutional principles, thereby showing that current pro-commons movements do not dispense with the law altogether but actually selectively appropriate and interpret the law that best supports their *commoning* projects.

The chapter is broadly divided into three parts: the first considers traditional common lands, emphasising the importance of custom in shaping their management and their diversity.[8] Historically, such diverse customary practices have been subjected to a simplification by the legislator with the law of 16 June 1927, n. 1766 (hereafter the 1927 law), which sought to erase diversity in order to fit the common lands into a rigid and single-property legal category. If customary laws reflected the practices on the common lands, it will be argued that the 1927 law reflected a capitalist logic indifferent to maintaining a close link between the commoners and their land.[9] This led to the disappearance of many common lands and management practices, though some examples of common lands in contemporary Italy, which have been able to maintain close ties to customary law, are visible, especially in the northern mountainous regions of the country, taking the form of communal property. The second part of the chapter considers the new wave of Italian commons, where the concept of the commons is politicised through direct action (occupation of urban spaces such as the Valle Theatre in Rome), coupled with attempts at reforming property law to disentangle ownership of goods from their categorisation as commons using, *inter alia*, expansive readings of the Italian Constitution and bringing into the discussion procedural questions about deliberation. The third part provides concluding remarks focused on the changing role and use of law on commons to shape the types of property and property relations in traditional and new commons and the difficulty in subjecting them to similar legal principles and rules. What will emerge from the analysis below is that, rather than being a fixed legal category, property is relational and fluid in the context of Italian commons.

Traditional commons and agrarian practice in Italy

The first part of this chapter is concerned with property relations in traditional commons in Italy, pointing to their heterogeneity, close link to agrarian practice and custom and their relationship with statutory law. It starts by providing a historical excursus into the emergence of traditional common lands in Italy and

[8] Editors' note: For further discussion of the role of custom in commons management, see Rodgers in this volume.

[9] Editors' note: Compare the situation in contemporary China where the law reinforces the link between community members and their land. See Xu and Gong in this volume.

a consideration of the way in which national law re-thought property relations in commons. During medieval times, commons flourished, but with the end of the *ancien régime* and the rise of new conceptualisations of property based on the primacy of individual ownership, the commons suffered. However, this has not meant a complete disappearance of traditional commons from the Italian landscape today, and the case of northern mountain communal properties will be considered to understand the relevance of customary law in regulating property rights and its difficult relation with constitutional principles.

Traditional commons through history

The birth of traditional common land in Italy can be traced back to the Middle Ages, though it is possible to speak about shared grazing rights on pastoral land since Roman times, with the *ager compascuus*, where the owners of lands adjacent to grazing land could exercise rights of common of grazing. However, the predominant conception of property in Roman times was that of the *dominium*, i.e. the quiritarian ownership of a thing.[10] As the legal historian Grossi observed, it was only in the Middle Ages that the concept of the *dominium* was devitalised in Italy, privileging a direct and more communitarian relationship with the land, based on use rather than title.[11] The devitalisation of the *dominium* was partly due to changing socio-economic and environmental conditions, but also to the influence of Germanic juridical practices (*Gewere*) emphasising the physical possession of the land and the direct, concrete relationship with it, rather than abstract title. During the Middle Ages, we see the compression of the *dominium* due to the number of new uses and entitlements limiting the owner's freedom and favouring the redistribution of the resources.

The commons in the Middle Ages comprised both communal properties and private manorial lands over which rights of common (e.g. *ius lignandi, ius herbandi, ius pascendi, ius venandi et piscandi*) existed. Local customs played a fundamental role in governing property relationships on commons, rendering very arduous any attempt at categorising and mapping agrarian commons within a single framework.[12] The state, which in the nineteenth and twentieth centuries became a fundamental force in the regulation and suppression of the commons, played only a marginal and discontinuous role until the end of the *ancien régime*. Indeed, the state regulated only certain aspects[13] without repealing the local norms produced,

[10] In Roman law, full ownership over a thing held under a legal title by Roman citizens, known as *quirites*.
[11] Grossi, *Un altro modo di possedere*.
[12] Dani, 'Il concetto giuridico di "beni comuni" tra passato e presente', 22.
[13] For example, prohibiting rights of common of hunting in areas valuable to the king. See A. Dani, 'Pluralismo giuridico e ricostruzione storica dei diritti collettivi', *Archivio Scialoja-Bolla*, 1 (2005), 61–84.

inter alia, by municipal statutes, uncodified agrarian practices, corporations, religious communities and feudal partnerships. A pluralist juridical framework therefore existed determining property relations in commons.[14] Nevertheless, two general points can be made: first, that the rights of common belonged to a restricted identifiable community (e.g. members of a *villa*, of a municipality, or of a restricted circle of families); and second, that the rights of common were based on custom and agrarian practices and therefore were directly linked with the use of the resources. Guaranteeing to the community the right to satisfy its basic needs was the purpose of the commons in medieval times. This means that the key issue for the communities holding rights of common was the concrete possibility of exercising them, rather than questions over ownership.

This juridical pluralism and direct link between the user and the resource in question in the articulation of entitlements began to be suppressed with the legal codifications of the nineteenth century, the rise of the centralised state and individual private property, and the loss of regulatory powers of the municipalities. The commons came to be linked to the agrarian feudal past, which was to be rejected in the name of economic and political liberalism. English empiricism and the French Enlightenment influenced European (Italian included) understandings of property to a great extent, positioning individual private property as the model that could best guarantee economic efficiency and productivity. The French *Code civil* strongly presented a model of property centred on individual and exclusive rights. This is also visible in the Italian Civil Code of 1865, derived in large part from the French model and consequently adopting a similar conceptualisation of property. Nevertheless, two laws concerning formal papal provinces were passed by Parliament that recognised the commons and cooperative management practices as part of agricultural policy (law of 24 June 1888, n. 5841 and law of 4 August 1894, n. 397). However, these laws were never implemented due to the difficulty encountered in paying the compensation settlements and therefore were suspended a few years later by the law of 8 March 1908, n. 76.

Common land then became the subject of the 1927 law and the implementing regulation (Regal Decree of 26 February 1928, n. 332, hereafter the 1928 decree). Due attention will be paid to this law here because it is the only national statute on common land and it is still in force today. The law was drafted during Mussolini's rule and reflected the agrarian capitalist logic of the time. Its aim was to provide a single legislative framework for both the enclosure of certain commons and the regulation of the remaining ones within the sphere of public law. In doing so, it proposed a simplified and unified vision of the commons, primarily based on the experiences of southern Italy. In southern Italy *civic uses* were rights of common exercised on manorial lands, disentangled from manorial lands by early

[14] Dani, 'Pluralismo giuridico e ricostruzione storica dei diritti collettivi', 12.

nineteenth-century laws related to the abolition of feudalism. Such nineteenth-century legislation influenced the 1927 legislator. The *civic uses* of southern Italy were very different from typologies of commons existing in northern and central Italy, which included also communal properties. However, the 1927 law did not make such a distinction, extending the southern Italian model to the whole country. Such monolithic representation of common land by the 1927 law has been amply criticised in the literature.[15]

Under the 1927 law, a distinction was made between *civic uses* on private property (defined as *jura in re aliena*) and *civic uses* on communally-owned lands (*jura in re propria*). *Civic uses* on private property were subject to dissolution (*liquidazione*), thereby banning situations in which a property would be 'shared' between the owner and the commoners. Article 5 of the 1927 law sets out the method to be used to dissolve the *civic uses*, mainly borrowed from the nineteenth-century laws of southern Italy. The land in question is divided into two parcels (quotas), one of which is left to the owner where no *civic uses* can be exercised, while the other is transferred to the relevant municipality where the rights of commons remain exercisable by the residents (Article 1). The parcel assigned to the municipality has to be commensurate to the value of the *civic uses* dissolved on the quota retained by the owner. The law specifies that compensation should be higher if the *civic uses* are for economic purposes rather than just for subsistence. As an exemption, lands that had been improved and developed can be enjoyed by the owner in perpetuity on condition of paying a stated yearly rent to the municipality (i.e. emphyteusis). The yearly rent should be commensurate to the value of the rights of common previously exercised on the land (Article 7). Although the 1927 law treated this as an exemption, it became the standard procedure to dissolve rights of common due to pressures from agricultural policy.[16] The 1927 law required the *civic uses* to be declared within six months of the publication of the law, hence the timeframe in which to operate was very tight.

As for the community-owned lands (*jura in re propria*), the 1927 law uses the terminology of *civic uses*, which, as already observed, is a distortion and simplification of the varied constructions and practices of property relations in Italian commons. Communal properties are subject to the same regulation as those portions of lands assigned to the state and municipality as per Article 1. All of these communal properties are subdivided into two categories under Article 11. Category A comprises the lands suitable for pasture and forest use, and category B those suitable for cultivation. Category A's lands are defined as inalienable, not acquirable by prescription, indivisible and to be left as forests and grazing lands

[15] See, for example, V. Cerulli Irelli, *Proprietà pubblica e diritti collettivi* (Padova, CEDAM, 1983); and P. Grossi, 'Assolutismo Giuridico e Proprietà Collettive', *Quaderni Fiorentini per la storia del pensiero giuridico moderno*, 19 (1990), 505–556; Marinelli, *Gli usi civici*.

[16] M. A. Lorizio, 'Usi civici', *Enciclopedia Giuridica*, vol. XXXII (Roma, Treccani, 1994), pp. 1–23.

where rights of commons could be exercised within the limits of Article 521 of the 1865 Civil Code, now Article 1021 of the current 1942 Civil Code (i.e. for satisfying the needs of the users and their families). Changes of use for category A lands are only permitted in the name of the public interest under Article 41 of the 1928 decree. Category B's lands are subdivided into parcels (quotas) assigned to individual farmers and therefore privatised.

Finally, the 1927 law has introduced the principle of legitimate occupation, i.e. the occupier *sine titulo* could become the single owner of the land if he/she had occupied the common land for at least ten years and made substantial developments on it (Article 9). The *civic uses* Commissioners, magistrates with administrative and legal functions, were responsible for implementing the 1927 law and settling any disputes regarding the dissolution. The law did not enclose all common lands, but in an effort to prioritise agricultural capitalism and private property, it aimed at abolishing *civic uses* on private land and privatising those commons (category B) that could be used for agriculture. As a consequence of the 1927 law, only category A (non-agricultural commons) should have persisted, to be owned and regulated primarily by state bodies (e.g. the municipality) on behalf of the local community entitled to exercise rights of common over them.

Overall, the 1927 law can be seen as an attempt at subsuming all commons under a single public law regime, derived from the experience of southern Italian states. By including also mountain communal properties within the conceptual parameters of *civic uses*, the law had the effect of undermining the diversity characterising property relations on Italian commons and risked transforming the remaining commons into goods to be owned by the state and subject to public law requirements.

Such public law characterisation of mountain communal properties that the 1927 law called for was strongly opposed by some jurists (notably Gian Gastone Bolla)[17] and by the commoners themselves, whose aim was to prove common ownership of these resources and to be recognised as a private body. Such struggles initially saw some local-level victories (e.g. the legislative decree of 2 May 1948, n. 1105, on the *Regole* of Cadore, recognising that the 1927 law did not apply to these *Regole* and that they could manage the commons according to their own local statutes and by-laws). At the national level, Article 34 of the law of 25 July 1952, n. 991, Article 10 of the law of 3 December 1971, n. 1102 (hereafter the 1971 law) and Article 3 of the law of 31 January 1994, n. 97 (hereafter the 1994 law) recognised that mountain communal properties were to be regulated following their own by-laws and have the juridical status of a private association. The lands were to be used exclusively for agricultural, forest and grazing activities (known in Italian

[17] For a description of the work of Bolla, see C. Trebeschi and A. Trebeschi, 'Appunti per un ricordo di Gian Gastone Bolla', *Archivio Scialoja-Bolla*, 1 (2003), 15–34; and P. Grossi, *Nobiltà del diritto: Profili di giuristi* (Milano, Giuffrè Editore, 2008), pp. 13–18.

law as *agro-sylvan-pastoral* uses) with a view to protecting the environment. This is in line with the law of 8 August 1985, n. 431 (known as the Galasso law) which includes Italian common lands within the list of lands bound by environmental and landscape considerations, therefore limiting their use to agro-sylvan-pastoral activities and assigning them a public interest (environmental) function. Also the Constitutional Court has confirmed the contribution common lands make to environmental protection and therefore their fulfilment of a public interest function.[18]

There is another legislative development that is worth noting as an attempt to overcome the simplifying ethos of the 1927 law. The law of 15 January 1972, n. 11 transferred the administrative functions of the Regional Commissioners and the Commissioners retained only jurisdictional functions to resolve disputes regarding *civic uses*. Assigning the administration of common lands to the regions has contributed to partially overcoming the reductive monolithic conception of the commons endorsed by the 1927 law since each region issues a regional law for the governance of common land reflecting regional and local priorities. However, such devolution has meant that in some cases regions have dedicated only intermittent attention to the subject, and some have used the *change of use* provisions of Article 41 of the 1928 law or the principle of legitimate possession to reduce the number of lands falling within category A.

Traditional commons today

As a consequence of the legislative history of traditional commons, three main typologies of commons exist in Italy today: (1) lands owned by public administrations and in a few cases by private entities[19] over which the local community can exercise rights of common; (2) 'open' collective properties, i.e. civic lands attributed to the community of residents within a municipality or fraction (an administrative unit smaller than the municipality) and often administered by the municipality on behalf of the community; and (3) 'closed' communal properties, i.e. land owned by a specific community with the legal status of a private association. In the first and second cases, all the residents of the municipality or the fraction can exercise rights of common on the lands. The rights of common can therefore be acquired and exercised by those who are not the original inhabitants of the lands but have become residents of the municipality/fraction where the common lands are. The rights of common, which include rights of estovers (the right to cut wood), grazing rights, the right to cut grass, the right to gather wild plants, etc., can be exercised only in so far as they serve to satisfy the vital needs of the rights holders and their families, hence within the limits of Article 1021 of the 1942 Civil Code.

[18] Corte cost. sent. n. 156/1995 and n. 310/2006.

[19] *Civic uses* on private land are however subject to dissolution as per the 1927 law.

In the third case, the status of rights holders is granted to those who are the descendants of the ancient inhabitants of the land. Therefore, rights of common on 'closed' communal properties depend on family lineage. Such 'closed' communal properties are registered under different categories in Italy, reflecting their historical diversity (e.g. *Regole*, *Comunanze*, *Vicinie*, *Partecipanze*, *Corporazioni*). 'Closed' communal properties are very interesting because they have been able to maintain an appropriate degree of political and legal autonomy, being regulated by customary law to be found in local by-laws and statutes, some dating back to the Middle Ages. The majority of 'closed' communal properties today are in the mountain areas of Italy. To a certain extent they represent the quintessential form of communal property and the emblem of successful common-pool resources as defined by Ostrom in her well-known 1990 study.[20] Ostrom, drawing on empirical case studies from different regions of the world, demonstrates how certain commons were able to self-regulate and had strong internal rules that allowed their proper functioning. Ostrom's famous design principles include well-defined boundaries around a community of users, and boundaries around the resource system used, collective choice arrangements, rules governing the use of commons that fit the local needs and conditions, graduated sanctions in case of disobedience, accessible and low-cost means for dispute settlement, etc.[21] Italian 'closed' communal properties satisfy most of these principles which are well set out in their local by-laws and statutes.

To provide an example, the *Regole* d'Ampezzo, a 'closed' communal property in the Veneto region, is governed by local by-laws, known as *Laudi*, dating back to the thirteenth century.[22] There is a general, overarching community *Laudo* as well as a number of more specific ones covering different areas within the communal property. The *Laudi* specify rules regarding the appropriation of resources on the land. The community *Laudo*, approved and modified by the general assembly of the *Regolieri* (the name by which commoners are known in the area), contains norms related to the institutions, decision-making processes and the limits and conditions for the exercise of rights of common. However, rights of common are inherited only by male children of the *Regolieri*, when they turn 25 years old. Women can inherit rights and are registered in the *Regole* Community Land Registry as rights holders only in the event that there are no male descendants in the family (Article 7 of the community *Laudo*). Moreover, if they marry, they can maintain and pass their rights to their offspring only if their husbands are themselves *Regolieri*; otherwise they will lose their rights (Article 7 of the

[20] E. Ostrom, *Governing the Commons: The Evolution of Institutions for Collective Action* (Cambridge, Cambridge University Press, 1990).
[21] Editors' note: For further discussion of Ostrom's design principles, see also Rodgers in this volume.
[22] M. Pieraccini, 'A Politicized, Legal Pluralist Analysis of the Commons' Resilience: The Case of the Regole d'Ampezzo', *Ecology and Society*, 18 (2013): www.ecologyandsociety.org/vol18/iss1/art4/.

community *Laudo*). This gender discrimination is by no means exclusive to the *Regole* d'Ampezzo; it characterises many mountain communal properties.[23] Indeed, the *Laudo* of the *Regole* d'Ampezzo is more open to females than are other *Laudi* of neighbouring communal properties. For example, in the communal property of the *Regole* of Comelico, rights of common are granted to women only if they are widows and have at least one son.[24]

A recent study by Casari and Lisciandra[25] argues that gender discrimination in communal property management in Italian alpine regions[26] has become more intensified in the modern period (since the eighteenth century), while in the late medieval period there were a number of ways in which community members could acquire rights of common, including egalitarian inheritance systems. The switch from an egalitarian to a patrilineal system in inheritance regulations emerged, according to the authors, as an attempt to limit the size of the community, controlling net migration through marriage, and to protect the economic value of communal properties.

Aside from the economic reasons behind the development of patrilineal systems, the problem is that such gender discrimination clashes with Article 3 of the Italian Constitution, which guarantees equal rights to all Italian citizens irrespective of race, gender, language, religion, political inclination and personal and social conditions. This issue has been reviewed by the Constitutional Court.[27] The Court was asked to rule on the constitutional legitimacy of the *Laudo* of the *Regole* d'Ampezzo. The Court ruled that the question was inadmissible taking into account that the *Regole* have the legal status of a private entity and are regulated by norms and customs which are not constitutionally recognised laws. Nevertheless, the *Regole* and other communal properties have a powerful public administrative function considering they have to manage their forests and grazing lands to fulfil environmental protection standards. This is required by national laws (the 1971 law, the Galasso law and the 1994 law), as explained above, and in the specific case of Veneto by the regional law of 19 August 1996, n. 26. These laws, however, though recognising the public interest function of the commons, have not turned the communal properties into an entity regulated by public bodies. Consequently the rules of communal properties cannot be subject to controls of constitutional legitimacy.

[23] Editors' note: For further discussion on gender discrimination in communal property management, see also Xu and Gong in this volume, for examples in the Chinese context, and Pienaar in this volume, for examples in the South African context.

[24] A. Menardi, 'Il Ruolo della donna nelle Regole d'Ampezzo', Regole d'Ampezzo 2002: www.regole.it/DocAppr/ruolodelladonna.pdf.

[25] M. Casari and M. Lisciandra, 'Gender Discrimination in Property Rights: Six Centuries of Commons Governance in the Alps', *Journal of Economic History*, 76 (2016), 559–594.

[26] Their study is primarily concerned with the rights of common in the Trentino region.

[27] Corte cost. sent. n. 917/1998.

From the brief overview of traditional agrarian commons presented above, a number of general considerations emerge. First, the strong link between local customary practices and regulations for commons governance has led to a heterogeneous property rights landscape in Italy. Second, the attempt to simplify such heterogeneity by the 1927 law and repositioning common lands within the parameters of public law has been noted. Third, there are certain legal developments post-1927 that have attempted to overcome the levelling philosophy of the 1927 law. Notable in this respect is the transfer of the administrative functions of common lands to the regions, which, at least theoretically, enables regulatory diversification and more attentiveness to local contexts. Also, it is worth stressing the recognition of mountain communal properties' private juridical status as well as their public interest function under the 1994 law, discussed above. This leaves the traditional common lands somewhere in between the public and private, rendering the justiciability of customary laws a difficult matter in a civil law system, as exemplified by the Constitutional Court ruling on the gender discrimination of the *Regole* d'Ampezzo. It is therefore evident that common lands occupy a complex juridical space, not reconcilable with the orthodox property tradition based on a simplistic civil law distinction between the private–individual and the public–state. The next section introduces the new commons in Italy in order to understand the extent to which they share any traits with traditional agrarian common lands.

The new commons in Italy

'Water as a commons' and the Rodotà Commission[28]

In recent years, the question of the commons (in Italian, *beni comuni*) has become revitalised in political and juridical debates in Italy. Bottom-up movements for the legitimisation of commons have taken concrete forms. Examples include the 2011 referendums where citizens voted, *inter alia*, against the privatisation of water services; the occupation by a diverse range of activists (students, lawyers and artists) of urban cultural spaces such as the Cinema Palazzo and the Valle Theatre in Rome; and the occupation of abandoned and degraded buildings such as former hospitals and monasteries, in Naples and Messina. Another example is the protest movement against the construction of a high-speed rail system in the Susa Valley (Piedmont), seen as an infrastructure project *un-commoning* the alpine landscape. These movements, all employing the discourse of the commons, are explicitly positioning themselves as collective attempts to fight against neoliberal policies and laws. Commons discourses are used as a check on government attempts to sell

[28] 'Acqua bene comune' (translation: 'Water as a commons') is the slogan of the Italian forum against the privatisation of water services. See: www.acquabenecomune.org/.

natural and cultural resources. So, for example, the occupation of the Valle Theatre was a protest against the municipality's decision to lease the theatre to a private operator as a result of the economic crisis. It is not the aim of this section to provide an overview of the varied movements and *commoning* practices currently emerging in Italy, but to provide a few remarkable examples engaging with the notion of property that show how discourses on new commons help to reframe the notion of property, and what role law performs in this reframing.

These examples demonstrate the way in which official law is contested yet at the same time strategically employed, as well as the way in which the discourses on the new commons push for both substantive and procedural changes in an attempt to democratise property.

At the core of the new commons movement in Italy there is a rejection of anachronistic and rigid legal frameworks. The discussions regarding the Civil Code's chapter on property (Chapter 3, Title 2) are emblematic in this respect. The Civil Code defines property according to title, distinguishing between private and public property. The simplistic public/private dichotomy linked to the equation of property with title is rejected by the commons activists promoting a different conceptualisation of property. This different conceptualisation is not only endorsed by dissident marginal groups and counter-hegemonic social movements, but it has been articulated in reformist proposals advanced by the Rodotà Commission in 2007 and even internalised by the Italian Supreme Court (Corte di Cassazione) in 2011, as discussed below. A Commission headed by the jurist Stefano Rodotà was appointed by the Ministry of Justice decree in 2007 with the task of drafting a proposal to reform the Civil Code's provisions on public property (Chapter 3, Title II), never modified since its initial publication in 1942. The obsolete character of Chapter 3 was evident for instance in the lack of inclusion of immaterial goods, explicable because the notion of property in 1942 was anchored to real property, and in the lack of strong protection measures for natural resources (such as water, forests, endangered species and habitats). The reform was also considered as a method to limit the incremental privatisation of public assets in Italy. According to a study carried out by the Accademia Nazionale dei Lincei, between 1992 and 2000 Italy was the leading country worldwide in privatising assets.[29]

Innovatively, the Rodotà Commission proposed a reclassification of property, which abandoned the formal link between property and title, giving prominence to the purpose/function of property and including the commons as a new category.[30] The argument was that the commons did not fit within the category of public

[29] S. Bayley and U. Mattei, 'Social Movements as Constituent Power: The Italian Struggle for the Commons', *Indiana Journal of Global Legal Studies*, 20 (2013), 965–1013.

[30] Article 1(3)(c) of the Commission Bill, Delegated Legislation to Reform the Civil Code Articles Concerning Public Property, Atto Senato n. 2031, XVI Legislatura proposta legislativa: www.senato.it/service/PDF/PDFServer/DF/217244.pdf.

goods. This was because commons should be defined by their social/public function, and hence could also be owned by private bodies as long as they fulfilled a social/public function. According to the Rodotà Commission, the commons are those goods enabling the exercise of fundamental rights, both substantive and procedural, sanctioned by Articles 2 and 3 of the Constitution. The commons are also informed by the principle of intergenerational justice as they involve the interests of future generations. Archaeological, cultural, landscape, and a number of natural resources (air, lakes, forests, etc.) are listed in the Rodotà Commission proposal as commons in what is stated to be a non-exhaustive list. It is worth remarking that ownership is not in question: the commons can be privately owned or property of the state as long as the public use and social function of the commons are guaranteed.

The Rodotà Commission forged strong links between the concept of the commons and the Italian Constitution, not only by referring to Article 3 to emphasise the importance of an egalitarian society, but also by emphasising that the Constitution does recognise the social function of property in Article 42. Article 42 of the Italian Constitution does divide property into public and private but it also states that 'Private property is recognised and guaranteed by the law, which prescribes the ways it is acquired, enjoyed *and its limitations so as to ensure its social function and make it accessible to all*' (emphasis added). Even though the Rodotà proposal has never been discussed in Parliament, one could infer that it was Rodotà's creative reading of the Constitution and its reformist attempts that greatly influenced the judgment of the Supreme Court in the case concerning the fishing valleys of Venice, discussed below.

The new commons in court

The case discussed here relates to the disputed juridical nature of fishing valleys on the margins of the Venetian lagoon. Fishing valleys are areas of land with bodies of water surrounded by barriers. The public administration claimed that the valleys were state property as they are part of the maritime domain, as sanctioned by Article 28 of the Italian Navigation Code. Under the Italian Civil Code, the goods of the public maritime domain are not available for purchase and are under state ownership (Article 822 and Article 823). On the other hand, fish farming companies claimed ownership of those valleys on the basis of a title of ownership registered in the land registry since the nineteenth century. The legitimate expectation of the companies was also validated by the customary practice of granting individuals title to the fishing valleys and tolerating their continued occupation and use of them since the fifteenth century. This conflict was resolved by the Italian Supreme Court in 2011 by reference to the commons. It was the first time that the Court had engaged with the concept of the commons to resolve an ownership dispute.[31] What is interesting in this case is that the Italian Supreme Court provided an expansive reading of the meaning of property, drawing on the concept of the commons and key constitutional principles. However, despite the innovative reasoning, the Court's answer was not entirely satisfactory, remaining trapped in the existing property categories defined in the Civil Code and deciding that the valleys were under state ownership. The possible limitations of the Court interpretation are highlighted by a subsequent decision reached on the same issue by the European Court of Human Rights (ECHR).[32]

When deciding the case, the Supreme Court drew on the commons discourse to disentangle property from title and therefore, apparently, to overcome the private/public dichotomy sanctioned by the Civil Code. The Court concluded that the valleys have a public-collectivist function and purpose and, as such, are commons regardless of their private or public ownership. The judgment, as translated by the author, reads:

> A real estate (immovable property), independently of the title, due to its intrinsic connotations, in particular the environmental and landscape ones, is aimed at the realisation of the social state. Such a good, beyond the outdated perspectives of the Roman law *dominium* and of the Civil Code, is a commons, i.e. it is instrumentally connected to the realisation of the public interest, independently of its title.

This purpose-oriented reading of property was supported in the Supreme Court's judgment by reference to key constitutional principles, namely fundamental rights (Article 2), landscape protection, today interpreted as including the environment (Article 9), and property rights (Article 42), thereby giving rise to an understanding of the public good, 'not only as an object of the state but as an instrument aimed at the realisation of the constitutional values'.

It was on this basis that the Supreme Court confirmed that the fishing valleys are state property, as the state-collectivity (in Italian, *stato-collettivita*), not the state-apparatus/institution (in Italian, *stato-apparato*), is the best institution to represent the public interest and protect the valleys' social and environmental functions as constitutionally acknowledged. Therefore, the Supreme Court rested its reasoning on overcoming the outdated private/public distinction by emphasising the purpose of a good over its formal categorisation according to title in the Civil Code and emphasised the role of the state in representing the collectivity and the public interest. Nevertheless, de facto it opted for and confirmed state ownership, requiring the fishing company to pay compensation to the public authorities.

Subsequently, one of the fishing companies (Valle Pierimpiè S.p.a.) alleged a violation of Article 1, Protocol 1 ECHR before the ECHR, arguing that it had

[31] Cass. civile sez. un., n. 3665/2011.

[32] *Valle Pierimpiè Società Agricola S.p.a. v Italy*, application no. 46154/11 (23 September 2014). The judgment is available only in French and in Italian.

been deprived of its property without being compensated for the expropriation and actually having to pay compensation to the public authorities for unlawful occupancy of the valley.[33] Although the Strasbourg Court, similarly to the Italian Supreme Court, recognised the importance of protecting the environment and the 'public-facing' purpose of the valleys (para 67), thereby finding legitimate the action of the state, also in light of Article 28 of the Navigation Code, the transfer of the valley to state ownership was found to constitute a manifestly disproportionate interference with Article 1, Protocol 1. The ECHR further held that the state had not struck a fair balance between the public and private interests at stake and that an excessive and impracticable burden had been imposed on the company. Taking the point of disentangling property from title seriously, the ECHR pointed out that it is not important whether a good is characterised as privately or state owned; what matters is whether it can fulfil its public-facing purpose. Therefore, the key for the ECHR is to resolve the issue not by opting for the state ownership of the good, as the Italian Supreme Court did, but by making sure that the management system places obligations and restrictions on the owner to safeguard the public interest.

In a sense, we could argue that the ECHR goes a step further than the Supreme Court in overcoming outdated and rigid understandings of property and refocusing the discourse on management rather than ownership. At the same time, the Italian Supreme Court, by explicitly invoking the commons, and providing an expansive reading of property, also broke new ground. Besides, it could be argued that by speaking about the 'state-collectivity', it proposed an understanding of the state not so removed from that found in the doctrine of public trust, where the state holds the natural resources in trust for the public. Moreover, the Italian Supreme Court reliance on constitutional principles to justify a new understanding of property beyond title is clearly reminiscent of the Rodotà Commission proposed reform of Chapter 3 of the Civil Code.

'Like water and like air. Let's free culture'[34]

The discourse of the commons in Italy, however, also moves beyond these reformist attempts and constitutionally-based readings of property. The more radical proponents in the commons movement, possibly sceptical of unsuccessful reformist attempts (e.g. lack of discussion in Parliament of the Rodotà Commission proposal), propose that one should not assume certain ontological characteristics determining what commons are, as the commons derive from contexts and prac-

[33] *Valle Pierimpiè Società Agricola S.p.a. v Italy*.
[34] Slogan used by the Valle Theatre occupants.

tices of commoning, practices of sharing and participatory initiatives.[35] The accent is therefore squarely placed on processes of commons' emergence, and a link made between property and deliberative democracy. The commons cannot be essentialised and reduced to a tangible proportion of the external world, and the aim is to enable their emergence via deliberative participatory decision-making practices and shared governance to fulfil their social functions. Right of access to the goods therefore is not the only variable to be taken into account, as rights of access to decision-making are also important in processes of *commoning*. As one of the main radical proponents of the commons writes: 'the commons project must be as much about a new framework for participatory government as alternative property rights arrangements'.[36]

For Mattei what distinguishes the commons from state and private goods is their inclusive character, both procedurally and substantially. The commons, unlike private goods and some public goods, are not commodities and cannot be reduced to the language of ownership. They express a qualitative relation.[37] The relational character of the commons that defies Cartesian dualisms of the subject (private owner, state) and object (territory) no longer sees the commons as a third way, alongside state and private property. The commons are conceptualised as 'a weapon of revolutionary theory and praxis' to develop a new vision rooted neither in the positivistic world of the 'is' nor in the ideological world of the 'ought to be' but in the creative and generative world of the 'could be'.[38]

To a certain extent, this revolutionary potential is embodied in urban occupations carried out in the name of cultural commons, for example the Cinema Palazzo and Valle Theatre in Rome, the Macao in Milan and the Marinoni Theatre in Venice. There, the occupiers are not contesting the property title but are interested in affirming these spaces as cultural commons in the sense of guaranteeing collective/public use determined through participatory decision-making. Interestingly some of these spaces have developed, or at least have aimed to develop, their own internal rules, their own by-laws, as in the case of the Foundation established in the Valle Theatre in Rome, which drafted a Statute to legitimise its legal status as a not-for-profit organisation as defined in Article 10 of the legislative decree of December 1997, n. 460.[39] The Statute was written through participatory mechanisms, with drafts discussed online, to make it a collective writing effort. The Statute defines the Foundation's aims and activities, membership rules, and bodies operating as part of the Foundation, and contains articles related to the drafting of

[35] U. Mattei, 'I beni comuni fra economia, diritto e filosfia', *Spazio Filosofico* (2013), 111–116: http://labont.it/wordpress/wp-content/uploads/2013/01/Mattei.pdf.

[36] Mattei, *Beni comuni*.

[37] Mattei, *Beni comuni*.

[38] Mattei, 'I beni comuni fra economia, diritto e filosfia'.

[39] Statuto Fondazione Teatro Valle Bene Comune: www.teatrovalleoccupato.it/wp-content/uploads/2013/10/STATUTO-FONDAZIONE-TEATRO-VALLE-BENE-COMUNE.pdf.

internal regulations and administration of funds. It is therefore possible to witness the attempt to develop a new internal normative order for the self-organisation of the Foundation. Such a normative order is however very porous, selectively borrowing from existing legal orders. The Preamble of the Statute indeed refers to the principles of the Italian Constitution to guide the work of the Valle Theatre as a commons. Article 43 of the Italian Constitution on the establishment of new enterprises for the common good is considered as the legal basis for the creation of the Foundation.[40] Interestingly, therefore, even these more radical *commoning* movements do not reject the law altogether, but attempt to engage with key constitutional principles.

To give another example, in Naples the occupation of an abandoned building, the former kindergarten Filangeri (*ex-asilo Filangeri*), which was then transformed into a cultural commons, was legitimised by the local administration with a municipal resolution of 2012.[41] The municipality recognises the former kindergarten as a space dedicated to democratic and participative cultural expression, defining culture as a commons. More recently, a second resolution of the municipality of Naples recognised the self-governmental arrangements of the former kindergarten, as established in a Declaration written collectively over three years by the occupants.[42] Not dissimilarly from the Statute of the Valle Theatre, the Declaration of the former kindergarten Filangeri engages creatively with constitutional principles.[43]

Conclusion: properties of Italian commons

This chapter has attempted to investigate the meaning of property and property relations in Italian commons, considering both traditional agricultural commons and new commons. There are a number of similarities between traditional and new commons that can be discerned. First, the model of property proposed by both traditional and new commons departs from an ownership model based on the right to exclude and an economic view of property as alienable commodity. Second, sustainability is a core element in both traditional agrarian and new commons. In traditional Italian commons this is visible in the principle of inalienability and indivisibility of the land; in the requirement to use commons to satisfy agro-sylvan-pastoral needs; and in the legal recognition of the environmental protection

[40] Article 43 of the Constitution reads: 'For the purposes of the common good, the law may establish that an enterprise or a category thereof be, through a pre-emptive decision or compulsory purchase authority with provision of compensation, reserved to the Government, a public agency, a workers' or users' association, provided that such enterprise operates in the field of essential public services, energy sources or monopolies and is of general public interest.'

[41] Resolution of the Municipality of Naples of 24 May 2012, n. 400.

[42] Resolution of the Municipality of Naples of 27 December 2015, n. 893.

[43] Dichiarazione d'uso civico dell'Asilo 2016: www.exasilofilangieri.it/regolamento-duso-civico/.

functions the commons fulfil. In the discourses of new commons, sustainability also figures predominantly as the commons are suitable spaces to satisfy essential human needs (whether access to vital resources such as water, or human dignity).

In regard to the differences between traditional and new commons, the key issue is the type of actors involved and their substantive and procedural property rights. The traditional commons are an example of limited-access commons where the key actors/beneficiaries are the members of a restricted community, identified through residence requirements or determined by agnatic relationships. Although some mountain communal properties satisfy Ostrom's design principles, considerations of democratic decision-making and equality do not necessarily come into play, as exemplified by gender discrimination in regard to the distribution of rights of common in northern alpine common properties. By contrast, the beneficiaries of the new commons are the public as a whole (the rights of access to the commons are to be held by all, irrespective of *ius solis* or *ius sanguinis*), and they therefore represent an example of open-access commons. Deliberative democracy, as much as distributive justice, is a key consideration in the formation and management of the new commons. In the new commons the public at large are not only entitled to have use rights but also democratic control over decision-making.[44] The fusion between the substantive and procedural dimensions in the conceptualisation of rights in new commons derives from the social function that is attributed to property. As the commons are to be a form of property that fulfils human rights, involves the interests of future generations, and enables collective access and protection of resources valuable to all, it follows that democratic and inclusive decision-making procedures are needed to achieve such aims. The new commons' understanding of property therefore has deliberative democracy built-in because the commons are resources that are fundamental not to a particular individual or a specific, geographically bounded group, but to all, and they therefore need to be managed by all. The discourses and practices of new commons attempt to democratise property, both substantially and procedurally.

To a certain extent the Italian new commons wave can be understood as a form of open commons as discussed by the scholarship on knowledge/cultural commons.[45] Such scholarship has explored knowledge commons such as Wikipedia and open source software, stressing their openness to an undefined class of users, in contrast to limited-access commons where a defined set of claimants lay claims in common. As Frischmann et al. explain,

[44] A. Di Robilant, 'Property and Deliberation: A New Type of Common Ownership', in S. Bailey, G. Farrell and U. Mattei (eds), *Protecting Future Generations through Commons* (Strasbourg: Council of Europe, 2013), pp. 61–79.

[45] See, for example, Y. Benkler, 'The Political Economy of Commons', *Upgrade*, 4 (2003), 6–9; B. Frischmann, M. J. Madison and K. Strandburg (eds), *Governing Knowledge Commons* (New York, Oxford University Press, 2014); M. J. Madison, B. Frischmann and K. Strandburg, 'Constructing Commons in the Cultural Environment', *Cornell Law Review*, 95 (2010), 657–709.

> unlike commons in the natural resource environment, knowledge commons arrangements usually must create a governance structure within which participants not only share existing resources but also engage in producing those resources and, indeed, in determining their character. In fact, knowledge commons members often come together for the very purpose of creating particular kinds of knowledge resources.[46]

However, there is a key difference between knowledge commons and the Italian new commons. Whereas knowledge commons are generally intangible commons and the community of users is produced by abstract connection to the resource (i.e. knowledge) rather than by physical proximity to the resource, the new Italian commons are embodied in physical spaces, be these theatres, hospitals, or former monasteries. The occupation of physical spaces and the use of these spaces for cultural activities is a fundamental prerequisite for the creation of the commons. Whereas, for knowledge commons, the embodiment of knowledge in tangible products is a challenge, embodiment in material spaces is fundamental to the very existence of Italian new commons.[47] In Italy, the very act of occupying physical spaces is part of the commoning project so that the spaces can be opened up to the public and fulfil their social function.

This by no means should be interpreted as claiming that only new commons fulfil a social function. As has been stated, the environmental protection function of traditional commons is recognised in Italian law. However, this is not their primary and only function considering that historically they have developed to fulfil the essential needs of a given, bounded community. Besides, traditional commons are not so preoccupied with procedural democracy and constitutional principles, which are foundational issues for proponents of Italian new commons.

The new commons lack a precise juridical base and the attempt at inserting the category of the commons into the property chapter of the Civil Code has not been successful. Clearly a legal clarification of the new commons would considerably strengthen their position. Consequently, some Italian scholars have proposed the application of key principles governing *civic uses* (such as sustainable access to the resource, collective belonging, inalienability of the good, etc.) to new commons.[48] However, applying traditional commons principles to new commons risks conflating different ways of constructing property relationships, one primarily based on regulating common rights to land with a view to promoting the sustainability of the local community and local resources, and the other based on a political effort to democratise property, both substantially and procedurally. Applying property law principles from traditional commons to new commons can therefore

[46] B. Frischmann, M. J. Madison and K. Strandburg, 'Governing Knowledge Commons', in Frischmann et al., *Governing Knowledge Commons*, pp. 1–44 at p. 16.
[47] Frischmann et al., 'Governing Knowledge Commons', p. 17.
[48] Marinelli, 'Usi civici e beni comuni'; Cerulli-Irelli and De Lucia, 'Beni comuni e dirittti collettivi'.

turn into a reductionist endeavour, which would undermine the democratic efforts championed by the new commons movement.

This chapter has exposed the fundamental traits of traditional and new commons in Italy to provide a comprehensive overview of the field and to search for similarities and differences. Points of contact between traditional and new commons exist, first and foremost the attempt to transcend the public/private dichotomy to be found in the Civil Code and to propose alternative property relations based on sustainable use, rather than title. However, the chapter has stressed that there are also key differences related to the actors involved, the weight assigned to democratic decision-making, as well as the relationship with constitutional principles. These differences render any attempt at subsuming traditional and new commons under a unified normative framework problematic, leaving open the search for a normative framework, or better normative frameworks, for new commons. As has been considered above, a key problem of the 1927 law on traditional commons has been its simplifying philosophy. It would therefore be paradoxical if a similar reductionism were to be applied to new commons.

4

Property in the Kibbutz: Old and New

ABRAHAM BELL, GIDEON PARCHOMOVSKY
AND BENJAMIN WEITZ

Introduction

The kibbutz, while bearing resemblance to communes that can be found around the world, is a uniquely Israeli invention.[1] Kibbutzim (kibbutzim is plural for kibbutz, which translates, literally, as 'collective') are agricultural communes that first developed in the land of Israel a century ago, before the establishment of the state. Traditionally, a kibbutz was made up of a limited number of families gathered to live communally and operate a collective farm. Martin Buber, a renowned Israeli philosopher and ideologue, famously stated that a kibbutz should never grow beyond the point at which every member knows every other member.[2] In 1920, there were only twelve kibbutzim in Israel with a total membership of roughly 800 people (which represented 1.5 per cent of the Jewish population at that time). According to the most recent census data, in 2005, there are roughly 270 kibbutzim in Israel, with a total population of approximately 118,000 (which equals 2.2 per cent of the Jewish population of Israel) and land holdings of about 550,000 acres.[3] The largest kibbutz in terms of its population was Maagan Michael with 1,340 members, and the smallest was Kibbutz Natur with a membership of only 48 people.[4]

The traditional kibbutz was Marxist in orientation. It operated on the principle of 'from each according to his ability, to each according to his needs'.[5] Later, as society changed throughout the initial pioneering generations into the 1980s, and

[1] D. Gavron, *The Kibbutz: Awakening from Utopia* (Lanham, MD, Rowman & Littlefield, 2000), p. 5.
[2] B. Zimmerman, 'A Kibbutz Cannot Be Larger Beyond the Size That Every Member Knows Every Other Member' (7 February 2008): www.kibbutz.org.il/cgi-webaxy/sal/sal.pl?lang=he&ID=3&act=show&dbid=pages&dataid=itonut_2008_dafyarok_080207_buber&findWords=%D7%92%D7%93%D7%99 (Hebrew). Editors' note: For a discussion on communes in China, see Xu and Gong in this volume.
[3] 'Kibbutzim and Their Population: Demographic Change from 1961–2005' (June 2008): www.cbs.gov.il/publications/kib05/pdf/h_print.pdf (Hebrew).
[4] Kibbutzim and Their Population: Demographic Change from 1961–2005, pp. 51–52.
[5] R. Russell, R. Hanneman and S. Getz, *The Renewal of the Kibbutz* (Brunswick, NJ, Rutgers University Press, 2013), p. 2.

Proceedings of the British Academy, **216**, 58–78.

the kibbutzim fell into a deep economic crisis, they endorsed a more free-market, capitalist way of thinking, with some kibbutzim, such as Kfar Ruppin, going as far as turning themselves into limited liability companies (LLC) with shares distributed to members.[6] Over time, most kibbutzim have adopted new economic and property arrangements as part of the so-called 'renewed kibbutz' movement, which is not so much a renewal as a reinvention. Today, most kibbutzim allow for private ownership of houses, and private ownership of kibbutz assets, while still providing an economic and social safety net for their members.

From the outset, kibbutzim developed a diverse set of property institutions in order to allocate use rights to their members. While the kibbutz was a collective legal entity that owned all kibbutz assets, kibbutzim had to develop some means of allocating asset-related rights and duties among members. The internal property arrangements of kibbutzim are a striking example of a localised property arrangement – a ubiquitous phenomenon of limited, non-standard property regimes that coexist alongside and within state property laws.[7] The existence of these unique property arrangements tasked the Israeli courts with the need to decipher, construe and enforce them within the official state system, whenever disputes transcended the boundaries of the kibbutz. We collectively refer to these tasks as the challenge of translation.

Disputes about kibbutz rights that have reached Israeli courts provide some excellent examples of translation problems. To give just one example by means of introduction, in *Rotem v Kibbutz Sdot Yam*, the Supreme Court of Israel ruled that beneficiaries of a testamental gift of all the testatrix's possessions could claim no rights in her house in the kibbutz because the kibbutz owned all rights in the realty, and the internal kibbutz property arrangements 'owned' by the testatrix consisted solely of temporary, personal use rights.[8] In other words, whatever rights the deceased may have had under the kibbutz's internal system for allocating property rights, the court found that the rights had neither value nor effect within broader Israeli laws of inheritance and property. The surviving daughter was thus left homeless.[9]

Over time, many of the internal norms and allocations have changed, as kibbutzim have become less 'collectivised' and economic forces have prompted most kibbutzim to alter their internal property arrangements and adopt, in their stead, the conventional property rules of the state. This trend has led to the emergence of the 'renewed kibbutz'. Yet, even the 'renewed kibbutz' features a set of unique

[6] Gavron, *The Kibbutz*, pp. 216–218.

[7] A. Bell and G. Parchomovsky, 'Property Lost in Translation', *University of Chicago Law Review*, 80 (2013), 515–573 at 516.

[8] *Rotem v Kibbutz Sdot Yam*, CA 5747/08 21 (2010): http://elyon1.court.gov.il/files/08/470/057/t04/08057470.t04.pdf.

[9] *Rotem v Kibbutz Sdot Yam*.

internal property institutions worthy of examination. Furthermore, as we will show, property disputes arising out of the unique rules and allocations that have been adopted by kibbutzim continue to preoccupy Israeli courts and challenge Israeli judges. Finally, the economic realignment of kibbutzim has itself been a major source of litigation in Israel, with the Supreme Court approving some,[10] but not other economic arrangements.[11] Throughout, the issue of translating internal property rights has remained at the forefront.

In this chapter, we explore the internal property arrangements of kibbutzim and the way in which they interact with the property arrangements of the wider society. We begin by looking at the evolution of the property regime in kibbutzim from communal property to private property. After turning to the particulars of internal property arrangements, we examine the limits that the Israeli Supreme Court placed in 2004 on the power of kibbutzim to develop their land, as well as cases that have followed this important decision and have attempted to solve some of the translation problems that the renewed kibbutz poses in regard to the relationship between labour and property rights, and individual property rights in kibbutz homes. A short conclusion ensues.

The traditional collective kibbutz

Traditional kibbutz life was austere. Kibbutz members were rotated through all jobs, from accounting to dishwashing.[12] Children were raised communally, spending relatively little time with their biological parents.[13] Clothing was simple and provided by the kibbutz.[14] Members were given a small allowance for basic needs, unconnected to the work they performed or the value they produced for the kibbutz.[15] All members were entitled to housing, food, clothing, and educational and cultural activities.[16] Kibbutz life was animated by an ideology of radical formal equality, patriotism, Marxism, romantic attraction to 'working the land', and self-

[10] *United Mizrahi Bank v Migdal Cooperative Village* (CA 6821/93, 1908/94, 3363/94) (1995) (Hebrew).
[11] *Association for a New Discourse for a Democratic Discourse in Israel et al. v The Minister of National Infrastructure* (HCJ 244/00).
[12] T. Simons and P. Ingram, 'Enemies of the State: The Interdependence of Institutional Forms and the Ecology of the Kibbutz, 1910–1997', *Administrative Science Quarterly*, 48 (2003), 592–621 at 593, citing A. D. Gordon, *Selected Essays*, 63 (League for Labour Palestine, 1938; trans. Frances Burnce).
[13] B. Bettelheim, *Children of the Dream* (New York, Simon & Schuster, 2001), pp. 31–34 ; S. L. Maital and M. H. Bornstein, 'The Ecology of Collaborative Child Rearing: A Systems Approach to Child Care on the Kibbutz', *Ethos*, 31 (2003), 274–306 at 277.
[14] See M. E. Spiro, 'Utopia and Its Discontents: The Kibbutz and Its Historical Vicissitudes', *American Anthropologist*, 106 (2004), 556–568 at 557.
[15] See Spiro, 'Utopia and Its Discontents', 557. See also B. Turniansky and J. Cwikel, 'Volunteering in a Voluntary Community: Kibbutz Members and Voluntarism', *Voluntas*, 7 (1996), 300–317 at 302.
[16] Gavron, *The Kibbutz*, p. 2.

sacrifice. While communes are not unknown to the world, the kibbutz was unique because of its centrality to life in Israel: '[w]here other communes rejected society and retreated from it, the kibbutz embraced society and sought to lead it'.[17] In Israel, 'kibbutz members played crucial roles in every sector of life in the Jewish community in Palestine . . . and, later on, in the state of Israel, including in the legislative and executive branches'.[18] Kibbutz members were viewed in Israeli society as both highly patriotic and as salt of the earth; they were historically overrepresented in the most demanding and dangerous army units and quite a few ascended to key roles in Israeli politics. In the early years of the state, kibbutzim enjoyed rapid growth, growing to 67,550 members and 214 kibbutzim by 1950.[19] At the height of the kibbutz movement, the percentage of the national population that lived on kibbutzim was 7 per cent, but the 7 per cent who lived on kibbutzim had a disproportionate influence on the affairs of the country.[20] However, by the 1960s, the rapid growth began to stall.[21]

The kibbutz was traditionally run in a completely collective manner in which 'the kibbutz belonged to all its members, and each member was personally responsible to the collective'.[22] Rather than putting the decision-making power in the hands of one person, decisions were made by a general assembly, in which all members could participate, and which was run based on a managerial rotation.[23] A unique property regime lay at the heart of the kibbutz movement and undergirded its economic operation. The traditional kibbutz was predicated on 'common-property holding and communal way of life'.[24] Kibbutz members were to 'hold and manage all property . . . together and share its benefits equally with no direct link to their labour or any other contribution to communal life'.[25] Ownership of private property was prohibited and the members' income from all jobs, both within the kibbutz and outside of it, went to a common account.[26] In the model by-laws created by the kibbutz federation in the 1970s, there was a prohibition against individuals owning assets separable from collective kibbutz property.[27] Article 53 stated that kibbutz members had to transfer their property to the kibbutz upon

[17] Gavron, *The Kibbutz*, p. 4.
[18] T. Dagan and A. Margalit, 'Tax, State, and Utopia', *Virginia Tax Review*, 33 (2010), 549–578 at 562.
[19] R. Edwards, *Kibbutz Movement*, in S. C. Tucker (ed.), *The Encyclopedia of the Arab-Israeli Conflict: A Political, Social, and Military History* (Santa Barbara, CA, ABC-CLIO, 2008), p. 581.
[20] Gavron, *The Kibbutz*, p. 4.
[21] Gavron, *The Kibbutz*, p. 6.
[22] Gavron, *The Kibbutz*, p. 2.
[23] U. Leviatan, 'Kibbutzim as a Real-Life Utopia: Survival Depends on Adherence to Utopian Values', *Psychology and Developing Societies*, 25(2) (2013), 249–281 at 252.
[24] Dagan and Margalit, 'Tax, State, and Utopia', 562.
[25] Dagan and Margalit, 'Tax, State, and Utopia', 562.
[26] Dagan and Margalit, 'Tax, State, and Utopia', 562.
[27] R. Russell, R. Hanneman and S. Getz, *The Renewal of the Kibbutz* (New Brunswick, NJ, Rutgers University Press, 2013), p. 83.

becoming members and Article 42 stated that a member had no capital rights in the kibbutz.[28] In the traditional kibbutz, resources were distributed based on members' needs and the kibbutz's financial health. The primary goal of the kibbutz was to give its members a high quality of life, as opposed to making a profit.[29] The kibbutz thus blended several ideals held dear by early twentieth-century Zionists: the return of the Jewish people to the land, connecting with the land by non-exploitative labour, and communism.[30] The property regime adopted by kibbutzim made it very difficult for members to leave the kibbutz as they had no property or savings they could take with them. It also made it nearly impossible for individual members to secure funding from banks or financial institutions as they had no privately owned assets they could use as collateral for loans. So while the property regime of the kibbutz was consistent with the overarching ideology of the kibbutz movement, it also had the effect of locking members in and stifling the potential for private entrepreneurship and enterprise.

The renewed kibbutz and privatisation

In the 1980s, the kibbutzim fell into a deep economic crisis.[31] Several factors contributed to the crisis, including longstanding economic mismanagement, and a changed social environment in which the younger generation of kibbutz-dwellers lost their parents' ideological commitment to a communist lifestyle, leading to the greying of the kibbutz population.[32] There was a great 'brain drain' in the kibbutzim as many of the more talented members left, while the weaker members remained and took advantage of the support networks of the kibbutz.[33] The kibbutzim had run into economic difficulties before, and, in fact, had been bailed out by the government in the 1950s.

The 1980s crisis was different, however, as it came against the background of a national economic crisis characterised by hyperinflation. In 1985, the national government adopted an austerity plan that proved successful in ending the hyperinflation.[34] While the plan saved Israel's national economy, as in all cases where runaway inflation is successfully combated, it hurt massive debtors, as they lost the ability to escape debts by relying on a devalued currency. The kibbutzim were

[28] Russell et al., *The Renewal of the Kibbutz*, p. 83.
[29] Dagan and Margalit, 'Tax, State, and Utopia', 566.
[30] Gideon Witkon, '"Allocating Assets" in the Kibbutz – A False Illusion, or Unpreventable Structural Changes', The Ben-Shemesh Institute for the Study of Land Policy and Land Use (2001), 18–38 at 20 (Hebrew).
[31] E. Ben-Rafael, 'Kibbutz: Survival at Risk', *Israel Studies*, 16(2) (2011), 81–108 at 82.
[32] Gavron, *The Kibbutz*, pp. 143–146.
[33] Russell et al., *The Renewal of the Kibbutz*, p. 76.
[34] Gavron, *The Kibbutz*, p. 145.

particularly vulnerable, as they had incurred many fixed interest loans at high interest rates on the assumption that inflation would continue to rise.[35] During the 1980s the debts of many kibbutzim quickly doubled, forcing them to take out even more loans, and thereby increasing their debt.[36] Worse yet, kibbutzim were often guarantors of the debt of other kibbutzim, which only served to exacerbate the crisis.[37]

The government bailed out the kibbutzim with debt restructuring plans adopted in 1989[38] and then again in 1994–1996,[39] after the first proved insufficient. The plans included several elements, the most important of which was debt forgiveness, accomplished by a combination of 'haircuts' to creditor banks' loans and government repayment from state funds in lieu of payment by the kibbutzim. Other elements of the plans included refinancing kibbutz debts at lower interest rates and over longer periods of time, and the surrender of some kibbutz assets. Both the kibbutzim and the banks were forced to accept some degree of oversight to prevent recurrence of the financial crisis, and the kibbutzim gave up some of the inter-kibbutz subsidies that had obscured identification of the most poorly managed kibbutzim. One of the most important aspects of the 1996 agreement was the surrender of kibbutz lands in high value areas back to the Israel Lands Authority which had original ownership over the kibbutz land.[40]

Even with the government bailouts, the kibbutzim had to make significant changes. Many kibbutzim could no longer afford the generous package of social services they had previously offered their members, and it was no longer possible to finance day-to-day operations with credit. Faced with this new economic reality, most kibbutzim were forced to adopt new models of economic activity that would allow them to operate in accordance with their means. The kibbutzim developed new methods of economic management, together with partial privatisation. These changes, which constituted a substantial retreat from the original Marxist vision of kibbutzim, were labelled a 'renewal', and today, many kibbutzim are officially labelled 'renewed' kibbutzim.[41]

The renewed kibbutz abandoned the historic property regime that was the hallmark of kibbutzim, and replaced it with private ownership of houses and kibbutz assets. It also adopted individualised salaries, and cut back on the social services offered to members. These reforms, and in particular the adoption of individualised salaries, enabled the stronger and younger members of kibbutzim to stay in the

[35] Gavron, *The Kibbutz*, p. 145.
[36] M. H. Ashkenazi and Y. Katz, 'From Cooperative to Renewed Kibbutz: The Case of Kibbutz "Galil", Israel', *Middle Eastern Studies*, 45(4) (2009), 571–592 at 576–577.
[37] Russell et al., *The Renewal of the Kibbutz*, p. 40.
[38] Ashkenazi and Katz, 'From Cooperative to Renewed Kibbutz', 578.
[39] Ashkenazi and Katz, 'From Cooperative to Renewed Kibbutz', 579.
[40] Gavron, *The Kibbutz*, p. 145.
[41] R. Russell, R. Hanneman and S. Getz, 'The Transformation of the Kibbutzim', *Israel Studies*, 16(2) (2011), 109–126 at 115.

kibbutz by guaranteeing that their higher earnings would primarily benefit them and would not be evenly distributed among all members of the kibbutz. At the same time, kibbutzim continued to provide a social safety net to members 'and an internal redistribution scheme through a community tax imposed on members who earn higher wages'.[42] The new approach was in stark contrast to the idea of the traditional kibbutz in which all property was common property owned by the kibbutz. While the traditional kibbutz had been defined as 'a cooperative society that is a separate settlement, organised on the basis of collective ownership of assets, self-employment, equality and cooperation in production, consumption, and education',[43] the renewed kibbutz was defined as:

> A cooperative society that is a separate settlement, organised on the basis of collective partnership in assets, self-employment, equality and cooperation in production, consumption and education, that maintains mutual responsibilities among its members and whose articles of association include some or all of the following:
>
> (1) Relative wages according to individual contribution or seniority;
> (2) Allocation of apartments;
> (3) Allocation of means of production to its members, excluding land, water and production quotas, provided that the cooperative maintains control over the means of production and that its articles of association restrict the negotiability of allocated means of production.[44]

A third type of kibbutz also emerged over time and is now recognised under Israeli law – the 'mixed' kibbutz, which is partially privatised, and contains elements of both the collective and renewed kibbutz.[45] The mixed kibbutz has not become popular as it remains stuck between the traditional collective kibbutz, and the renewed kibbutz, taking pieces from the ideologies of each.[46] Overall, the mixed kibbutz has failed as a viable alternative to the collective kibbutz, and, at best, can be seen as a transitional step for kibbutzim who make the change from collective to differential salaries.[47]

Regardless of whether they are collective or renewed, kibbutzim continue to enjoy the benefit of favourable regulatory treatment by the state in many areas. For instance, kibbutz members are exempt from the payment of individual income tax. Instead, the kibbutz as a whole pays taxes on behalf of all its members, with each member being imputed an equal share of the total kibbutz income.[48]

The movement towards capitalism on kibbutzim has been rapid. In 1995, of 249

[42] Dagan and Margalit, 'Tax, State, and Utopia', 552.
[43] Russell et al., 'The Transformation of the Kibbutzim', 115.
[44] Russell et al., 'The Transformation of the Kibbutzim', 115–116.
[45] Russell et al., 'The Transformation of the Kibbutzim', 113.
[46] Russell et al., *The Renewal of the Kibbutz*, p. 88.
[47] Russell et al., *The Renewal of the Kibbutz*, p. 88.
[48] Dagan and Margalit, 'Tax, State, and Utopia', 568.

kibbutzim, two were classified as 'renewed', and all the others as traditional.[49] By 2010, however, of 248 kibbutzim, only 53 were traditional cooperative kibbutzim; 186 were renewed kibbutzim; and nine were mixed.[50] While privatisation appears to have staved off economic collapse, the demographic challenge remains, with the younger generation lacking the commitment to kibbutz life displayed in the earliest years of kibbutzim.[51]

The introduction of differential payments and safety net budgets

In one of the earliest steps towards privatisation, members of kibbutzim were awarded personal cash allowances that they could spend in any way they desired, rather than just receiving all of their services for free. These 'salaries', however, were awarded on the basis of need, or given on a completely egalitarian basis. In the early 1990s, the kibbutzim Ein Zivan and Snir broke this model by granting members differential salaries based on the jobs they performed.[52] The differential salaries were also influenced by seniority and overall contribution to the kibbutz.[53] By 2010, 72 per cent of kibbutzim had adopted differential salaries for members. The blow represented by differential salaries was softened by the simultaneous adoption of a 'safety net' budget.[54] By 2010, 75 per cent of kibbutzim had safety net budgets.[55] These safety net budgets were created by taxes collected from working kibbutz members, with rates progressively increasing with the members' incomes.[56] The safety net budget was also used to subsidise the salaries of kibbutz members whose incomes fell below the national minimum.[57] Safety net budgets usually go along with other important changes to kibbutz communal property rights including the closing of dining halls and laundry services, as well as reducing or ending distributions to members for medical, educational, and celebratory expenses (such as bar mitzvah and wedding celebrations).[58]

[49] R. Russell, R. Hanneman and S. Getz, 'Antecedents and Consequences of the Adoption of Market-Based Compensation', in T. Eriksson (ed.), *Advances in the Economic Analysis of Participatory and Labor-Managed Firms* (Bingley, UK, Emerald, 2010), p. 229.
[50] Russell et al., 'The Transformation of the Kibbutzim', 113.
[51] C. McGreal, 'Israel's Kibbutzim Swap Socialist Ideals for Personal Profit in Struggle to Survive', *The Guardian* (2014): www.theguardian.com/world/2004/aug/31/israel.
[52] Russell et al., 'The Transformation of the Kibbutzim', 111.
[53] A. Lehavi, 'Mixing Property', *Seton Hall Law Review*, 38 (2008), 137–212 at 169.
[54] Russell et al., 'The Transformation of the Kibbutzim', 111.
[55] Russell et al., 'The Transformation of the Kibbutzim', 113.
[56] Russell et al., 'The Transformation of the Kibbutzim', 111.
[57] Russell et al., *The Renewal of the Kibbutz*, p. 85.
[58] Russell et al., 'The Transformation of the Kibbutzim', 113–114.

Changing models of housing and labour

When the kibbutz movement started in the 1920s, kibbutzim were created as cooperatives reliant on the labour of members. They made an effort not to make use of hired outside labour. This changed, however, as kibbutzim turned away from purely agricultural pursuits. As they built factories to go along with their farms, kibbutzim began hiring outside labour, and moving away from lockstep obedience to the traditional cooperative system.[59] The number of non-member workers on kibbutzim began to rise rapidly, drawing in outside employees even for agricultural work, leading to a labour force in the 1970s of which 52 per cent were non-members. An attempt to return to more traditional kibbutz values drove down outside labour to as low as 23 per cent by 1992. However, the financial crisis and demographic changes forced the kibbutzim to return to hiring from outside the membership. By 2004, once again 52 per cent of workers on kibbutzim were non-members, while 35 per cent of members and adult residents of kibbutzim commuted to jobs outside the kibbutz.[60]

The changing role of workers was naturally accompanied by changes in residential arrangements as well. Several factors contributed to this. First, kibbutz members sought to acquire the ability to ensure that their residences would pass along to the next generation, even if the younger generation left the kibbutz, or no longer lived with their parents (in the earliest generation of some kibbutzim, children never lived with their parents, and were instead raised communally). This desire translated itself into 'returning sons' programmes adopted by many kibbutzim. These programmes entitle children of kibbutz members to preferential allocations of land and membership rights. In 2007, 60 per cent of new kibbutz members were so-called 'returning sons', who took advantage of this preferential treatment. In renewed kibbutzim, where private ownership of land exists, these programmes allow the second generation to secure private property rights in formerly state-owned land at a below market price. For this reason, 'returning sons' programmes attracted criticism from other factions in Israeli society for legitimising 'conversion' of state land by kibbutz members, at the expense of other groups, and the public at large.[61] Second, with the workloads in the kibbutz no longer distributed on an egalitarian and Marxist basis, it became necessary to find a different basis on which to allocate rights to the kibbutz's assets and profits. Third, and perhaps most important, kibbutzim in many cases possess extremely valuable land, and in light of financial pressures, the kibbutzim sought to realise greater return from their real assets.

[59] Russell et al., 'The Transformation of the Kibbutzim', 117.
[60] Russell et al., 'The Transformation of the Kibbutzim', 117.
[61] M. Amor, '"Returning Sons" and "Continuing Sons": Thus the Israeli Land Aristocracy Was Built': www.haokets.org/2009/08/22/.

Today, renewed kibbutzim permit outsiders to take part in management decisions regarding many economic aspects of the kibbutz. Additionally, non-members of the kibbutz can live on the kibbutz and send their children to school on the kibbutz.[62] However, finding ways to translate kibbutz realty rights into profits for the kibbutzim has proved challenging.

The change of the kibbutz from a traditional, collective kibbutz to a renewed kibbutz presented many challenges for the relationship between labour and property rights. While in a traditional kibbutz the labour of a member and his or her personal budget which he or she received from the kibbutz were not related, the renewed kibbutz brought with it differential salaries, and new conflict for kibbutzim, and ultimately courts.

The case of *Ben Aharon v Kibbutz Tel Yosef*,[63] decided by the High Court for Justice in 2015, provides a vivid illustration. The case presented the question of whether members of a renewed kibbutz were subject to the general labour laws of Israel or to specific kibbutz regulations. In a traditional kibbutz, employees, who were also kibbutz members, fell outside of normal labour laws and were subject to kibbutz regulations. This was due to the unique relationship and ownership rights members had to their kibbutz. On a traditional kibbutz, a member worked because he or she was a member, and was a member because he or she worked.[64] The petitioner in *Ben Aharon* had been fired from his job as director of the fish farm on Kibbutz Tel Yosef, which had become renewed and switched to differential salaries in 2002. He sued for severance pay and damages in the amount of 704,000 shekels. Under Israeli labour laws, he was entitled to severance pay; but under the kibbutz regulations, he was not. The Israeli Supreme Court overturned the lower court and held that even though Tel Yosef, as a renewed kibbutz, differed from a traditional kibbutz, its labour and employment relations with members were governed by kibbutz regulations. The court recognised that the renewed kibbutz held onto many of the same ideals and structures as the traditional kibbutz. It pointed out that renewed kibbutzim: (1) financially helped members who did not receive a minimum wage, via the safety net budget; (2) offered a pension for members; and (3) provided departing members with services such as certain health and education services, as well as a form of severance. The court also recognised that the kibbutz had a framework for resolving disputes internally.

Due to the importance of this case, the Court decided to solicit the opinion of the heads of the cooperative organisation in charge of the kibbutzim. This group argued successfully that even on a renewed kibbutz, the kibbutz regulations should cover labour issues. The court agreed. *Inter alia*, the court explained that kibbutz

[62] McGreal, 'Israel's Kibbutzim Swap Socialist Ideals for Personal Profit in Struggle to Survive'.

[63] *Ben Aharon v Kibbutz Tel Yosef* (HCJ 2037/14) (2016) (Hebrew).

[64] *Ben Aharon v Kibbutz Tel Yosef* (HCJ 2037/14) (Hebrew).

members are partial owners of the factories, plants and assets, and have an ability to affect decision-making through voting.

Despite the fact that the court ultimately ruled in favour of the kibbutz, it noted the need for more clarity in this area and called on the legislator to find a comprehensive solution that would give workers on a renewed kibbutz appropriate protection, while upholding kibbutz values.

Traditional kibbutzim, for their part, have also had disputes relating to the connection of work to budget in the changing conditions of the twenty-first century. In *Micha Karu v Kibbutz Geva*,[65] the court of peace in Nazareth confronted such an issue. In a traditional kibbutz, members worked, and while they did not get a salary, they received a budget from the kibbutz. The budget a worker received was not connected to the type of work he or she performed. This was in accordance with the traditional kibbutz moto, 'To each according to his need, from each according to his ability'. The petitioner in this case was a member of Kibbutz Geva and the son of two of its founders. He worked in the kibbutz factory until 1988, when he was fired. From 1988 until 2007, he worked in other jobs, both on and off the kibbutz. Since 2007, he had been unemployed, and therefore unable to contribute to the collective kibbutz budget. In 2012, the kibbutz general assembly approved new work regulations that held that each member must work full-time (five days per week). The new regulations further provided that members are responsible for finding their own work, and members who do not work will be sanctioned. Since the petitioner was unemployed, the general assembly instructed the kibbutz secretariat to reduce his budget. The petitioner challenged this decision in court. Siding with the petitioner, the court ruled that the reduction of his budget was illegal. First, the court recognised that the new work order conflicted with the kibbutz regulations, which take precedence. The kibbutz regulations state that economic sanctions can only be imposed on a member for immoral behaviour, and the court said that the secretariat is not allowed to impose this kind of penalty as it is beyond the scope of its authority. The court reasoned that the new order went against the basic principles of the kibbutz, as well as against the principles of justice and equality. The order discriminated on the basis of age, and conflicted with section 71 of the kibbutz regulations which clearly states that the kibbutz is responsible for finding suitable work for its members based on their age, skills, and desires.

The court reasoned that the kibbutz regulations are a statutory agreement that sets up the relationship and legal duties between the kibbutz and its members. The basis of the collective kibbutz is that every member contributes according to his or her ability and takes according to his or her need. Matching personal budget to work conflicts with this foundational principle. The court ultimately held that the general assembly has no power to make a decision that (1) requires each member

[65] *Micha Karu v Kibbutz Geva 8362-08-14* (2015) (Hebrew).

to find their own work; (2) makes a general requirement to work full-time; (3) creates a direct relationship between work and budget; and (4) allows sanctions to be placed on members that reduce their budget. The court held that the general assembly can only make decisions that relate to the goals and authority of the kibbutz and that do not go against the general principles of the kibbutz. The only way to make the changes Kibbutz Geva wanted to make would be to amend the kibbutz regulations (which is a different process altogether).

The Israel Lands Authority during the 1990s and changing property rights

As is the case with most lands in Israel, the land possessed by kibbutzim is actually owned by the state of Israel, and the kibbutz merely leases the land from the Israel Lands Authority (formerly known as the Israel Lands Administration – ILA), which is the public body responsible for administering state-owned lands.[66] This national ownership of land is in contrast to the land policies of most other Western countries.[67] The Basic Law of Israel defines nationally owned lands as lands owned by the state, the Development Authority, and the Jewish National Fund (JNF). This law states that land may not be transferred and must remain under national ownership.[68] The ILA was established through the Israel Lands Administration Law of 1960 to administer these nationally owned lands and has since served as the administrative and regulatory body in charge of national land.[69] Typically, leases are for a short period – three years – and tightly restrict the uses to which the land can be put, specifying the use of the land as agricultural, commercial, residential, etc. Thus, where a kibbutz wants to change the use of land under its possession from agricultural to residential, for example, it must not only obtain changes in the relevant land use regulation, it must also obtain the permission of the Israel Lands Authority. Historically, since the kibbutz was communal in nature, individual members were not part of the lease and had no individual land rights or rights to kibbutz houses.[70]

During the 1990s, the kibbutzim successfully lobbied the ILA for several changes in the leasing arrangements that would improve their ability to earn

[66] *Association for a New Discourse for a Democratic Discourse in Israel et al. v The Minister of National Infrastructure* (HCJ 244/00).

[67] D. Barak-Erez, 'Law and Politics in Israel Lands: Towards Distributive Justice', *Israel Affairs*, 14(4) (2008), 662–680 at 662.

[68] The Israeli Lands Law, also of 1960, recognises seven exceptions, but despite these exceptions 93 per cent of the land is under national control.

[69] R. Hananel, 'Zionism and Agricultural Land: National Narratives, Environment Objectives, and Land Policy in Israel', *Land Use Policy*, 27 (2010), 1160–1170 at 1161.

[70] Lehavi, 'Mixing Property', 170.

profits from kibbutz lands. Decision 717 of the ILA from 1995 allowed kibbutzim to repurpose agricultural land for internal industry or business use, and, as part of a separate contract, to lease it to outsiders in an effort to bring in outside partners to their factories and businesses.[71] The kibbutz would then be able to lease this land from the ILA at a great discount (of up to 49 per cent). Decision 727 allowed kibbutzim to profit from reclassification of their land from an agricultural purpose to a residential or industrial purpose by allowing the kibbutz to receive compensation based on the increased value of the land as an industrial zone or residential community rather than as agricultural land. The kibbutzim would cooperate in the rezoning of the land, and then benefit from a percentage of the profits from development. In 1995, decision 737 was also passed, allowing kibbutzim to create an additional residential area for residents who would get to use kibbutz facilities and participate in the life of the kibbutz, but would be non-members.[72] The decision was meant to enable the kibbutz to rent repurposed land to these non-members at a severely discounted rate. The idea behind decision 737 was to strengthen the kibbutz by helping it attract a younger population, while also assisting the kibbutz sector financially during a time of great economic difficulty.

Supreme Court oversight of the changing kibbutz

Shortly after the Israel Lands Authority began the process of liberalising controls over kibbutz land, it found itself in court. In 2000, *Hakeshet Hademokratit Hamizrahit*, a self-described 'apolitical, non-parliamentary social movement whose goal is to affect the current public agenda in the aim of bringing . . . about a meaningful change among the Israeli society and implement[ing] values of democracy, human rights, social justice, equality and multi cultures',[73] spearheaded a lawsuit against the ILA for granting excessive property rights to the kibbutzim. *Hakeshet Hademokratit Hamizrahit* believed that the decisions of the ILA were a perpetuation of the injustice caused by the original allocation of lands, in which most of the immigrants from Arab countries did not participate. In its 2000 decision *Association for a New Discourse for a Democratic Discourse in Israel et al. v The Minister of National Infrastructure*,[74] the Supreme Court sided with *Hakeshet Hamizrahit* and overturned decisions 717, 727 and 737 of the ILA. As described above, each of these decisions dealt with the ability of kibbutzim to repurpose

[71] Avi Lapidot et al., 'The Kibbutz in a Changing Environment – Between Survival and Preserving Values', *Geographic Perspectives*, 66 (2006), 7–27 at 13 (Hebrew).

[72] Witkon, '"Allocating Assets" in the Kibbutz', 30.

[73] Hakeshet Hademocratit Hamizrahit: www.ha-keshet.org.il/english/english_index.html.

[74] *Association for a New Discourse for a Democratic Discourse in Israel et al. v The Minister of National Infrastructure* (HCJ 244/00).

their land and to be compensated for the repurposing. All three decisions were also aimed at giving kibbutzim the ability to extract greater profit from the realty they controlled.

The petitioners (in the consolidated cases) challenged decisions 717, 727 and 737, based on two theories. First, they claimed that while the decisions were formally within the legal authority of the ILA, their scope was such that they implemented large-scale policy decisions that ought to have been made by the Knesset (the Israeli Parliament). The petitioners thus claimed that the decisions were *ultra vires*. The court was not terribly sympathetic to this argument. It was much more receptive, however, to the second claim of the petitioners, namely that the decisions were grossly unreasonable and unfair. The court ended up overturning all three decisions based on declaring them to be grossly unreasonable because they were insufficiently sensitive to the needs of distributive justice. The petitioners claimed that the kibbutz population were receiving benefits that the rest of the population were not getting, and that the decisions therefore harmed the principles of equality and of equal distribution of resources. To understand the court's ruling, it is necessary to take note of three important background facts.

First, the decisions were adopted against the backdrop of not only the kibbutzim's severe economic crisis, but also a severe housing crunch that Israel was suffering at the time. The housing crunch was the result of massive immigration of Jews from the former Soviet Union, following the collapse of the Soviet regime.[75] For decades, the Soviet regime had strongly restricted the emigration of Jews from their country. When the Soviet Union collapsed, hundreds of thousands of Jews took advantage of the opportunity to move to Israel. Israel's housing market was not ready to provide the required new housing. Israeli land use controls are exceptionally cumbersome, and obtaining the necessary regulatory permissions for new construction was not easy.[76] Additionally, formal state ownership of most of the country's land, and cartels in the construction industry, created further barriers to rapid construction to meet consumer demand.[77] The ILA decisions were meant to kill two birds with one stone. They would free up lands for rapid construction for new residential housing, and also provide an influx of cash to the still-struggling kibbutzim.

Second, the decisions were made against the backdrop of tight Israeli governmental control over land. Israel has one of the highest degrees of state ownership and control of lands in the Western world: over 90 per cent of the lands of Israel are owned or controlled by the state. The ILA controls lands owned by the state of Israel (more than 80 per cent of the land in Israel) as well as those owned by

[75] Hananel, 'Zionism and Agricultural Land', 1163.

[76] *Association for a New Discourse for a Democratic Discourse in Israel et al. v The Minister of National Infrastructure* (HCJ 244/00).

[77] R. Alterman, 'Land Use Law in the Face of a Rapid-Growth Crisis: The Case of Mass-Immigration to Israel in the 1990s', *Washington University Journal of Law & Policy*, 3 (2000), 773–840.

the Development Authority and the Jewish National Fund. Several laws in Israel restrict the ability of the state to sell state lands.[78] The ILA's management of agricultural lands has long been a priority. Decision 1 of the ILA from 1965 stated that land for agricultural use would be transferred to kibbutzim only by lease and would be for the sole purpose of working the land and living on the land. Prior to decision 727, if the ILA decided to change the zoning of land from agricultural to residential or industrial, the kibbutz would not see any of the benefits of development. The ILA would transfer possession of the land to the development company and the kibbutz would receive compensation based on the pre-development value – the value of the land under agricultural purposes and the improvements made to the land. Naturally, the result of this system was that kibbutzim would have no incentive to initiate or cooperate in repurposing their lands for development.

Third, the case took place against the backdrop of an increasingly activist Supreme Court in the realm of public law, and in particular administrative law. Throughout the 1980s and 1990s, the Supreme Court expanded judicial authority generally, and its own authority in particular. One of the most unusual powers of the Israeli Supreme Court is to sit as a court of first instance in matters of administrative law. Sitting as a High Court of Justice, the Supreme Court can hear petitions against actions by state authorities and fashion relief as necessary for 'justice'. Decisions of the High Court of Justice cannot be appealed by right, and where leave for appeals is granted, the appeals are heard by an additional hearing of a larger panel of the Supreme Court. The 1980s and 1990s witnessed a broad expansion of the High Court of Justice's authority to hear cases, as the court essentially eliminated all standing requirements and invited petitions from parties whose only interest in the case was political. Today, any person who dislikes the activity of a government agency can file a petition to the Supreme Court, sitting in its capacity as a High Court of Justice, and ask it to intervene on his or her behalf. At the same time, the court expanded its substantive powers of administrative review, giving itself the authority to strike down state actions that were plainly within the formal powers of the state agency, but whose wisdom the court found wanting, or 'unreasonable'. The court has been accused of using its newly asserted authority ideologically, in support of left-wing political causes and economic populism.

Ultimately, the court decided to strike down all three ILA decisions. Describing the ILA as the trustee of public lands, the court found the decisions defective for failing to take proper account of the public interest in lands.

In overturning decision 717, the court held that allowing kibbutzim to benefit from the repurposing of their land was 'unfair' and at odds with principles of 'distributive justice'. Likewise, in rejecting decision 737, the court found the decision 'unfair'. While the court recognised that decision 737 would help

[78] *Association for a New Discourse for a Democratic Discourse in Israel et al. v The Minister of National Infrastructure* (HCJ 244/00).

kibbutzim with their residential issues as well as with their demographic issues, the court ultimately ruled that allowing kibbutzim to make agricultural land available for residential use at a highly discounted rate gave the kibbutzim unfair benefits. Additionally, the court noted that lessees of the kibbutz land at the discounted rate might (and often did) decide to sublet the residences on the open market, leading to 'speculation' and 'profit', which the court found undesirable. Finally, the court rejected decision 727, stating that the compensation provided to kibbutzim for repurposing was unreasonable and unfair. The court found the compensation to discriminate unfairly, both by giving larger compensation for more valuable land (and thus unfairly discriminating against kibbutzim in remote areas with less valuable lands), and by giving compensation to kibbutzim who were giving up their lands, while not offering the same programme of development and compensation to non-kibbutz land-holders.

Much of the rhetoric of the court was backward-looking. The Supreme Court noted that the kibbutzim had benefited from receiving large amounts of land from the government for agricultural purposes. Thus, reasoned the court, it would be unfair to allow the kibbutz to share in the profits from converting the land to commercial purposes; it would be more 'fair' to other Israelis who had not received land from the state to ensure that the land continued to be used efficiently for agriculture.

The results of the court's decision continue to be felt. As Israel's population grows, urban areas continue to expand into formerly agricultural areas. However, development has taken place mostly outside of kibbutzim. Kibbutzim are reluctant to cooperate with development plans that do not guarantee them a share of the profits, but it is not clear that the ILA can develop a comprehensive method of ensuring the kibbutz's share without running afoul of the law. Ironically, the interests of the groups the Supreme Court sought to protect in the name of distributive justice were harmed by the decision. The Supreme Court's decision contributed to a rise in housing prices, making it nearly impossible for members of disempowered groups to find affordable housing.

Following the decision of the Supreme Court, the ILA adopted decisions 949, 959 and 969 that set forth much stricter criteria for converting agricultural land. They also reduced the financial compensation for converting.[79] These transitional decisions helped ease the repeal of decisions 717, 727 and 737.

[79] Hananel, 'Zionism and Agricultural Land', 1164.

Decision 751 and challenges surrounding individual property rights in kibbutz homes

Traditionally, the kibbutz leased all of its agricultural and residential property from the ILA, and allowed its members to live in the kibbutz houses, even though the members themselves were not the holders of the leases and did not have property rights in the homes they lived in. During the mid-1990s there was a strong push for individual home ownership amongst kibbutz members. One of the leading factors pushing individual home ownership was the desire to transfer houses to offspring, especially when individual kibbutz members have made major improvements to their homes over the years.[80] In 1996, the ILA adopted decision 751 and for the first time granted kibbutz members property rights in their homes, while the kibbutz still maintained the leases over the agricultural land of the kibbutz. Technically the kibbutz member could cease to be a member of the kibbutz, but could remain in his or her house.[81] This, however, required a high capitalisation fee that would have to be paid up front that most kibbutz members could not afford.[82]

In 2007, the ILA expanded on decision 751, decreeing that 'each family would be allocated one housing unit for a capitalisation fee of 3.75% of the tract's full market value and could make the tract fully alienable for an additional payment of 29.25%'.[83] The housing rights are an 'alienable, inheritable right of a long-term capitalised leasehold, and in some cases full ownership'.[84] The renewed kibbutz must also have effective restraints on alienation of houses. Either the kibbutz must have a provision in its by-laws that allows the house only to be transferred to members of the kibbutz, or the housing can be transferred to non-members as long as they are members of the cooperative organisation of the kibbutz (different from being members of the kibbutz).[85] In any case, at all times 50 per cent of the houses must be owned by members.[86] The kibbutz also has right of first refusal to purchase the housing unit at the market price if there is to be a transfer.[87]

Individual kibbutzim which had decided to go through the process of renewal were expected to validate the adoption of decision 751 for their specific kibbutz, and then determine how the process of house allocation would take place on their specific kibbutz based on their own unique circumstances. This created many legal

[80] Russell et al., 'The Transformation of the Kibbutzim', 121.

[81] Witkon, '"Allocating Assets" in the Kibbutz', 21.

[82] Lehavi, 'Mixing Property', 170–171.

[83] A. Lehavi, *The Construction of Property: Norms, Institutions, Challenges* (Cambridge, Cambridge University Press, 2013), pp. 116–117.

[84] Lehavi, *The Construction of Property*, p. 117.

[85] Eliezer Ben-Rafael et al., "Law and Order in the Matter of the Kibbutz: Report of the Public Committee for the Kibbutzim" (Jerusalem, 2003), 6 (Hebrew).

[86] Lehavi, 'Mixing Property', 170–171.

[87] Lehavi, 'Mixing Property', 170–171.

issues for kibbutzim to determine and for courts to interpret in the implementation of decision 751.

The first question the kibbutzim had to answer was: who is entitled to possession of a house? In *Ilan Levy v HaGoshrim*, the district court of Nazareth was confronted with how to allocate homes to a separated, but not legally divorced couple.[88] In 2000, Kibbutz HaGoshrim amended its regulations in accordance with decision 751 and allowed members of the kibbutz to possess a leasehold for their house directly from the ILA. When the regulations were first amended, the kibbutz allowed each family unit to bequeath only one house to its heirs. The kibbutz defined family unit to include both divorced and separated couples, meaning that even if a couple had been separated and were living in separate houses, upon their death they could only pass one house to their descendants. While this rule changed in 2003 to allow more than one house to be bequeathed per family unit, the change came too late for the petitioners in *Ilan Levy v HaGoshrim*. The petitioners were the children of a couple who had been separated for 16 years, without officially divorcing. Although the couple were recognised as separated by kibbutz members and lived in different houses, when the kibbutz made a list of those entitled to house ownership in 2002, they were listed as a couple, rather than as singles, and therefore were entitled to bequeath only one house to their heirs. The petitioners argued that since the current rule allowed more than one house per family unit, they should be entitled to the rights to both the mother's and the father's homes as their heirs. The court upheld the kibbutz's decision and reasoned that since at the time of the mother's death the kibbutz regulations stated that each family unit was entitled to one house only, the petitioners were only entitled to one house.

It is important to note that in a different decision, *Navat Ben Haim v Kibbutz Givat Haim*,[89] the court rejected a formalistic test in determining whether a separated couple counted as married or as singles for the purposes of house allocation. The court instead adopted a substantive test that would examine the realities and circumstances of each individual dispute, focusing on the realities of the relationship of the couple as of the date the kibbutz adopted private house allocation under Decision 751. This would allow a separated couple to potentially be considered as singles for the purposes of house allocation under decision 751, depending on the specific circumstances of the case and the relationship.[90]

In *Parlamotor v Kibbutz Ramat HaKovesh*, the court of peace of Tel Aviv was presented with the question of when precisely house allocation, per decision 751, becomes effective.[91] On 21 January 2005, Kibbutz Ramat HaKovesh passed, through its general assembly, its basic principles of private ownership. The

[88] *Ilan Levy v HaGoshrim 58-10* (2014) (Hebrew).

[89] *Navat Ben Haim v Kibbutz Givat Haim* (HCJ 5271/10).

[90] *Navat Ben Haim v Kibbutz Givat Haim 1501-06* (2010) (Hebrew).

[91] *Parlamotor v Kibbutz Ramat HaKovesh 10680-11-09* (2010) (Hebrew).

principles outlined a plan for the renewal of the kibbutz and established a steering committee to develop a more detailed plan. On 2 February 2006, the general assembly passed guidelines that detailed how the renewal would work procedurally. On 4 April 2006, the kibbutz voted on a plan for allocation of houses. The plan attempted to create a more up-to-date balance between the ideals of freedom and individual rights, on the one hand, and the desire to hold on to a strong sense of community, on the other. Specifically, members would be allocated 'residential property stock' based on the number of years the member had been a member of the kibbutz. The maximum for a couple was set at 448,000 shekels and the maximum for a single person was set at 224,000 shekels. While this plan was originally rejected, it was put up for a vote again and passed. The petitioners in *Parlamotor* were the widow and children of the deceased founder and member of the kibbutz, who died on 6 June 2006, nine days before the final house allocation plan finally passed. The kibbutz decided to treat the widow as single, and gave her 'residential property stock' of only 224,000 shekels, as opposed to 448,000 shekels.

The petitioners argued that the cut-off date for determining the value of the stock should have been 21 January 2005, as this date created the property rights that would eventually be allocated on 15 June 2006. But to no avail. The court upheld the decision of the kibbutz and stated that the date of the final vote served as the date for determining the allocation of property rights. On this date, eligible members received their allocation and since the deceased had passed away nine days earlier, he should not be factored into the calculation. The court pointed to the communal organisations regulation that states that the right to ownership of property transfers to members on the date of the final decision establishing private ownership of property, and that one's status as a member ends with one's death. While the court noted the revolutionary impact of the kibbutz's decision to begin the process of renewal, it argued that this had no legal implications for the allocation of property rights, which was instead set in motion after the death of the deceased. The court also pointed to a number of precedent cases such as *Harstein v Kibbutz Tel Yosef*,[92] *Shefek Shoval v Kibbutz Neot mordecai*,[93] *Zinger v Kibbutz haSolelim*[94] and *Hen v Kibbutz Tel Katzir*,[95] all of which came out in favour of the kibbutz based on similar facts.

A second difficulty that kibbutzim and courts have faced in the implementation of decision 751 is the question of who is an official kibbutz member, and therefore eligible for property rights in their kibbutz home. In *Kibbutz Gesher HaZiv v Ron and Talia Dotan*,[96] the court addressed the question: to which property rights are former kibbutz members entitled when they leave the kibbutz? The respondents in

[92] *Harstein v Kibbutz Tel Yosef 555/06* (Hebrew).
[93] *Shefek Shoval v Kibbutz Neot mordecai 549/07* (Hebrew).
[94] *Zinger v Kibbutz haSolelim 249/99* (Hebrew).
[95] *Hen v Kibbutz Tel Katzir 529/05* (2010) (Hebrew).
[96] *Kibbutz Gesher HaZiv v Ron and Talia Dotan 735-08* (2010) (Hebrew).

this case were a married couple who had been members of Kibbutz Gesher HaZiv. In 2002, the kibbutz general assembly adopted organisational change regulations which provided the guidelines for how members would be able to acquire property rights in accordance with decision 751. In 2003, the couple signed an agreement with the kibbutz, which allowed them to sign a lease with the ILA, and, in 2004, the couple signed a lease with the ILA. In 2006, the couple were convicted of possession and sale of illegal drugs. As part of the organisational change regulations, the kibbutz had reserved the right to take possession of a leaving member's house either by paying him or her market value, or by selling it to a new, incoming member, and compensating the leaving member with the proceeds of the sale. The kibbutz argued that since the lease the couple had signed was subject to the terms of the organisational change regulations, the kibbutz was completely within its rights to repossess the house and compensate the couple accordingly when they ceased to be members. The court agreed. It proceeded to explain that the damage to the couple was minimal since they would receive market value for their house.

Privatisation today

Even before privatisation, kibbutzim had a variety of different internal property arrangements, and the variety has grown in the aftermath of the 'renewal'. Today, many kibbutz members make their own arrangements for employment and simply pay fees for kibbutz services.[97] Kibbutz members receive payment for their work on the kibbutz, and such payments reflect the differing skill levels and demands of the employment tasks. Privatisation is most striking in the case of kibbutz-owned enterprises – not only agricultural businesses but also other kibbutz-owned ventures, such as small manufacturing plants. While the kibbutz continues to own the businesses, their management has been professionalised, and the membership at large can no longer make operational and other business decisions.[98] In one particularly striking example, Kibbutz Shamir had its main corporation, Shamir Optical Industry, listed on NASDAQ. These changes have been adopted at different paces in different kibbutzim, but the overall trajectory is clear.[99]

In nearly all kibbutzim, while the kibbutz retains formal title over realty in the kibbutz, members have recognised protected rights to individual units.[100] Kibbutz members no longer yield all outside property rights to the collective, and members

[97] Spiro, 'Utopia and Its Discontents', 561.

[98] See E. Ben-Rafael, *Crisis and Transformation: The Kibbutz at Century's End* (New York, State University of New York Press, 1997), pp. 109–110.

[99] See A. Cnaan, 'Holy Land of Aliens: Formal Governance Mechanisms in Israeli Alternative Communities', unpublished PhD dissertation (Rensselaer Polytechnic Institute, 2007) (on file at Rensselaer Polytechnic Institute), pp. 69–73.

[100] See Spiro, 'Utopia and Its Discontents', 561.

therefore own pieces of realty outside the kibbutz. Kibbutz members can and do use their personal assets to acquire chattels and realty to which they then hold sole title.[101] Kibbutz Merom Golan is a good example of a modern, privatized kibbutz. Of the 500 residents of Kibbutz Merom Golan in the Golan Heights, only 150 are voting members of the kibbutz.[102] The vast majority of residents do not work on the kibbutz, but instead have outside professions and retain their salaries, paying a fee for use of kibbutz resources such as a pool or daycare. Plots of land must be developed according to kibbutz specifications, but cost up to $150,000 per plot.[103]

Conclusion

In this chapter, we have detailed the unique property arrangements that developed in the Israeli kibbutz. From a property perspective, the kibbutz constitutes a legal laboratory where extensive experimentation with localised property norms has been carried out for nearly a full century. Over time, the collective property regime that was once the hallmark of all Israeli kibbutzim has been abandoned and replaced with more familiar property settings that rely on private property rights. Yet, to this day, most kibbutzim hold steadfastly to property arrangements that have no parallels in the broader Israeli society. Our study of the changing nature of the institution of property in kibbutzim offers a fascinating picture of the interplay among law, ideology and economic forces. It also highlights the challenges that unique property settings adopted by a certain group or sector within a society present for the broader legal system.

[101] See Spiro, 'Utopia and Its Discontents', 561.

[102] L. McLaren, 'Privatizing the Modern-Day Kibbutz', *MacLeans* (2014): www.macleans.ca/news/world/privatizing-the-modern-day-kibbutz/.

[103] Dagan and Margalit, 'Tax, State, and Utopia', 568.

5

Community Rights in Scots Property Law

MALCOLM COMBE

Introduction

On 16 March 2016, the Scottish Parliament at Holyrood voted through what is now the Land Reform (Scotland) Act 2016 (asp 18) ('the 2016 Act') by 108 votes to 14. This was the second statute branded as land reform passed at Holyrood since the millennium, with the Land Reform (Scotland) Act 2003 (asp 2) ('the 2003 Act') preceding it (by a slightly less comprehensive 101 votes for and 19 against).

The short titles of those two statutes, not to mention the generally cross-political party support for the contents of them, ably demonstrate that land reform is in the air in Scotland. Both statutes contain provisions that aim to facilitate or, in some cases, compel transfer of land from an existing landowner to a community body. The 2016 Act also contains provisions about engaging communities in decisions relating to land that may affect them. Away from the land reform brand, the Community Empowerment (Scotland) Act 2015 (asp 6) ('the 2015 Act') also introduced new rights of community acquisition that can be deployed against private landowners, together with a scheme that allows communities to take on assets from the public sector. That there has been so much recent legislation makes Scotland a prime candidate for examining legal strategies for the development and regulation of communal property.

These measures are ripe for analysis, but such analysis should not exclude the distinctive features of the well-developed system of property law that existed in Scotland before the recent legislation was passed. Scots law is generally described as being a 'mixed' legal system, formed of a civilian (Roman) foundation that has been overlaid by common law (English) influence. It would be fair to say that the mixture of Scots property law has more of a civilian flavour to it. Within that, a strong right of ownership gives much autonomy to the owner of a thing, but there are aspects of Scots law that can also give communities certain rights in relation to property. This chapter will set out some key points of Scots property law and where

Proceedings of the British Academy, **216**, 79–101. © The British Academy 2018.

concepts of community feature within it, before explaining why new community rights were introduced, where the new rights slot into the Scottish system, and offering some observations about what the rights mean for Scottish communities.

Scots property law and community generally

In common with most civilian traditions,[1] Scots property law is unititular.[2] That is to say, there is only one title of ownership in any thing at any one time. With the exception of indivisible common or joint ownership by more than one individual (discussed below), the Scottish concept of ownership 'necessarily excludes every other person but the proprietor'.[3] This concept of ownership has not been changed by any of the recent reforms brought in by the Scottish Parliament. As we shall see, the land reform measures that communities can benefit from operate within a single title per asset system,[4] allowing community members to associate together into a suitable body and then in turn allowing that body to acquire sole title to local assets.

To set the scene, it might be helpful to clarify a number of aspects of Scots law that are of at least tangential relevance to conceptions of property and community. These clarifications relate to: the recent abolition of feudal tenure and title conditions; regulation of co-ownership; and the idiosyncratic systems of commonty, common grazings and common good property.

Feudalism and title conditions

Not much needs to be said about the system of feudal tenure that used to prevail in most of Scotland, save to note that it was swept away by the Abolition of Feudal Tenure etc. (Scotland) Act 2000 (asp 5).[5] It merits a brief mention here because

[1] Consider R. Zimmermann, K. Reid and D. Visser, *Mixed Legal Systems in Comparative Perspective: Property and Obligations in Scotland* (Oxford, Oxford University Press, 2005).

[2] On Scots property law generally, see K. G. C. Reid, *The Law of Property in Scotland* (Edinburgh, LexisNexis Butterworths, 1996); and G. L. Gretton and A. J. M. Steven, *Property, Trusts and Succession*, 3rd edn (Haywards Heath, Bloomsbury, 2017).

[3] J. Erskine, *An Institute of the Law of Scotland*, 1st edn (Edinburgh, 1773; reprinted as *Old Studies in Scots Law*, vol. 5, Edinburgh, Edinburgh Legal Education Trust, 2014), II, 1, 1. This was confirmed in *Burnett's Tr v Grainger*, 2004 SLT 513.

[4] Or, as noted in an earlier article, 'Scottish land reform is taking place within a decidedly unititular regime.' M. M. Combe, 'Parts 2 and 3 of the Land Reform (Scotland) Act 2003: A Definitive Answer to the Scottish Land Question?', *Juridical Review*, 2006, 195–227 at 225.

[5] K. G. C. Reid, *The Abolition of Feudal Tenure in Scotland* (Edinburgh, LexisNexis Butterworths, 2003). Incidentally, the Norse-influenced Northern Isles, Orkney and Shetland, did not receive feudalism to the same extent as the rest of Scotland.

there used to be different levels of land tenure, with a vassal holding from a feudal superior who ultimately held from the Crown.[6] This created something of a hierarchical community, in which those towards the bottom of the feudal chain could be held to account for their actions by those above them. On 28 November 2004 all vassals who held the *dominium utile* of the land – i.e. the substantial right in land enjoyed by the vassal, roughly equivalent to the Anglo-American fee simple[7] – were converted into outright owners, so this is now largely of historical interest.

One reason that feudalism lingered for so long in Scotland was because of its important role in the regulation of land use. This allowed real burdens to be imposed on areas of land for the benefit of a feudal superior (or, in some circumstances, another area of land). Where a large area of land was subject to the same or similar burdens, there was something of a community in existence, with shared obligations and rights relating to other members of that community.

Real burdens – which might alternatively be referred to as real conditions or (in English terminology) restrictive and positive covenants – attach to immoveable property, binding the current owner and any successors in title to do, or not to do, certain acts in situations defined in their title deeds. These might operate to oblige the landowner to (for example) build using granite, but not above a certain height. These devices were important to the modern development of Scotland's cities, most notably Edinburgh's New Town.[8] Traditionally these obligations would have been enforced by a feudal superior, serving as a pseudo-planning regime in the absence of a modern system of public control,[9] but following the decline and now abolition of feudalism in Scotland real burdens tend to be enforced by neighbouring proprietors. One term used in the Title Conditions (Scotland) Act 2003 (asp 9), the framework Act that regulates real burdens and contains important provisions for the law relating to servitudes (easements), is 'community burden'.[10] What might make this relevant to those interested in community management of assets is that this statute was enacted following a major study into the utility of real obligations,

[6] Gretton and Steven, *Property, Trusts and Succession*, Appendix.

[7] An example of this equivalence was provided by UK tax legislation. Before its amendment to reflect the abolition of the feudal system in Scotland, section 96(1) of the Value Added Tax Act 1994 provided '"fee simple" . . . in relation to Scotland, means the estate or interest of the proprietor of the dominium utile . . .'.

[8] See Reid, *The Law of Property in Scotland*, paras 376–385. As Reid notes (para. 376), their importance was not restricted to Edinburgh, with a key early case relating to Bon Accord Square in Aberdeen: *Tailors of Aberdeen v Coutts*, 1840 1 Rob 296, HL.

[9] See K. G. C. Reid, 'Real Rights and Real Obligations', in S. Bartels and M. Milo (eds), *Contents of Real Rights* (Nijmegen, Wolf Legal Publishers, 2004), pp. 25–45 at pp. 35–37. On the transition away from feudalism, see Reid, *The Abolition of Feudal Tenure in Scotland*. As for the current non-pseudo-planning regime in Scotland, the primary statute is the Town and Country Planning (Scotland) Act 1997. That regime, to a certain extent, allows communities to be involved in the planning process, but that is beyond the scope of this chapter.

[10] Section 25.

and it was recognised that these obligations could have a positive role to play in a modern system of property law.[11] Members of (ownership) communities can have a role within that.

Co-ownership – common and joint property

As noted already, Scots law is unititular. That does not prevent shared ownership of an asset. This is often encountered with spouses, civil partners or cohabitants co-owning a family home. Another example of people associating together to manage property would be where such property is within the patrimony of a trust and those people administer it as trustees.[12]

Different regimes prevail to regulate those exemplar situations in Scots property law. Since the important case of *Magistrates of Banff v Ruthin Castle Ltd*,[13] it is generally accepted that there is a binary structure of co-ownership in Scots property law. The first exemplar would see people co-owning on the basis of 'common property', the latter being 'joint property'. The terminology is suboptimal, although fittingly common property is the more common situation. '"Joint ownership" is the special case, the main example being in the law of trusts.'[14]

Comparison with another legal system is instructive: in South Africa the equivalent to common property is referred to as 'free co-ownership', while joint property can be juxtaposed with 'bound co-ownership'.[15] This highlights the key distinction between the two Scots systems of co-ownership: in a situation of common property an owner has a right to sell her share and indeed insist on a court action to

[11] See, for example, the observations of the Government-formed Land Reform and Policy Group in their papers Identifying the Solutions (September 1998) at paragraph 5.1 and Recommendations for Action (January 1999) at paragraph 2.4. The Scottish Law Commission Report on Real Burdens (Scot Law Com No. 181, 2000) considered the arguments in favour of abolishing real burdens entirely, but rejected them: at paragraphs 1.14–1.21. See also Scottish Law Commission Discussion Paper on Real Burdens (Scot Law Com DP No. 106, 1998). Both papers are available at www.scotlawcom.gov.uk.

[12] The Scottish device of trust is similar but different from the English device with the same name. See further G. L. Gretton, 'Trusts without Equity', *International and Comparative Law Quarterly*, 49 (2000), 599–620. The Scots law approach to trust property is that the trustees own that property and the beneficiaries of the trust have a strong right (but not an ownership right) to hold those trustees to account.

[13] 1944 SC 36. See Reid, *The Law of Property in Scotland*, paragraph 17.

[14] Gretton and Steven, *Property, Trusts and Succession*, paragraph 10.2. The other example normally given is of unincorporated associations, i.e. clubs. It might also be noted that partnerships in Scots law have a distinct legal personality (in terms of the Partnership Act 1890) and can own property outright without routing that directly through a co-ownership regime, although relationships within that partnership would then be governed by the partnership deed and the prevailing law relating to partnerships.

[15] D. Kleyn and S. Wortley, 'Co-ownership', in R. Zimmermann, D. Visser and K. Reid (eds), *Mixed Legal Systems in Comparative Perspective: Property and Obligations in Scotland and South Africa* (Oxford, Oxford University Press, 2004), pp. 703–734.

divide the asset or sell the asset and divide the proceeds,[16] but such a route is not ordinarily available for a trustee in a trust.[17]

The relevance of this for the present discussion is that a loose community of interest (that is to say, individuals with a common purpose) of potentially any number of people[18] could come together to buy an asset on a shared basis, and if they did so via the simple expedient of sharing a title they would default into a situation of common property. In that circumstance, use (and overuse) of the asset and exit routes from ownership of it would be regulated by the rules applicable to that regime.[19] However, the susceptibility of the relationship to being ended by a disgruntled co-owner at any time renders this an inappropriate mechanism for long-term community ownership.[20] Alternatively, they might form a specific trust, perhaps for a charitable purpose or another public goal relating to the target asset, and in those circumstances the trustees would find themselves in the regime governed by joint property. Both those situations would require a willing seller and a mutually agreeable price, which is no small assumption to make. As has been hinted above, Scottish land reform legislation steers communities into neither situation. Rather, it asks members of a community to form themselves into a legal vehicle – traditionally a company limited by guarantee[21] – that does not have anything to do with co-ownership. Certain stipulations are made in relation to that vehicle's constitutional documents to make it community-oriented and

[16] By way of an action of division and sale (sometimes called an action of division or sale, or known by the Latin *actio communi dividundo*), as confirmed by *Upper Crathes Fishings Ltd v Bailey's Executors*, 1991 SC 30. See also *Morrison v Kirk*, 1911 2 SLT 335. English law observers may find some help from an analogy between common property and tenants in common.

[17] English law observers may find help here from an analogy between joint property and joint tenancy. Editors' note: For a discussion of co-ownership in England, see Abram and Blandy in this volume.

[18] Theoretically, there is no upper limit to the number of co-owners: *Menzies v Macdonald*, (1854) 16 D 827 affd (1856) 2 Macq 463, HL, discussed (and critiqued) in Reid, *The Law of Property in Scotland*, paragraph 28.

[19] With agreement amongst the co-owners, any otherwise lawful use would be possible; without such agreement, only ordinary use would be acceptable and no co-owner would be entitled to gain any excessive benefit: *Carmichael v Simpson*, 1932 SLT (Sh Ct) 16. Consider also *Bailey's Executors v Upper Crathes Fishing Ltd*, 1987 SLT 405, where one co-owner successfully obtained an interdict (injunction) to stop another co-owner's excessive use of fisheries.

[20] The denouement in the *Bailey's Executors v Upper Crathes Fishing Ltd* saga was the already referenced case of *Upper Crathes Fishings Ltd v Bailey's Executors*. The co-owner who had been interdicted (enjoined) from that excessive use then raised an action to sell the asset, which the other co-owner could not object to. This highlights why this model can only work for as long as the parties are generally in agreement, and the absolute nature of the escape route means the standard situation of common property is not a realistic model for strategic community projects.

[21] 'Traditionally' might be too strong a word here, as the tradition only started in the 2003 Act (sections 34 and 71). The 2015 Act now allows Scottish charitable incorporated organisations (SCIOs) and community benefit societies to represent the community. The earlier Transfer of Crofting Estates (Scotland) Act 1997 (discussed below) was more flexible about the community bodies that the public sector could transfer its crofting assets to.

representative, which will have implications for membership, office-holding and running of the entity, but otherwise matters of governance are left to the standard position for such entities.

Commonty, common grazings and common good

Tantalising as the above heading is, hinting as it does at three Scots institutions that revolve around common rights, the regimes for commonty, common grazings and common good are probably more of academic than practical interest. That is not to say they are completely irrelevant to modern Scotland (common grazings being particularly relevant to the system of landholding known as crofting), but it is to say they are idiosyncratic, and it is not possible to give them more than a passing comment here.[22]

Commonty is worth mentioning in the light of the foregoing discussion of co-ownership as a 'peculiar' right in common lands.[23] Gordon and Wortley describe this as a right attached to a holding of separate property, giving holders of such property an additional right to the land comprising the commonty. They also note that in many instances the use of a commonty was such that it was 'difficult to determine whether the right held was the proprietary right of commonty, or merely a servitude of pasture or cutting peat'.[24] Whilst the latter situation would clearly be important to those able to exercise such rights, and (as discussed above) title conditions – of which servitudes (together with real burdens) are a subset – can play a role in the regulation of land in or by a community, it would not strictly be an example of communal ownership.[25]

Commonties were of a certain historic importance to Scotland, but since the Division of Commonties Act 1695 it has been possible for landowners abutting

[22] Editors' note: For a discussion on grazing rights over common land in England and Wales, see Rodgers in this volume.

[23] W. M. Gordon and S. Wortley, *Scottish Land Law*, 3rd edn (Edinburgh, Thomson Reuters, 2009), paragraph 15–179.

[24] Gordon and Wortley, *Scottish Land Law*, paragraph 15-180. On servitudes (the Scottish equivalent term for 'easement'), see D. J. Cusine and R. R. M. Paisley, *Servitudes and Rights of Way* (Edinburgh, W. Green/Sweet & Maxwell, 1998).

[25] There could be some functional equivalence between mutual servitude holders and those having an ownership right in a thing. Such servitude holders would not have *carte blanche* to do what they want. Co-dominant benefited proprietors (that is to say, dominant proprietors making use of the same servient tenement) have to sensibly manage their shared rights, both to not act to the detriment of the servient proprietor (through increasing the burden) and to avoid disputes between themselves. See G. J. Bell, *Principles of the Law of Scotland*, 4th edn (Edinburgh, 1839; reprinted as *Old Studies in Scots Law*, vol. 1, Edinburgh, 2010), § 988; and *Alvis v Harrison*, 1991 SLT 64; and consider *Carstairs v Spence*, 1924 SC 380; and the related discussion in Cusine and Paisley, *Servitudes and Rights of Way*, paragraphs 12.196–12.201. For co-dominant proprietors, see *Agnew v Lord Advocate*, 1871 11 M 309; *Yeaman v Mathewson*, 1896 12 Sh Ct Rep. 354; and the related discussion in Cusine and Paisley at paragraph 12.20.

a commonty to have that commonty apportioned amongst them (after which the portions would be owned outright by the apportioned owner and no longer treated as part of a commonty). The activist Andy Wightman singled out this legislation in his land reform polemic, with chapter 7 of his book being dedicated to what he calls 'The fourth land grab – the commonties'.[26] Whilst erosion of the commonties had taken place before that legislation, it was designed to achieve (and achieved) the acceleration of a move from land being held as commonties to pockets of outright ownership.

Although rarely encountered,[27] there are occasional examples of commonties that escaped division, plus the seventeenth-century legislation allowing for division did not apply to burgh (i.e. municipal) property.[28] The exact extent of such land is not clear and there have been calls for further research into commonties.[29] As it happens, the Scottish Government has tasked the Scottish Law Commission to look at commonties (and specifically the 1695 Act).[30] Be that as it may, commonties are not common enough and probably not understood enough to provide a useful modern Scottish example of a practical open-access resource.[31]

What is relevant in the present day is crofting law and, within that regime, the regulation of common grazings. These common grazings form a shared resource

[26] A. Wightman, *The Poor Had No Lawyers: Who Owns Scotland (and How They Got It)*, 4th edn (Edinburgh, Birlinn, 2015), ch. 7.

[27] Writing in 1996, Professor Reid noted that 'Commonty is, or, perhaps more accurately, *was* a form of shared ownership of land for the purposes of grazing cattle or cutting peats' (emphasis added). He went on to say, 'It became rare in the modern period and it is not known whether any examples still survive.' Reid, *The Law of Property in Scotland*, paragraph 37.

[28] See the discussion in A. L. Jarman. 'Customary Rights in Scots Law: Test Cases on Access to Land in the Nineteenth Century', *Journal of Legal History*, 28 (2007), 207–232. In terms of municipal resources, common good land will be considered below.

[29] One recent call came from Professor Gretton, in a book review of Wightman's aforementioned polemic: G. L. Gretton, 'Review: Andy Wightman, *The Poor Had No Lawyers: Who Owns Scotland (and How They Got It)*', *Edinburgh Law Review*, 15 (2011), 329–331. Jarman also bemoans the lack of Scottish research into commonties as compared to what has taken place in England, noting that, 'Today the subject of common land in Scotland is largely the purview of the informed activist and local authority lawyers rather than the academic scholar.' Jarman, 'Customary Rights in Scots Law', 211–212.

[30] On 31 August 2016, Andy Wightman MSP (the same person who wrote *The Poor Had No Lawyers*, and now a Member of the Scottish Parliament for the Scottish Green Party) lodged a parliamentary question (S5W-02239) asking 'what progress it is making with the review of the Division of Commonties Act 1695, and what discussions it has had with the Scottish Law Commission regarding the matter'. The relevant Cabinet Secretary responded (on 20 September 2016) to note that 'the Scottish Law Commission has agreed to consider the Division of Commonties Act 1695 as part of its next tranche of statute law repeals work'. See www.parliament.scot/S5ChamberOffice/WA20160920.pdf.

[31] A brief mention should be made of lands held runrig, a largely historic form of landholding that used to operate on a rotational basis. Runrig can be distinguished from commonty in that separate rights to the rigs (also called ridges, i.e. cultivation areas) were allocated to holders, but there are some similarities: runrig lands were also legislated for in 1695, by the Runrig Lands Act, which allowed for similar division and apportionment to take place; and runrig lands are also of limited importance in the present day. See Gordon and Wortley, *Scottish Land Law*, paragraphs 15-181–15-182.

that crofters can use along with other members of a crofting locale. Used in this context, 'crofters' has a very specific statutory meaning. In statutory terms, crofting began in the late nineteenth century in the Scottish Highlands and Islands,[32] with crofters and (landless) cottars being organised into townships with shared common grazings. The entitlement to use those common grazings flows as a pertinent (which is a perk, or appurtenance, to use land based on a right in other land) from a (very) secure croft tenancy.[33] Traditionally, grazings would indeed have been used for the grazing of livestock, but with agreement amongst relevant parties these can be put to a variety of different uses, including forestry.[34] Whilst there are just over a thousand of these common grazings in Scotland,[35] it would be fair to say that the model is somewhat *sui generis*, and it can be noted that recent land reform measures have not embraced a wider application of the common grazings model for community rights in land.

Another potential point of interest relates to common good land, that is to say land that falls to be administered by a local authority in a certain capacity.[36] The issue of common land around burghs has been touched on above, in the context of commonties that could not be subject to division in terms of the 1695 Act, and it has been noted that this dodging of enclosure meant that urban commons 'were an important feature in the urban-rural economy which existed up to the late eighteenth century in the larger towns and even later in the small royal burghs'.[37] Division-proof as they were, they did not prove immune to erosion

[32] Crofting is a form of landholding associated with the so-called 'Crofting Counties' in the north and west of Scotland, which gives the crofter (tenant) almost absolute security of tenure. The legal framework that established crofters as creatures of statute began with the Crofters Holdings (Scotland) Act 1886 and is now found in the Crofters (Scotland) Act 1993. For an overview of the history of crofting, see J. Hunter, *The Making of the Crofting Community* (Edinburgh, Birlinn, 2000; first published 1976).

[33] Since 1976, it has been possible for crofters to compel a transfer of both a house and croft land, with the rules for doing so currently being found in the Crofters (Scotland) Act 1993, sections 12–19, but the regulation of owner-occupier crofters is not something that will be explored here. The only point that will be mentioned is that owner-occupier crofters, despite buying out their landlord and thus freeing themselves from obligations that follow on from being a tenant, continue to have duties in relation to their land and that land is still subject to regulation by the Crofting Commission (the statutory body that regulates crofting). In the event they are somehow remiss in their management of the croft, enforcement action can follow, including being asked to let the land to someone else: the Crofters (Scotland) Act 1993, section 26J.

[34] The Crofters (Scotland) Act 1993, sections 50, 50A and 50B. The relevant parties that would need to be involved in any decision would include other crofters, the owner, and the relevant statutory body.

[35] The Crofting Commission website notes there are 1,060 common grazings, covering over 500,000 hectares of land (approximately 6 per cent of Scotland's land mass). See www.crofting.scotland.gov.uk/facts-and-figures.

[36] A. C. Ferguson, *Common Good Law* (Edinburgh, Avizandum, 2006).

[37] Jarman, 'Customary Rights in Scots Law', 212, quoting I. H. Adams, 'The Legal Geography of Scotland's Common Lands', *Revue de l'Institut de Sociologie*, 2 (1973), 259–323.

over time,[38] with Wightman categorising the erosion of such land as another 'land grab'.[39]

In terms of what assets in modern Scotland fall to be administered by local authorities, as successors to the old burghs and in turn the owners of common good property that was transferred to them,[40] the Final Report of the Land Reform Review Group – a publication and a body that will be discussed further below – considered this and noted that in 2012 the combined value of Common Good Funds was considered to be over £300 million.[41] Of that, '[b]y far the largest component . . . is heritable [immoveable] property and while this mainly consists of public buildings and public spaces, such as parks, it also includes in some cases farm land and other heritable property, such as salmon fishings'.[42] Much recent reform has been aimed at establishing and publicising what the extent of these holdings is.[43] It is nevertheless clear that such assets are important to communities across Scotland. In turn, what the municipal embodiment of a community[44] is able to do with such property is important, and a specific and somewhat esoteric reform in the newest land reform legislation is designed to make it easier to change the use common good land is put to.[45]

As with the brief look at commonty and common grazings above, it is difficult to extrapolate lessons for community ownership as a whole from common good land, but it is clear that the use of such assets can be locally significant. There

[38] There was some notable resistance: consider A. C. Loux, 'The Great Rabbit Massacre – A "Comedy of the Commons"? Custom, Community and Rights of Public Access to the Links of St Andrews', *Liverpool Law Review*, 22 (2000), 123–155; and the related case of *Dempster v Cleghorn*, 1813 2 Dow 40 (HL).

[39] Wightman, *The Poor Had No Lawyers*, ch. 8. As to what caused this erosion, Wightman offers the view that there was corruption and bad governance, which (in property law terms) could result in gains for individual proprietors who benefited from the operation of rules of positive prescription (adverse possession) to validate acquisitions. (The modern equivalent rules of positive prescription are found in Part 1 of the Prescription and Limitation (Scotland) Act 1973.)

[40] By the Local Government (Scotland) Act 1973, sections 222(2) and (3).

[41] The Land Reform Review Group, *The Land of Scotland and the Common Good* (Edinburgh, The Scottish Government, 2014), Section 14 – Common Good Lands, paragraph 2.

[42] The Land Reform Review Group, *The Land of Scotland and the Common Good*, Section 14 – Common Good Lands, paragraph 1.

[43] The 2015 Act, Part 8. This is in line with the recommendation that 'the position over Common Good lands should be improved to ensure they are adequately safeguarded and appropriately managed. The Group recommends that a new statutory framework should be developed to modernise the arrangements governing Common Good property.' The Land Reform Review Group, *The Land of Scotland and the Common Good*, Section 14 – Common Good Lands, paragraph 21.

[44] It is acknowledged that treating local authorities as actually equivalent to an embodiment of a local community is a stretch, given the geographical size of some of Scotland's 32 local authorities.

[45] The 2016 Act, section 77. This reform was largely driven by a case to do with the siting of a new school on a park in Edinburgh: *Portobello Park Action Group Association v City of Edinburgh Council*, [2012] CSIH 69. See further M. M. Combe, 'Lessons in Scots Law: The Common Good School', *Edinburgh Law Review*, 17 (2013), 63–68.

are many other important reference points for community involvement in local land decisions, including community councils,[46] the wider planning process, and indeed the accountability of public bodies or the Crown that own or manage land in Scotland. Important as those and other features might be, this chapter will now consider the community rights found in Part 2, Part 3 and Part 3A of the 2003 Act and Part 5 of the 2016 Act, all of which seek to empower communities by giving a route to ownership of land. Before doing that, it will briefly explain why there has been a drive for such reform.

Community rights of acquisition

Why is land reform happening in Scotland?

To an extent, the appetite for Scottish land reform, and in turn the widening of community involvement with land, is amply demonstrated by the simple fact of the recent legislative steps. That still raises a few questions. Why is there such an appetite? Why now? What are the alternatives?[47]

Taking the 'Why now?' question first, as it is the most easily dealt with, a crucial factor was the establishment of the Scottish Parliament. The Scotland Act 1998 introduced a unicameral legislative forum with the time and the inclination to embrace land law reform when it brought devolution to Scotland. The new Parliament was spurred on by the formation of the Land Reform Policy Group[48] ('LRPG') chaired by Lord Sewel, at the instigation of the Labour government that was swept into power by the 1997 General Election.[49] The inaugural elections for a Scottish Parliament returned a Labour/Liberal Democrat coalition, who took the

[46] These are statutory bodies established by the Local Government (Scotland) Act 1973 that play a consultative role in the planning process. More recently, they and certain other properly constituted community bodies have been given a role where they can enter into devices reminiscent of title conditions called 'good neighbour agreements' in relation to land, in terms of the Town and Country Planning (Scotland) Act, section 75D. See further M. M. Combe, 'Good Neighbour Agreements – Bad Law?', *Journal of the Law Society of Scotland*, 52(8) (2007), 50–53.

[47] Questions such as this have been considered by the author elsewhere. See Combe, 'Parts 2 and 3 of the Land Reform (Scotland) Act 2003'; M. M. Combe, 'The Environmental Implications of Redistributive Land Reform', *Environmental Law Review*, 18 (2016), 104–125; and M. M. Combe, 'The Land Reform (Scotland) Act 2016: Another Answer to the Scottish Land Question', *Juridical Review*, 2016, 291–313.

[48] Three publications were produced by the Land Reform Policy Group and published by the Scottish Office: *Identifying the Problems* (1998); *Identifying the Solutions* (1998); and *Recommendations for Action* (1999).

[49] Of course, land reform literature pre-dates this era, including J. McEwen, *Who Owns Scotland* (Edinburgh, EUSPB, 1977). It would also be simplistic to attribute all relatively modern reforms to the Labour victory in 1997, as it was a Conservative government that implemented the Transfer of Crofting Estates (Scotland) Act 1997 discussed below.

LRPG's recommendations forward in a variety of legislative measures in the first term of the new devolved administration. The most important of these for present purposes was the 2003 Act, which brought two community rights of acquisition.[50] In this first wave of activity, the Scottish Parliament also legislated on matters relating to property law more generally and specifically in relation to the heavily regulated agricultural holdings sector.[51] That goes some way to explain why those initial years of devolution were so fertile for land reform, but why is there a continuing appetite for more?

The so-called Scottish land question, which essentially turns on how land in Scotland is owned and used, has lingered for many years. The occasionally turbulent history in (parts of) Scotland may have played a part in that,[52] but the manner in which the land of contemporary Scotland is owned and organised in the present day as measured against contemporary commitments to sustainability and sound land management for economic, social and environmental goals continues to cause comment.

Whilst history might be relevant to some, it has not been a major driver for contemporary Scottish land reform. There has been no overt attempt to right a historical wrong against an identifiable community.[53] Scottish land reform also contrasts with other jurisdictions that have sought to provide subsistence agriculture for those who are hungry, or shelter for those who are destitute, although notions about food security, sanitation and housing have been creeping into the Scottish debate, as a positive rights-based driver for land reform.[54]

[50] A number of related statutes were also passed, such as the already mentioned Abolition of Feudal Tenure etc. (Scotland) Act 2000 and the Title Conditions (Scotland) Act 2003.

[51] As regulated by the Agricultural Holdings (Scotland) Act 1991 and the Agricultural Holdings (Scotland) Act 2003 (asp 11).

[52] Many resources are available. For the Highlands and Islands, consider Hunter, *The Making of the Crofting Community*; and for the Lowlands, consider T. M. Devine, 'Social Responses to Agrarian "Improvement": The Highland and Lowland Clearances in Scotland', in R. A. Houston and I. D. Whyte (eds), *Scottish Society 1500–1800* (Cambridge, Cambridge University Press, 1989), pp. 148–168.

[53] This contrasts with, for example, one aspect of South Africa's land reform programme: D. L. Carey Miller with A. Pope, *Land Tenure in South Africa* (Cape Town, Juta, 2000), particularly ch. 7; J. M. Pienaar, *Land Reform* (Cape Town, Juta, 2014), p. 209 and ch. 9. Editors' note: See also Pienaar in this volume.

[54] To the extent that section 98 of the 2003 Act has been amended (by the 2015 Act) to make explicit reference to the International Covenant on Economic, Social and Cultural Rights, which in turn raises the issues of food, sanitation and housing. It can be noted that a rights-based argument for reform can quickly be met by a rights-based argument against reform, as a landowner has a human right to peaceful enjoyment of her possessions except where that is disturbed in the public interest (non-arbitrarily and generally with compensation). Two cases provide useful examples of what is and is not acceptable in human rights terms and (in turn) the devolution settlement established by the Scotland Act 1998. What is not acceptable is made clear in a series of cases about the Agricultural Holdings (Scotland) Act 2003, culminating in the UK Supreme Court case of *Salvesen v Riddell* [2013] UKSC 22. The various steps of that saga are analysed in M. M. Combe, 'Human Rights, Limited Competence and Limited Partnerships: *Salvesen v Riddell*', *Scots Law Times (News)*, 2012, 193–200; 'Peaceful Enjoyment of

The drivers towards land reform that have been used include arguments about local enterprise or complaints that the pattern of landownership in Scotland is such that there is dominance by major players in the land market.[55] To make a proper analysis of whether this is a problem for Scotland can be difficult or laborious, owing to the occasionally patchy information about who owns what available at present. That patchiness is twofold: clear data is not always available on public registers for land;[56] and there can be a lack of clarity about who controls the landholding entity that is registered as owner.[57] Meanwhile, a recent paper submitted to the Scottish Affairs Committee at Westminster suggests around 432 landowners own 50 per cent of the privately owned land in Scotland.[58] That is a striking figure,[59] which also raises issues, beyond the scope of this essay, of social

Farmland at the Supreme Court', *Scots Law Times (News)*, 2013, 201–203; and 'Remedial Measures in Agricultural Holdings', *Scots Law Times (News)*, 2014, 70–71. What is acceptable is a properly considered piece of legislation that provides for the reallocation of property rights within a statutory scheme that allows a landowner to make representations throughout: *Pairc Crofters Limited and Pairc Renewables Limited v The Scottish Ministers* [2012] CSIH 96. That saga is analysed in M. M. Combe, 'Ruaig an Fhèidh', *Journal of the Law Society of Scotland*, 56(5) (2011), 54–55; and 'Ruaig an Fhèidh: 3', *Journal of the Law Society of Scotland*, 58(2) (2013), 31–33.

[55] There are hints at a critical view of monopolies in the Final Report of the Land Reform Review Group, where it is noted that present voluntary good land management practices should not disguise the fact that they do so at their own discretion and that the present arrangements provide limited sanctions against those who do not. This situation arises because of the degree of 'monopoly' control large landowners effectively have over land and other community interests, in ways that can determine the future of whole localities. *The Land of Scotland and the Common Good*, Section 24 – Pattern of Rural Land Ownership, paragraph 25.

[56] Scotland has operated a system of deeds registration for the transfer of land since the Registration Act 1617, before moving to a map-based system of registration of title that has been phased in since the Land Registration (Scotland) Act 1979. The transition has been slow, but is perhaps nearing resolution, with both the Scottish Government and Registers of Scotland committing to a rapid completion of the coverage of the Land Register to the whole of Scotland, in line with the recent Land Registration etc. (Scotland) Act 2012. See further: http://news.scotland.gov.uk/News/Target-set-to-register-all-of-Scotland-s-land-cc8.aspx.

[57] In proceedings at the Rural Affairs, Climate Change and Environment Committee of the Scottish Parliament in the run-up to the 2016 Act, an estimate that some 750,000 acres of Scotland was owned via non-transparent entities was discussed and not doubted (Official Report of the Rural Affairs, Climate Change and Environment Committee, 7 September 2015, Report, Col 71 (Edinburgh, Scottish Parliamentary Corporate Body), at: www.scottish.parliament.uk/parliamentarybusiness/report.aspx?r=10075&mode=pdf. The figure appears in the magazine *Private Eye*, issue 1395 (26 June 2015). The transparency point has also been made by Wightman, *The Poor Had No Lawyers*, ch. 29. These concerns have led to legislation aimed at improving access to information about who controls land, in Part 3 of the 2016 Act.

[58] J. Hunter, P. Peacock, A. Wightman and M. Foxley (with a foreword by Ian Davidson MP), *432:50 – Towards a Comprehensive Land Reform Agenda for Scotland: A Briefing Paper for the House of Commons* (Scottish Affairs Committee, 2013), available at: www.parliament.uk/business/committees/committees-a-z/commons-select/scottish-affairs-committee/news/land-reform-inquiry/. By 'privately owned', state-owned land is excluded, so the land owned by Forestry Commission Scotland (via the Scottish Ministers) does not feature in that analysis.

[59] See A. McKee, C. Warren, J. Glass and P. Wagstaff, 'The Scottish Private Estate', in J. Glass, M. F. Price, C. Warren and A. Scott, *Lairds, Land and Sustainability* (Edinburgh, Edinburgh University Press,

justice and fairness across society. Another possibility is that reform is about the governance of land, which is particularly seen to be an issue when landowners are termed as 'absentee' (a point which can be compounded when a non-active, non-resident owner is also non-transparent). To simplify, the argument would be that land is better governed when those who live or work on the land have a stake in its governance. This might bring related benefits in terms of population retention or revitalisation. Whether a community is the best candidate to take on the governance of land is a tricky question. Organisations like Community Land Scotland strongly advocate the case for it,[60] but there are issues as to whether any incoming owner, community or otherwise, will have the necessary skills when it comes to land management, whilst some have cautioned against models of community ownership that trap communities into their own circumstances.[61]

All of this gives a flavour of what has fed into the land reform debate in Scotland. The next thing to consider is where the community features as a result of that debate.

Community-oriented Scottish land reform

As already noted, the 2003 Act brought in two rights of community acquisition which were innovative for Scotland. The measures gave rural communities[62] a right of first refusal over assets (Part 2) and crofting communities a right to force a sale of certain crofting assets (Part 3). Flagship as this legislation was, it was not actually the first statute to put local communities to the fore. The first real statutory intervention came in the form of the Transfer of Crofting Estates (Scotland) Act 1997. This legislation provides for transfer of crofting lands owned by the state, to a community body. That community body would then become a crofting landlord. The highly regulated crofting scheme that governs such land would mean no particular change of land use would be possible by the incoming owner in the event of a transfer, meaning the actual 'on the ground' land reform effect of this measure

2013), pp. 62–85 at p. 65, where it is observed (drawing on the work of Kevin Cahill and others) that 'Scotland has the most concentrated pattern of private ownership in Europe, and possibly the world.' A similar statement is made by Monbiot (also drawing on the work of Cahill) about Britain as a whole when he states that 'we have one of the highest concentrations of landownership in the world': G. Monbiot, *Feral* (London, Penguin, 2014), p. 107. See further K. Cahill, *Who Owns Britain* (Edinburgh, Canongate, 2002).

[60] See www.communitylandscotland.org.uk.

[61] Consider Antinori, who notes that 'devolving responsibility may "enslave" local indigenous groups to the natural environment'. C. Antinori, 'Governance and Resource Management in Mexico's Community Forestry Sector', in J. Holder and C. Harrison (eds), *Law and Geography* (Oxford, Oxford University Press, 2003), pp. 307–321 at p. 310.

[62] Rural communities were (initially) classed as those with a population of 10,000 people or less: see The Community Right to Buy (Definition of Excluded Land) (Scotland) Order 2004 (SSI 2004/296).

was always destined to be limited.[63] As it happens, its effect was limited anyway, as only one crofting community has availed itself of the legislative scheme.

That being said, a real impact of the 1997 Act was to propel community into the thinking of those framing legislative intervention, but that was not the only factor. Many important examples of community ownership in Scotland came about as a result of community action that did not wait for legislation.[64] The community acquisitions of the islands of Eigg and Gigha (amongst others) pre-dated such developments, and those trailblazing communities have generally fared well: both have witnessed population increases since transfer to their respective communities.[65] That is not to say communities are insulated from all challenges of land management. The Isle of Gigha Heritage Trust has faced some documented issues, particularly in relation to the debt owed by the community landowning entity (and secured on its land) post-acquisition.[66]

Mention of the Isle of Gigha Heritage Trust provides an opportunity for an important aside: as explained in the foregoing discussion about co-ownership, community landowners who have acquired land without reference to any statutory scheme have tended to channel that community through one landowning entity, with a structure and membership that can be tailored to suit them (and any funders) without any community property ownership legal constraints.

Taken together with the 1997 Act, these extra-statutory developments in Scotland, and the means by which they were achieved, showcased community models to the Land Reform Policy Group. The LRPG went on to embrace community models in its work, without any particular study of comparative models of land reform.[67]

[63] There are processes to remove land from the control of crofting law, known as resumption and decrofting, but both are somewhat convoluted and no analysis will be made of them here.

[64] See J. Bryden and C. Geisler, 'Community-Based Land Reform: Lessons from Scotland', *Land Use Policy*, 24 (2007), 24–34.

[65] J. Hunter, *From the Low Tide of the Sea to the Highest Mountain Tops: Community Ownership in the Highlands and Islands of Scotland* (Kershader, The Islands Books Trust, 2012). As regards the community acquisitions that have taken place under the 2003 Act, see C. Mulholland, G. McAteer, C. Martin, L. Murray, R. Mc Morran, E. Brodie, S. Skerratt and A. Moxey, 'Impact Evaluation of the Community Right to Buy' (Edinburgh, Scottish Government Social Research, 2015), at: www.gov.scot/Publications/2015/10/8581.

[66] 'A Tale of Two Islands as Gigha Dream Turns Sour', *The Sunday Herald*, 23 November 2014, at: www.heraldscotland.com/news/13190772.A_tale_of_two_islands_as_Gigha_dream_turns_sour/. I wrote a blog post in response to this: 'Gigha Dream Turns Sour? Community Ownership in Scotland', 23 November 2014, at: https://basedrones.wordpress.com/2014/11/23/gigha-dream-turns-sour-community-ownership-in-scotland/.

[67] International analysis was somewhat lacking in the work of the Land Reform Policy Group. More recently, Scottish civil servants have engaged in welcome comparative work: see the Scottish Parliament Information Centre Briefing 15/38, *International Perspectives on Land Reform* (Edinburgh, SPICe, 2015), at: http://www.scottish.parliament.uk/parliamentarybusiness/91179.aspx. Interestingly, the Executive Summary of that Briefing indicates that Scotland may be swimming against the tide in

Land reform did not particularly feature in the second and third terms of the Scottish Parliament,[68] but after the Scottish National Party won a majority in the 2011 election it appointed a group to look at land reform in 2012 to fulfil a manifesto commitment. This Land Reform Review Group ('LRRG') produced its Final Report in 2014, containing 62 recommendations as to what the Scottish Government should do,[69] but not before the then First Minister Alex Salmond announced (in 2013) a commitment to bringing 1 million acres of Scotland (approximately one-twentieth of its land area) under community ownership.[70]

With community having such a central role somewhat pre-judged at that highest level of government, with the groundwork of existing community landowners, and with those existing legislative schemes to look at, it is not surprising that the Final Report looked closely at community options. It did this in several ways. In addition to exhorting the Scottish Government to take steps to look after any lingering common land or commonties that come to light,[71] it suggested establishing a working group to find out what is owned by communities[72] and developing a 'strategic framework to promote the continued growth of local community land

its fondness for community ownership, which is 'in contrast to the apparent European trend towards increasing land consolidation. The Community Right to Buy and Crofting Community Right to Buy . . . are correspondingly unique pieces of existing legislation, despite the growing Community Land Trust movement in North America and Europe, and draft legislation in Kenya that seeks to restore and register community land rights.' Meanwhile, the Scottish Land Commission (a statutory body established by the 2016 Act) has taken further interest in comparative research, commissioning a report into interventions in land markets. This was published in March 2018: see J. Glass, R. Bryce, M. Combe, N. E. Hutchison, M. F. Price, L. Schulz and D. Valero, 'Research on interventions to manage land markets and limit the concentration of land ownership elsewhere in the world' (2018), Scottish Land Commission, Commissioned Report No. 1, at: https://landcommission.gov.scot/publications-consultations-research/research.

[68] Which is not to say no land-related statutes were passed: consider the Crofting Reform etc. Act 2007, the Private Rented (Housing) Scotland Act 2011 and the Wildlife and Natural Environment (Scotland) Act 2011.

[69] The Land Reform Review Group, *The Land of Scotland and the Common Good*. See further M. M. Combe, 'Land Reform Revisited: The Land of Scotland and the Common Good', *Edinburgh Law Review*, 18 (2014), 410–413. The author was appointed an Adviser to the Group in 2013.

[70] 'I believe it is possible, I believe it is necessary for us to set a target of one million acres of Scotland in community land ownership by 2020': Alex Salmond, speaking at the Community Land Scotland Annual Conference, 2013, quoted at: www.gov.scot/Topics/Environment/land-reform/MillionAcres. Further details of the Scottish Government's steps in this area can also be found at that link.

[71] 'The Group recommends that these distinctive forms of land tenure should be identified and safeguarded as part of modernising Scotland's system of land ownership.' The Land Reform Review Group, *The Land of Scotland and the Common Good*, Section 7 – Ownerless Land, paragraph 11. As noted above, steps are being taken by the Scottish Government to ascertain how relevant commonties continue to be in modern Scotland.

[72] The role of this group 'would be to improve existing information on the numbers and types of community land owners and the land that they own, and to develop a strategy for achieving this target'. The Land Reform Review Group, *The Land of Scotland and the Common Good*, Section 16 – Land and Community Development, paragraph 15.

ownership'.[73] It went on to suggest that community rights should be made less bureaucratic and expanded to urban areas,[74] and that

> statutory land rights of local communities should include a right to register an interest in land, the existing right of pre-emption over land and a right to buy land, as well as rights to request the purchase of public land and to request Scottish Ministers to implement a Compulsory Purchase Order.[75]

There was also a specific recommendation for a 'Community Land Agency, within Government, with a range of powers, particularly in facilitating negotiation between land owners and communities, to promote, support and deliver a significant increase in local community land ownership in Scotland'.[76]

Following this there was a further Holyrood consultation about what the promised Bill should include,[77] after which the Stage 1 draft of the Bill was released.[78] Not all of the recommendations of the Final Report of the LRRG were included. Some were destined for the separate but related statute on community empowerment. The 2015 Act amended the 2003 Act, widening the scope of its pre-emptive community right to buy to the whole of Scotland (rather than simply rural Scotland, in line with the recommendation of the LRRG)[79] and finessing the existing scheme to make it more user-friendly. It also introduced provision for communities to make 'asset transfer requests' from their local authority, which must be considered by that local authority in light of a statutory scheme and cannot simply be rejected

[73] The Land Reform Review Group, *The Land of Scotland and the Common Good*, Section 16 – Land and Community Development, paragraph 18.

[74] On less bureaucracy, there was a call for greater flexibility as to what comprised an appropriate community body, which has been catered for by moving beyond simply companies limited by guarantee. On the expansion to urban areas, see the 2015 Act, section 36, which amends the 2003 Act, section 33. These reforms came into force on 15 April 2016, under The Community Empowerment (Scotland) Act 2015 (Commencement No. 3 and Savings) Order 2015 (SSI 2015, No. 399).

[75] Section 17 – Local Community Land Rights, paragraph 27. A similar but slightly different recommendation also made in Section 17 was that communities 'should have the right to request that a local authority exercises a Compulsory Sale Order' (at paragraph 33).

[76] Section 19 — Community Support Services, paragraph 20. Reference can be made here to the Scottish Government-funded Community Ownership Support Service delivered by the Development Trusts Association Scotland, at: www.dtascommunityownership.org.uk.

[77] Consultation on the Future of Land Reform in Scotland (2014), at: www.gov.scot/Topics/Environment/land-reform/consultation.

[78] Intriguingly, the Scottish Affairs Committee got involved in the debate at a UK level. Although no Westminster legislation followed (or is likely to follow) from that intervention, the Committee gathered evidence and published two reports which add to the contemporary debate: see Scottish Affairs Committee, *Eighth Report – Land Reform in Scotland: Interim Report* (2014), at: www.publications.parliament.uk/pa/cm201314/cmselect/cmscotaf/877/87702.htm; and Scottish Affairs Committee, *Eighth Report – Land Reform in Scotland: Final Report* (2015), at: www.publications.parliament.uk/pa/cm201415/cmselect/cmscotaf/274/27402.htm. Its contribution to community ownership was to query 'whether parts of the tax system are pushing up land prices and undermining a commitment to increasing community land ownership': *Final Report*, Conclusion and Recommendation 7 and paragraph 26.

[79] The 2015 Act, section 36, which amends the 2003 Act, section 33.

out of hand.[80] Most importantly for present purposes, it introduced a new right of community acquisition where land has been 'wholly or mainly abandoned or neglected' or somehow managed in a way that was detrimental to a community's 'environmental wellbeing'.[81]

As regards the most recent Land Reform (Scotland) Bill, at Stage 1 it included a 'right to buy land to further sustainable development' for communities, whilst provision was made to give guidance to landowners about consultation with local communities when making decisions about land. A Call for Evidence about the actual terms of that Bill was made by the relevant scrutinising Scottish Parliament Committee, then three stages of parliamentary and related committee scrutiny followed.[82] Although there was some sculpting of the provisions about communities, the general model stayed the same throughout the legislative process.

How does this suite of legislation work?

First wave community rights of acquisition

The 2003 Act works by allowing a community body (i.e. members of a locality associated together in a suitable juristic persona) to acquire land in certain circumstances. For communities in crofting areas of the Scottish Highlands and Islands looking to acquire ownership of land under crofting tenure, common grazings and certain eligible additional land, a sale can be forced on an unwilling seller. For communities seeking to acquire land under Part 2 of the 2003 Act, there are two crucial differences. The right is of first refusal, meaning the owner cannot be forced to transfer and the community right will only trigger when the owner decides to transfer the land. Relatedly, a community must register an interest in the land it seeks to acquire in a public register, to put the landowner on notice of its plans.[83] Whilst the owner cannot be forced to sell under Part 2, this is still an important power for the community to have, and one that is stronger than the right to bid that applies in England and Wales as a result of Part 5 of the Localism Act 2011.[84] That

[80] The regime as a whole is found in the 2015 Act, Part 5. It commenced on 23 January 2017, per The Community Empowerment (Scotland) Act 2015 (Commencement No. 4 and Transitory Provision) Order 2016 (SSI 2016/363).

[81] The 2015 Act, section 74, introducing a new Part 3A to the 2003 Act.

[82] See Rural Affairs, *Climate Change and Environment Committee, Stage 1 Report on the Land Reform (Scotland) Bill* (2015), at: www.parliament.scot/S4_RuralAffairsClimateChangeandEnvironmentCommittee/Reports/RACCES042015R10Rev.pdf.

[83] The 2003 Act, section 36. The Register of Community Interest in Land is maintained by the Keeper of the Registers of Scotland and is available at: http://rcil.ros.gov.uk/RCIL/default.asp?category=rcil&service=home.

[84] Whilst the Scottish regime in Part 2 cannot force a sale to a community, as a landowner can choose to no longer sell at any point in the transaction, it does mean a properly constituted community body

legislation only provides a right to bid for a targeted asset of community value, whereas the Scottish legislation provides that a transferring landowner must sell to the community at an agreed or set price.

The schemes in Parts 2 and 3 both involve a number of preparatory steps, the first of which is incorporation of a suitable entity that acts as its embodiment. This body that community members are channelled into will then own the land outright, on a single title. Where the body is a company limited by guarantee, its articles of association must be tailored so as to have not fewer than ten members, provision that at least three-quarters of the members of the company are also members of the local community (with a related stipulation that those members have control of the company), and provision that any surplus funds or assets of the company are to be applied for the benefit of the community. If an alternative form of Scottish charitable incorporated organisation or community benefit society is opted for, then similar rules apply, *mutatis mutandis*. In all cases, the body must have been recognised by Scottish Ministers as having a commitment to sustainable development.[85] The community is then left to operate in a suitably sculpted regime under the Companies Act 2006, the Co-operative and Community Benefit Societies Act 2014 or the Charities and Trustee Investment (Scotland) Act 2005 (asp 10) (as applicable).

Whilst more flexibility has undeniably been introduced by allowing these two forms to be adopted by communities as alternatives to a company limited by guarantee, it can be noted that there are more flexible schemes in operation for certain community bodies recognised in other Scottish statutes. The most notable comparator is the Transfer of Crofting Estates (Scotland) Act 1997, section 2, which simply needs a body (corporate or unincorporated, to be approved by the Secretary of State, after consultation with the Crofting Commission) that is 'representative of the crofting interests in the property to be disposed of' and 'has the promotion of the interests of persons residing on such property as its primary objective'. There is similar flexibility in the 2015 Act, section 19, which allows a body (again, corporate or unincorporated) with certain simple constitutional requirements to make participation requests of certain public bodies (to allow it to get involved with the delivery of service) and asset transfer requests of a local authority in the aforementioned fashion.[86]

with a registered interest cannot be forced to contend with a new landowner for the asset it has targeted. This is because any transfer that did not first consider the community could be open to challenge. The moratorium under the Localism Act 2011 gives communities a (relatively weaker) right to bid.

[85] Sections 34(4) and 71(4) of the 2003 Act provide that Ministers must have given the body 'written confirmation that they are satisfied that the main purpose of the body is consistent with furthering the achievement of sustainable development'.

[86] Another less than favourable comparison for 2003 Act and 2016 Act community bodies is provided in relation to the bodies that can enter into good neighbour agreements, discussed in Combe, 'Good Neighbour Agreements – Bad Law?'

Once a suitable body has been formed, there must also be evidence of local support. In terms of the Part 2 right of pre-emption, evidence is needed at the beginning of the acquisition process,[87] followed by a ballot to ensure majority support before exercise of the right itself.[88] Even then acquisition will only be possible with the approval of the Scottish Ministers. That approval will only be forthcoming if the acquisition is in the public interest and compatible with furthering the achievement of sustainable development.[89] The (repeated) role of sustainable development in this statute has been described as a 'primary duty' on the decision-makers which 'has priority over any other duties or objectives',[90] so its application and interpretation are of crucial importance.[91] Assuming a community steers itself through these provisions, the land is then transferred at an agreed or independently valued price.[92] There are provisions that allow the owner to input into or appeal about the overall process throughout.

Second wave community rights of acquisition

The 2003 Act will soon have a new Part 3A, introduced by the 2015 Act.[93] Section 74 of the 2015 Act enshrines a right which goes beyond pre-emption, meaning this new entitlement has something in common with the crofting community right to buy in that it will not require a willing seller. Properly constituted community bodies, which track the requirements set out above, are to be given the right to acquire

[87] In most circumstances, support will be demonstrated when at least 10 per cent of the population approve, in terms of section 38. There are also special and more stringent rules in section 39 for 'late applications'. These are applications that are rushed by a community after land has been exposed for sale by the owner, and in those circumstances there is a higher threshold in relation to community support.

[88] Ballots are required for the ultimate exercise of a right to buy under section 52 of the 2003 Act. The approval process for crofting community bodies is in section 75.

[89] Section 51(3)(c) and (d) (for the Part 2 community right to buy) and section 74(1)(j) and (n) (for the Part 3 crofting community right to buy). There is also an extra requirement for sustainable development in Part 2 where a community seeks to register an interest to acquire land that is near (rather than within) that community: section 38(1)(b)(ii).

[90] A. Ross, *Sustainable Development in the UK: From Rhetoric to Reality?* (Abingdon, Earthscan, 2012), p. 191.

[91] In relation to sustainable development, see Combe, 'Parts 2 and 3 of the Land Reform (Scotland) Act 2003', 219–222. There has been litigation relating to what is expected of communities, with *Holmehill Limited v The Scottish Ministers*, 2006 SLT (Sh Ct) 79 making it clear that a community should tread carefully if a main driver for the attempt to acquire land is to thwart development, as discussed in M. M. Combe, 'No Place Like *Holme*: Community Expectations and the Right to Buy', *Edinburgh Law Review*, 12 (2006), 109–116.

[92] The 2003 Act, sections 59–60A and 88.

[93] See further M. M. Combe, 'Digesting the Community Empowerment Act', *Journal of the Law Society of Scotland*, 60(8) (2015), 40–41. The Scottish Government had initially suggested these would come into force in the summer of 2017 but at the time of press, these are still not in force. See https://beta.gov.scot/policies/community-empowerment/.

'eligible land' if (in the opinion of Scottish Ministers): '(a) it is wholly or mainly abandoned or neglected, or (b) the use or management of the land is such that it results in or causes harm, directly or indirectly, to the environmental wellbeing of a relevant community'. Again, there is a role for Scottish Ministers, who must consent to the acquisition and they will only do so when satisfied that the land is in fact eligible (i.e. abandoned, neglected or environmentally detrimental) and that the exercise of the right is both in the public interest and compatible with furthering the achievement of sustainable development.[94] These provisions are not yet in force.

Third wave community rights of acquisition

The 2016 Act contains a wide range of important measures, with much of it being dedicated to the matter of agricultural holdings reform and other provisions for diverse issues such as deer management, fiscal reform of the tax treatment of land used for shooting, and a new body called the Scottish Land Commission to monitor matters relating to land. In terms of community land specifically, Part 5 provides for a community right to acquire land to further sustainable development, again adopting a community-centric model not unlike Parts 2, 3 and 3A of the 2003 Act, albeit with an onerous process that communities might find it difficult to get through. The process is onerous because this right of acquisition does not require a willing seller: when the statutory tests are met, and subject to payment of an agreed or independently valued price, transfer is compelled.

Where the 2016 Act differs from the other community rights of acquisition is in asking that more hurdles than public interest and sustainable development are cleared. The transfer of land must also be likely to result in 'significant benefit' to the relevant community, and must be 'the only practicable, or the most practicable, way of achieving that significant benefit'.[95] There is then a further test that 'not granting consent to the transfer of land is likely to result in harm to that community'.[96] Those additional conditions bring the ideas of 'significant benefit' and 'harm' to the fore, both of which are to be determined by an analysis of a community's economic development, regeneration, public health, and social and environmental wellbeing.[97] Another innovative feature of Part 5 as compared to the other rights of acquisition is that a community may nominate a third party acquirer, albeit the transfer to such a nominee would still need to meet all the tests already mentioned, *mutatis mutandis*. Whilst this might not open up a form

[94] The 2003 Act, section 97H, to be introduced by the 2015 Act, section 74.

[95] The 2016 Act, section 56(2)(c).

[96] The 2016 Act, section 56(2)(d).

[97] The 2016 Act, section 56(12). None of these terms are defined, but environmental wellbeing features in the right of acquisition in part 3A of the 2003 Act, section 97C(2)(b), to be introduced by the 2015 Act, section 74.

of community ownership, it could open up funding and partnership arrangements that have not been possible under existing statutory schemes.

Also of interest from a community perspective is the way Parts 4 and 5 of the Act are tied together. Ministers can take into account the extent to which landowners have had regard to guidance issued under section 44 (about engaging a community with decisions affecting land) in determining whether an application to buy land under Part 5 meets the 'sustainable development conditions' for a community buyout.[98] This means the guidance could be important in certain contexts when a community tries to force a sale.

What effect have the measures had so far?

There have been a number of community transfers under the scheme of Part 2 of the 2003 Act, albeit the impact has not been profound in terms of numbers of activated community interests in the Register of Community Interests in Land.[99] In terms of qualitative rather than quantitative impact, recent Scottish Government-commissioned research seems to indicate positive trends for communities and other benefits across a range of aspects.[100] The scheme is not a one-way street for communities though: there have been occasions when communities have faced challenge in court, and indeed certain communities who thought they were progressing along the land reform process (having obtained Scottish Ministerial consent for that) have been challenged through litigation.[101]

The impact of the crofting community right to buy, or at least the potential spectre of it, has been more noticeable. This too has been the subject of litigation, but the one 'hostile'[102] buyout eventually resulted in a transfer to the relevant

[98] The 2016 Act, section 56(4).

[99] Nineteen of the 208 registered interests have been activated: http://rcil.ros.gov.uk/RCIL/default.asp?category=rcil&service=home. Perhaps this lack of profound impact should not be surprising, as it was noted prior to enactment of the 2003 Act (by Ross Finnie MSP, the then Minister for Environment and Rural Development) that this right was not designed for 'significant redistribution of land': Justice 2 Committee, Stage 1 Report, paragraph 75 (SP Paper 541 at: http://archive.scottish.parliament.uk/business/committees/historic/justice2/reports-02/j2r02-02-vol01-02.htm#2).

[100] See C. Mulholland, G. McAteer, C. Martin, L. Murray, R. Mc Morran, E. Brodie, S. Skerratt and A. Moxey, 'Impact Evaluation of the Community Right to Buy' (Edinburgh, Scottish Government Social Research, 2015), at: www.gov.scot/Publications/2015/10/8581. This looked at the impact of the legislation on local communities in the period from 2004 to 2014.

[101] Consider the cases of *Holmehill Limited v The Scottish Ministers*, 2006 SLT (Sh Ct) 79, and *Hazle v Lord Advocate* (Kirkcaldy Sheriff Court (ref B270/07), 16 March 2009), discussed and critiqued in Combe, 'No Place Like *Holme*'; and M. M. Combe, 'Access to Land and to Landownership', *Edinburgh Law Review*, 14 (2010), 106–113, respectively. See also *West Register (Property Investments) Ltd v Lord Advocate*, 11 March 2015, Selkirk Sheriff Court (unreported), discussed in K. G. C. Reid and G. L. Gretton, *Conveyancing 2015* (Edinburgh, Avizandum, 2016), pp. 37–39.

[102] Press and Journal, 'Pairc Estate in hands of community after Scotland's first hostile land buyout', 6 December 2015: www.pressandjournal.co.uk/fp/news/islands/771128/estate-in-hands-of-community-

community, after the landowner's challenge to the scheme of Part 3 based on the European Convention of Human Rights was unsuccessful.[103] It has also contributed to various transfers of land (particularly in the Western Isles) in the limited area where it operates without the need to resort to litigation.[104] All of this chimes with earlier commentary that Part 3 of the 2003 Act marks a 'fairly radical step away from the traditional protection afforded to Scotland's landowners'.[105] As for the provisions in Part 3A of the 2003 Act and Part 5 of the 2016 Act, time will tell.

Conclusion

There is no doubt that recent measures are making Scotland something of a contemporary case study for land reform. Its community-centric approach also makes it a case study for those interested in community rights.[106] Within wider questions of whether Scotland should engage in a land reform process at all, there are sub-questions about who gets to benefit. Whilst there are some individual rights of acquisition available to certain tenants in Scotland,[107] these are somewhat sidelined in comparison to the community-oriented approach.

It might be that Scotland stumbled into its particular model of community-oriented land reform, but this chapter should provide some detail about how it can work in theory and in reality. As to whether Scotland can be a model for other jurisdictions, an American professor's observations about the 2003 Act might be of interest at this juncture. This chapter has tried to demonstrate that the 2003 Act

after-scotlands-first-hostile-land-buyout/. The *Pairc* dispute also highlighted the need for remedial legislation, in the form of a new section 69A of the 2003 Act which was introduced by the Crofting Reform etc. Act 2007, following on from the case of *Scottish Ministers v Pairc Trust Ltd*, 2007 SLCR 166.

[103] *Pairc Crofters Limited and Pairc Renewables Limited v The Scottish Ministers*, [2012] CSIH 96. See further Combe, 'Ruaig an Fhèidh'; and Combe, 'Ruaig an Fhèidh: 3'.

[104] See Hunter, *From the Low Tide*.

[105] D. L. Carey Miller and M. M. Combe, 'The Boundaries of Property Rights in Scots Law', *Electronic Journal of Comparative Law*, 10.3 (December 2006), www.ejcl.org/103/art103-4.pdf, 6. Radical as that change is to a property lawyer, MacKenzie has argued that the real radical effect of Part 3 is the 'troubling of the norms of property law through which class interest is brokered', and it was the 'threat to the commodification of land' that was behind certain opposition to land reform. A. F. D. MacKenzie, *Places of Possibility: Property, Nature and Community Land Ownership* (Somerset, NJ, John Wiley & Sons, 2012), p. 48.

[106] Bryden and Geisler, 'Community-Based Land Reform: Lessons from Scotland'.

[107] Crofters have an individual right to buy in terms of sections 13–19 of the Crofters (Scotland) Act 1993. Tenants of agricultural holdings have a right of first refusal over that tenanted land (introduced by Part 2 of the Agricultural Holdings (Scotland) Act 2003), and will soon have an additional right to acquire from a landlord who has repeatedly done something wrong, namely when a landlord is in material breach of an order of the Scottish Land Court or an arbitral award: see the new Part 2A to the Agricultural Holdings (Scotland) Act 2003, introduced by section 100 of the 2016 Act.

(and indeed other legislation) was important for communities in Scotland, but the 2003 Act's provisions were also important for rights of responsible outdoor access in Scotland.[108] In an article that looked at the access rights introduced by Part 1 of the Land Reform (Scotland) Act 2003 in some detail, Lovett noted that the statute demonstrated:

> it is practically possible for a modern, democratic nation committed to the rule of law, the protection of private property, and open markets to create, if it wants, a property regime that to a considerable extent replaces the *ex ante* presumption in favor of the right to exclude that has come to be taken for granted in the United States with an equally robust, but rebuttable, *ex ante* presumption in favor of access.[109]

Similarly, it is submitted that the rights of community acquisition introduced into Scots law have not caused unwarranted or unjustified detriment to Scotland's rule of law, the protection of private property, and open markets. Just as recent land registration innovation has been heralded as 'evolution, not revolution',[110] the same could be applied to the community-oriented reforms Scotland has entered into to date. Observers from Scotland and beyond will be watching closely to see whether the same is true in relation to the new waves of land reform legislation that will be introduced in the coming months.

[108] See further R. R. M. Paisley, *Access Rights and Rights of Way* (Edinburgh, The Scottish Rights of Way and Access Society (Scotways), 2006); and M. M. Combe, 'Get Off That Land: Non-Owner Regulation of Access to Land', *Juridical Review*, 2014, 287–317.

[109] J. A. Lovett, 'Progressive Property in Action: The Land Reform (Scotland) Act 2003', *Nebraska Law Review*, 89 (2011), 739–818 at 816–817.

[110] G. L. Gretton, 'The Shape of Things to Come', *Journal of the Law Society of Scotland*, 55(3) (2010), 22–25 at 22 (the innovation being the Land Registration etc. (Scotland) Act 2012 (asp 5)).

6

The Legal Status of Customary Land Tenure Systems and the Protection of Communal Property in Cameroon

WALTERS NSOH[1]

Introduction

Present-day Cameroon, unlike many other states in Africa, has the 'mixed blessing' of having been shaped by the experiences of the German, French and British colonialists. It includes the British mandated territory of Southern Cameroons which was administered as part of British Nigeria prior to independence in the 1960s. One of the legacies of colonisation is the legal systems that were left behind in the nation-states that were created.[2] As a result of its colonial history, Cameroon is one of the few examples of countries with a dual legal system, the English common law and the French civil law operating in a somewhat feeble coexistence.

However, prior to colonisation, when there were no nation-states with national boundaries, communities often migrated, picking up customary practices along the way. Consequently, many nation-states are artificial creations made up of people of diverse ethnicity, cultures, languages, norms and expectations. For example, the establishment of the German colony of Kamerun in 1884 included all of present-day Cameroon and sections of several of its neighbours. Due to the historical links between Cameroon and Nigeria, and given the dual legal system that still operates

[1] I am particularly grateful to Professors Rosalind Malcolm and Alison Clarke for comments on the earlier drafts of this chapter. I am also grateful to the participants of the Workshop on Legal Strategies for the Development and Protection of Communal Property (Sheffield, May 2016), for their valuable contributions, and to the external peer reviewer and editors of this volume for their useful comments. The views expressed in this chapter are solely those of the author, as are any errors that have eluded scrutiny.

[2] V. J. Ngoh, *History of Cameroon since 1800* (Limbe, Presbook, 1996), pp. 7–10; M. D. DeLancey and R. N. Mbuh, *Historical Dictionary of the Republic of Cameroon*, 4th edn (Lanham, MD, Scarecrow Press, 2010).

Proceedings of the British Academy, **216**, 102–126. © The British Academy 2018.

in Cameroon, the evolution of the law in Cameroon has therefore been significantly influenced by the development of the law (i.e. both imposed Western legal systems and the local customary law) in Nigeria. This experience is not peculiar to Nigeria and Cameroon; the colonial history of most of Africa is littered with examples of similar such arrangements, demonstrating the relevance of the present discussion for the rest of sub-Saharan Africa.

One area of the legal system where colonisation has had an impact is in the land tenure system. The current land laws of most sub-Saharan African countries such as Cameroon are based largely on Western land law principles imposed by the foreign legal systems, including the German system (which was the system in place prior to the defeat of Germany in World War I). These legal systems have evolved against a background of the different kinds of customary communal property rights exercised by different ethnic groups, with the primary aim of harmonising/abolishing the customary land tenure systems that existed prior to colonisation. The development of the law in this way has, however, been without a full understanding of the role of custom in the ownership and use of communal property. This lack of understanding has resulted in huge gaps between approaches envisaged in the written law on the protection of communal property and local knowledge and understanding of the ownership and use of communal property. This approach to land reform prevents individuals and communities from making use of lands which they have traditionally occupied and used under custom, if they are not in possession of the required 'legal' documents. Such developments have also failed to recognise the link between customary land tenure, unsustainable resource exploitation and the structural inequality that this generates.

More recently, the role of custom in resource management has received some consideration, notably in relation to matters concerning the governance of commons in England and Wales, discussed elsewhere in this volume. Nevertheless, the ownership and use of communal property remains very much tied to the modern land tenure system, which still relies on the customary tenure system to operate effectively. For example, in relation to forestry resources, the law in Cameroon recognises the ownership of, and property rights in, forest, which is strictly governed by the land tenure system, as well as the rules set out in the forestry laws.[3] This means that, depending on the categorisation of the forests, 'the State, local authorities, village communities and private individuals may exercise on the forests all the rights that result from ownership, subject to restrictions laid down in the regulations governing land tenure and State lands'.[4]

But how exactly does the customary land tenure system which is still operational in many parts of the country fit into this contemporary land ownership

[3] Law No. 94-1 of 20 January 1994 to lay down Forestry, Wildlife and Fisheries Regulations (hereinafter, 1994 Forestry Law), section 6.
[4] 1994 Forestry Law, section 7.

and use structure? This chapter assesses the extent to which law and practice in Cameroon are developing and protecting communal property. Using the example of forestry resources, it examines in particular the meaning of customary land tenure, its elements, including its communal interest element (which is a main feature of the customary system for most of sub-Saharan Africa), and the extent to which successive land law reforms in Cameroon recognise customary notions of communal and/or community property ownership and use rights in forests. Before considering the restrictions on the ownership of communal property by the regulations governing land tenure and state lands in Cameroon, it is important to first look at what is meant by customary land tenure.

'African' customary land tenure and communal property

The term customary law is a very generic one. It is therefore useful to distinguish this type of law from the modern or Western law. Elias defines customary law as 'the body of rules which are recognised as obligatory by its members'.[5] Gluckman defines it as 'A set of rules accepted by all normal members of the society as defining right and reasonable ways in which persons ought to behave in relation to each other and to things, including ways of obtaining protection for one's rights.'[6] Both definitions highlight the element of consent, a point emphasised by the Privy Council in the *Eshugbayi Eleko v Government of Nigeria* case: 'It is the assent of the native community that gives a custom its validity, and, therefore, barbarous or mild, it must be shown to be recognised by the native community whose conduct it is supposed to regulate.'[7] Assante, in his study about customary rules in Ghana, characterises the system as a body of well-established rules of conduct 'usually enforced by the heads of fragmentary segments, and in rare cases, by spontaneous community action'.[8]

Another useful characterisation is contained in section 2 of the Customary Courts Ordinance, cap. 142 of the 1948 Laws of Nigeria, as amended by the Adaptation of Existing Laws Order, 1963, which defines customary law as:

> [A] rule or body of rules regulating rights and imposing correlative duties, being a rule or body of rules which obtains and is fortified by established usage and which is appropriate and applicable to any particular cause, matter, dispute, issue or question.

[5] T. O. Elias, *The Nature of African Customary Law* (Manchester, Manchester University Press, 1956), p. 55.
[6] M. Gluckman, *The Judicial Process among the Barotse of Northern Rhodesia (Zambia)* (Manchester, Manchester University Press, 1955), p. xv. Gluckman sets himself apart by limiting the consent to 'normal members', which means that consent does not need to be unanimous.
[7] [1931] 42 AC 662.
[8] S. K. B. Assante, *Property Law and Social Goals in Ghana* (Accra, University of Ghana Press, 1975), pp. 2–3. See also K. Akuffo, 'The Conception of Land Ownership in African Customary Law and Its Implications for Development', *African Journal of International and Comparative Law*, 17 (2009), 57–78.

This definition complements those proposed by Elias and Gluckman above by including the phrase 'fortified by established usage', which means that the (usually unwritten) rules of customary law must, in addition to the other factors, be recognised by the community. Customary law is therefore made up of customary practices that have been recognised by secondary rules of the legal order and thereby given formal normative effect.[9]

One characteristic that is also common in customary law is the community interest that appears in land tenure systems across Africa. The community interest refers to the customary collective rights of ownership and use that the community holds over the property. In this regard, the much referenced principle of customary land tenure[10] by a Nigerian chief, the *Elesi* of Odogbolo, before the West African Lands Committee – 'I conceive land belongs to a vast family of which many are dead, few are living and countless members are still unborn'[11] – is therefore not an empty statement. This suggests that customary communal property rights are exercised over all land under the customary land tenure system. This basic principle was accepted by the Committee in its Report[12] and has received judicial approval in several cases. For example, in the often-cited Nigerian case of *Amodu Tijani v Secretary, Southern Nigeria*,[13] the Judicial Committee of the Privy Council accepted as 'substantially true' the following statement of Rayner, CJ in 1898:

> Land belongs to the community, the village or family, never to the individual. All members of the community, village or family have an equal right to the land, but in every case the chief or headman of the community or village, or head of the family, has charge of the land, and in loose mode of speech is sometimes called the owner. He is to some extent in the position of a trustee, and as such holds the land for the use of the community or family. He has control of it, and any member who wants a

[9] Editors' note: See also Rodgers in this volume.

[10] Although different laws and customs obtain in various communities of Cameroon, the definitions of customary law cited above and other evidence indicate that it is possible to discern some general principles of customary land tenure law. For an authoritative and detailed discussion of customary land tenure systems, see C. K. Meek, *Land Law and Land Administration in Nigeria and the Cameroons* (London, HMSO, 1957); J. W. Bruce, *African Tenure Models at the Turn of the Century: Individual Property Models and Common Property Models*, vol. 1 (Rome, FAO, 2000); C. Lund, *African Land Tenure: Questioning Basic Assumptions* (London, IIED, 2000); M. Doumbé-Moulongo, *Les Coutumes et le Droit au Cameroun* (Yaoundé, Editions CLE, 1972); F. M. Mifsud, *Customary Land Law in Africa: With Reference to Legislation Aimed at Adjusting Customary Tenures to the Needs of Development*, vol. 7 (Rome, FAO, 1966); R. Debusmann and S. Arnold (eds), *Land Law and Land Ownership in Africa: Case Studies from Colonial and Contemporary Cameroon and Tanzania* (Bayreuth, Bayreuth University, 1996); C. N. Ngwasiri, 'The Impacts of the Present Land Tenure Reforms in Cameroon', *Cameroon Law Review* (Editions Clé), 28 (1984), 73–85; C. N. Ngwasiri and Y. N. Nje, *Advocacy for Separate Land Legislation for the Rural Areas of Cameroon*, ed. A. Ndeso-Atanga and others (Yaounde, A PVO-NGO/NRM Cameroon, 1995).

[11] C. J. Rayner, *Report of the Land Tenure in West Africa* (1898), Comnd. 1078, p. 183.

[12] Rayner, *Report of the Land Tenure in West Africa.*

[13] [1921] 2 AC 399.

> piece of land to cultivate or build a house upon, goes to him for it. But the land so given still remains the property of the community or family. He cannot make any important disposition of the land without consulting the elders of the community or family, and their consent must in all cases be given before a grant can be made to a stranger. This is a pure native custom along the whole length of this [West African] coast and wherever we find . . . individual owners, this is again due to the introduction of English [and French] ideas.[14]

In as much as the above statement of principle is true to some extent, it is also not without some dispute. For example, Elias,[15] Coker[16] and Lloyd[17] (all writing about family property rules in the Nigerian context) are all of the view that customary ownership of land is vested in individuals or in joint descendants of an individual owner, the family or extended family, not the community at large, which is made up of other families that are not necessarily part of that lineage. Although the family or extended family could, in itself, be regarded as a 'close-knit' community, the above argument appears to suggest that, in terms of resource control and use, customary ownership is still vested in individuals. The reason for this may lie in the 'patrilineal kinship systems'[18] which dominate traditional African extended family cultures. Under such systems, ownership remains with the family head of the lineage, although the members may share in the resources.[19] This is the very basis of individual ownership; a view also supported by Utuama[20] who maintains that Rayner's statement is incorrect in so far as it denies the existence of individual ownership of land. In another Nigerian case, *Balogun & others v Oshodi*,[21] decided ten years after the *Amodu Tijani* case, Webber, J. pointed out that the notion that individual ownership is quite foreign to native ideas has disappeared with the process of time, due to the spread of English ideas. This view was also shared by Speed, Ag. CJ in the case of *Lewis v Bankole*, who had observed that 'the institution of communal ownership has been dead for many years and the institution of family ownership is a dying one'.[22] However, in *Bujulaiye v Akapo*, Butler Lloyd, J. rightly rejected this observation, stating that 'the institution of family ownership is still a very live force in native tenure . . .'.[23] This statement

[14] Rayner, *Report of the Land Tenure in West Africa*.
[15] T. O. Elias, *Nigerian Land Law*, 4th edn (London, Sweet & Maxwell, 1971), p. 74.
[16] G. B. A. Coker, *Family Property among the Yorubas*, 2nd edn (London, Sweet & Maxwell, 1966), p. 29.
[17] P. C. Lloyd, 'Family Property among the Yoruba', *Journal of African Law*, 3 (1959), 105–115 at 105 and 115.
[18] G. Foster, 'The Capacity of the Extended Family Safety Net for Orphans in Africa', *Psychology, Health and Medicine*, 5 (2000), 55–62 at 56.
[19] Foster, 'The Capacity of the Extended Family Safety Net for Orphans in Africa', 56.
[20] A. A. Utuama, *Nigerian Law of Real Property* (Ibadan, Shaneson C.I., 1989), p. 6.
[21] [1931] 10 NLR 35, [50].
[22] [1908] 1 NLR 82, [84].
[23] [1938] 14 NLR 10.

suggests that customary land tenure is characterised by customary communal property rights exercised by all members of the family or extended family, living as a community. Irrespective of which side of the argument is correct, it suffices to say that the notion of customary law and ownership is an ever changing one,[24] and there is no dispute that the traditional basis of customary land tenure is private as well as communal ownership, whether it is within a family, extended family or a community.[25] As the search for a distinction between Western land law and customary land tenure continues, this qualification remains one of the distinctive features of customary land tenure systems, even up till this day.

Another distinctive feature lies in the role of control and management that is vested in the chief of the community/village or family head (in most cases, a member of the royal family of the community/village, or the family head as designated by the succession rules) in the administration of the communal land. In addition to the rules known to the entire group, he also allots or allocates portions of the land to members (or non-members in some cases, as customary tenants), for their individual use (mostly for subsistence farming or building residential houses). In every case, however, such land remains community/family land, except where under some custom or agreement the land has been partitioned. In those cases the individual members become absolute owners of their allotted portions (i.e. exclusive of the community/family).

It is worth emphasising that these distinctive features also apply to communities in Cameroon. For example, in villages of South Cameroon, plots with houses, farms and fallows, on the one hand, are owned by individuals. Ownership of land is acquired by effective use or occupation, recognised by all Bantu-speaking communities in Cameroon[26] and the 1974 Land Ordinances.[27] On the other hand, land reserves made up of forests that have never been cleared belong to the customary domain of the village and have the status of communal property. Indeed, they belong to the entire group in a village and each member of the group has the right to take a portion in accordance with rules that are known to the entire group (such as clearing). The group has the authority to exclude non-members of the community from forest land that extends to the borders with neighbouring villages.[28] Thus to them, there is no such thing as vacant or unoccupied land.

[24] On how time has affected the notion of customary law and ownership, see for example M. Gluckman, *Ideas and Procedures in African Customary Law* (studies presented and discussed at the Eighth International African Seminar at the Haile Sellassie I University, Addis Ababa, January 1966), pp. 9–15.
[25] H. W. J. Sonius, *Introduction to Aspects of Customary Land Law in Africa as Compared with Some Indonesian Aspects* (Leiden, Universitaire Pers Leiden, 1963), p. 19.
[26] Bantu-speaking peoples are the largest group in Cameroon and are spread into other African countries: Ngoh, *History of Cameroon since 1800*, pp. 31–33.
[27] See below, 'Ownership and the Land Ordinances of 1974'.
[28] According to some authors, this system is based on the colonial practice in which 'community was conflated with tribe and "strangers" were seen as having no traditional access to land whereas in most

To some groups, such as the indigenous Pygmy[29] communities, with different approaches to land and natural resource usage, land is a zone of influence, where their hunting and gathering activities take place.[30] However, as Lewis asserts, there is a 'long-standing and widespread perception by local, national and international non-hunter-gatherers that hunting and gathering does not confer rights over land'.[31] In line with Pemunta, this is because of the undue importance that colonial and post-colonial land tenure attaches to agriculture when determining rights over land, thereby downplaying other local forms of land and resource use.[32] Such perceptions help explain the 'casualness with which governments and other outsiders have appropriated Pygmy peoples' lands'.[33] Notwithstanding, the notion remains amongst the Pygmy groups that land is communal property on which their hunting and gathering activities take place. This difference in perceptions between the Pygmy groups and non-hunter-gatherers, and the implications this has for land and resource use, supports the argument that the development of the law has been without a full understanding of the role of custom in the ownership and use of communal property.

The right of control and management vested in the community chief or family head ensures that legally, nobody, not even a member of the community or family, can make use of the community or family land in any way whatsoever, without

of pre-colonial Africa, strangers were considered as members of the kinship network . . . thus enhancing the prestige and labour force of a household, kin group or community': N. V. Pemunta, 'The Governance of Nature as Development and the Erasure of the Pygmies of Cameroon', *GeoJournal*, 78 (2013), 353–371 at 363–364. See also M. Mamdani, *Citizen and Subject: Contemporary Africa and the Legacy of Late Colonialism* (Princeton, Princeton University Press, 1996), pp. 139–146.

[29] The term 'Pygmy' or 'Pygmies' may have derogatory connotations, but is used here as a term externally imposed but now reclaimed by some indigenous groups and support organisations as a term of identity to encompass different groups of central African hunter-gatherers and former hunter-gatherers, and to distinguish them from other ethnic groups who may also live in the forests, but who are reliant on farming, and who are economically and politically dominant. See, for example, Survival International, 'The Pygmies' (*Survival International*, 2017): www.survivalinternational.org/tribes/pygmies.

[30] For more on the customary land usage amongst Pygmy populations, see, for example, K. Biesbrouck, 'Agriculture among Equatorial "Hunters-Gatherers" and the Process of Sedentarization: The Case of the Bagyeli in Cameroon', in K. Biesbrouck, S. Elders and G. Rossel (eds), *Central African Hunter-Gatherers in a Multidisciplinary Perspective: Challenging Elusiveness* (Leiden, CNWS, 1999); K. Biesbrouck, *Bagyeli Forest Management in Context* (Wageningen, Tropenbos-Cameroon Programme, 1999); Valérie Couillard and others, *Land Rights and the Forest Peoples of Africa: Historical, Legal and Anthropological Perspectives* (Moreton-in-Marsh, Forest Peoples Programme, 2009), pp. 12–14.

[31] J. Lewis, 'Technological Leap-Frogging in the Congo Basin, Pygmies and Geographic Positioning Systems in Central Africa: What Has Happened and Where Is It Going?' *African Study Monographs Supplementary Issue*, 43 (2012), 15–44 at 18.

[32] Pemunta, 'The Governance of Nature as Development and the Erasure of the Pygmies of Cameroon', 364.

[33] Lewis, 'Technological Leap-Frogging in the Congo Basin, Pygmies and Geographic Positioning Systems in Central Africa', 18.

the consent or concurrence of the community chief or family head. This position, however, has never been respected by everybody, including the government, right from the colonial days, especially in French Cameroon between 1959 and 1963.[34]

It has been pointed out that, in such a system, any proceeds or money, whether arising from sale, compensation, or rent of the communal or family land, received by the community chief or family head must be shared within the community or family.[35] This is because, in the actual sense, the chief or family head holds the land as a custodian and manages it in consultation with principal elders of the community. In theory, this means that as the custodian of the land, they hold the land in a fiduciary capacity, and are accountable to members of the community to whom the land belongs.[36] From every indication, it seems this is the very idea of communal ownership. According to some sources, it is not an idea peculiar to the people of South Cameroon or the west coast of Africa; it is an African idea.[37] So how does this prevailing model of customary land tenure fit with the statutory ownership of land in Cameroon?

Ownership of communal land in Cameroon

In 1974, the divergent systems of land tenure in Cameroon were brought into parity by the enactment of the 1974 Land Ordinances. These Ordinances, which are considered in detail in the next section, still form the foundation of the present law. They generally nationalise all land and are strikingly similar to the pre-existing

[34] C. F. Fisiy, *Power and Privilege in the Administration of Law: Land Law Reforms and Social Differentiation in Cameroon* (Leiden, African Studies Centre, 1992), p. 32.

[35] Per Endeley, J. in the case of *L.E. Agbortar J.A. Oben v Chief M.M. Besong*, [1968] 43 WCLR 45, [45]. See also C. Anyangwe, 'Land Tenure and Interest in Land in Cameroonian Indigenous Law', *Cameroon Law Review*, 27 (1984), 29–41 at 31–38; and J. G. Frynas, *Oil in Nigeria: Conflict and Litigation between Oil Companies and Village Communities* (London, Transaction Publishers, 2000), p. 73.

[36] See, for example, D. Fobih, *The Significance of Secure Access to Land for the Livelihoods and Food Security of Africa's Farmers and the Urban Poor* (Proceedings and Summary of Conclusions from the Land in Africa: Market Asset, or Secure Livelihood? Conference, London, 8–9 November 2004) (writing about customary land rules in the Ghanaian context).

[37] L. Hangula, 'People's Rights to Land and Natural Resources', in K. Fischer-Buder (ed.), *Human Rights and Democracy in Southern Africa* (Windhoek, New Namibia Books, 1999), p. 84; J. M. Sarbah, *Fanti Customary Laws: A Brief Introduction to the Principles of the Native Laws and Customs of the Fanti and Akan Districts of the Gold Coast with a Report of Some Cases Thereon Decided in the Law Courts*, 3rd edn (London, Cass, 1968); N. A. Ollennu, *Principles of Customary Land Law in Ghana*, vol. 2 (London, Sweet & Maxwell, 1962). Interestingly, this is also the system of landholding among the Maori indigenous people of New Zealand. See Frédéric Sautet, *Once Were Iwi? A Brief Institutional Analysis of Maori Tribal Organisations Through Time*, New Zealand Business Roundtable Working Paper, 2008.

Land Tenure Laws of the Francophone regions of Cameroon.[38] In fact, the 1974 Land Ordinances have been aptly described as the successors of the 1963 Decree-law and other laws from colonial days.[39] So the 1974 land reforms have not brought about any real change either to the Western value system aspects of the land tenure system, or in the efforts to erode and replace the customary land tenure systems of the country.[40] But who owns what, and to what extent are customary communal property rights over land and resources still recognised, under the 1974 Land Ordinances and customary laws?

Ownership and the Land Ordinances of 1974

The Land Ordinances were promulgated in 1974 following a successful referendum on a unitary state in 1972. By these Ordinances (the '1974 Ordinances') the land tenure systems in the French- and English-speaking parts of Cameroon were brought into parity. Based on what was framed as a public consultation,[41] they are:

- Ordinance No. 74/1 of 6 July 1974 to establish rules governing land tenure;
- Ordinance No. 74/2 of 6 July 1974 to establish rules governing state lands; and
- Ordinance No. 74/3 of 6 July 1974 concerning the procedure governing expropriation for a public purpose and the terms and conditions of compensation.

Following their enactment, these Ordinances could only be made operational after a decree of application had been enacted. It took another two years for these procedural rules to be elaborated.[42] On 27 April 1976, three decrees of application laying down the conditions for obtaining land certificates, the management

[38] Before the 1974 Land Ordinances, many other laws, decrees and orders had been enacted after 1963, all aimed at consolidating the state's grip on land. For example, Law No. 66-3-COR of 7 July 1966 and its decree of application, Decree No. 66-307 of 25 September 1966, emphasised that there must be what was called '*la mise en valeur des terres*', requiring every individual, including the customary 'holders', to apply for a land title, irrespective of the nature of the tenure.

[39] R. S. Mbatu, 'Forest Exploitation in Cameroon (1884–1994): An Oxymoron of Top-Down and Bottom-Up Forest Management Policy Approaches', *International Journal of Environmental Studies*, 66 (2009), 747–763 at 754.

[40] A. J. Njoh, 'The Political Economy of Urban Land Reforms in a Post-Colonial State', *International Journal of Urban and Regional Research*, 22 (1998), 408–424 at 411–412.

[41] A. D. Tjouen, *Droits domaniaux et techniques foncières en droit camerounais: étude d'une réforme législative* (Paris, Economica, 1982), p. 84. The legitimacy of such public consultation has however been questioned. See, for instance, Fisiy, *Power and Privilege in the Administration of Law*, p. 38.

[42] Tjouen has suggested that this delay was caused by the opposition that followed the enactment of the Ordinances, especially from traditional authorities and landlords in the southern parts of Cameroon who perceived the law as a covert form of expropriation of their land: Tjouen, *Droits domaniaux et techniques foncières en droit camerounais*, pp. 85–87. This argument conflicts with the view that the people were adequately consulted using questionnaires and had given their full support for the reforms.

of national lands, and the management of the private property of the state, were finally published. Although the 1976 decrees of application rendered the 1974 Land Ordinances operational, their application soon revealed gaps in the conception and procedural requirements of the land reforms. The result of this was another round of amendments and facilitating legislation, and by the end of 1985 at least 57 normative texts relating to land tenure had been published in the Official Gazette. Since their enactment, the 1974 Land Ordinances have remained the subject of much debate in the country. Their various shortcomings have been highlighted and they can be described as revolutionary, reformative,[43] controversial, and impactful, especially on customary land rights.[44] They certainly form a complex piece of legislation, with far-reaching consequences.

Apart from the overarching need to harmonise, rationalise and consolidate the various legislations[45] (especially those of land and forestry), it is difficult to fully explain the real motives of the sweeping measures contained in such a rapidly changing body of legislative enactments, especially as the 'land tenure legislation was enacted without the full knowledge of the indigenous land tenure systems in the country'.[46] Significantly, it seems in no area is the complexity of the legislation more pronounced than on the issue of ownership of land. For that, one can only gain a better insight into how the law is structured and operates by focusing on the three Ordinances and how they are applied. The common feature here is the division of land into three broad categories, private property (Article 2 of Ordinance No. 74/1), public property,[47] and national lands (Articles 14, 15 and 16). 'National lands' refers to land that has not been registered as private or public property. This is the area that has generated much controversy and is the focus of the present enquiry.

Patterns of access to land under Ordinance No. 74/1

Although Ordinance No. 74/1 significantly distinguishes between private and public property rights, it also declares in Article 1 that:

> (1) The State guarantee to all natural persons and corporate bodies having landed property the right to freely enjoy and dispose of such lands.

[43] Anyangwe, 'Land Tenure and Interest in Land in Cameroonian Indigenous Law', 29.

[44] Ngwasiri and Nje, *Advocacy for Separate Land Legislation for the Rural Areas of Cameroon*, pp. 3–15; Njoh, 'The Political Economy of Urban Land Reforms in a Post-Colonial State', 411. See also the case of *Amidu Lukong v Razel Road Construction Co. Ltd and MINAT*, [2001] 1 CCLR Part 7, 81.

[45] That is, the battered remains of English, French and local customary land laws.

[46] Ngwasiri and Nje, *Advocacy for Separate Land Legislation for the Rural Areas of Cameroon*, p. 7. See also Ngwasiri, 'The Impacts of the Present Land Tenure Reforms in Cameroon', 76.

[47] See 'Public property rights' below.

(2) The State shall be the guardian of all lands. It may, in this capacity, intervene to ensure the rational use of land or in the imperative interest of defence or the economic policies of the nation.

By this provision, the state recognises the rights of individuals and corporate bodies to privately own land, but also reserves the right to intervene in the public interest to ensure rational use of such lands. Article 1(2) also makes the state guardian of all land, i.e. public lands and national lands as well, and may dispose of it as it sees fit in accordance with established guidelines.[48]

According to Article 2 of Ordinance No. 74/1:

> The following categories of lands shall be subject to the right of private property:
>
> a) registered lands; b) freehold lands; c) lands acquired under the transcription system; d) lands covered by a final concession; e) lands entered in the Grundbuch.

These were lands already registered under the preceding state land administration systems as privately owned. These included those that were registered under the 1932 Act (for those parts of the country that were under French colonial rule);[49] those for which a Certificate of Occupancy (which was the recognised document of title in parts of the country under British colonial rule) had been issued;[50] lands under the *Grundbuch*;[51] lands registered under the transcription system; and those that were covered by final concessions.

There is no doubt that those who held such rights were those who had connections with the colonial and post-colonial legislation. Nevertheless, for those holders of documentary titles in land, a timeframe of ten years, starting from 5 August 1974, was provided to allow them to convert their previous interests in the land into land certificates under the new law. A land certificate is what confers ownership under the 1974 Land Ordinances. Failure to convert these old interests within the specified timeframe amounted to forfeiture and the land reverted to the common pool of 'national lands'.[52] Therefore, private property now covers only land for which a land certificate has been issued. In practice and in law, no customary communal property rights are exercisable over these private lands, unless the private property is registered in the name of the community.

[48] See further below, 'Implications for customary communal property rights in Cameroon'.

[49] This consisted of two decrees enacted on 12 July 1932. The first decree was aimed at the collective recording of land rights by corporate groups for lands which had no document of title. The second introduced the registration of individual interests in land. Holders of interests in land could have them registered and a document of title issued.

[50] Issued under the Land and Native Rights Ordinance of 1927 that was applicable in parts of the country that were under British colonial rule.

[51] The German land register in which a systematic registration of all interests in land was recorded, specifying the location and the dimensions of the interests in land.

[52] Ordinance No. 74/1 of 6 July 1974, articles 3 and 4.

To define 'national lands', Articles 14 and 15 of Ordinance No. 74/1 state that:

> 14. (1) National lands shall as of right comprise lands which at the date on which the present Ordinance enters into force, are not classed into the private or public property of the State and other public bodies. (2) National lands shall not include lands covered by private property right as defined in Article 2 above.
>
> 15. National lands shall be divided into two categories:
> (1) Lands occupied with houses, farms and plantations and grazing lands, manifesting human presence and development; (2) Lands free of any effective occupation.

This means that occupied and unoccupied lands that are not registered are included in the category of national lands. It is this provision that has raised concerns in local communities that their lands are being nationalised. Instead of being vested in the community chief or family head, the control and management of 'national lands' is now by the state. Specifically, Article 16 of Ordinance No. 74/1 provides that:

> (1) National lands shall be administered by the State in such a way as to ensure rational use and development thereof. (2) Consultative boards presided over by the administrative authorities and necessarily comprising representatives of the traditional authorities shall be established for this purpose.

The role of the Consultative Board is to investigate developments on a specific plot of national land, so the involvement of the traditional authorities gives them a real voice in practice over what happens to the customary communal property rights. The one question, though, that arises is whether the 'vesting provisions' (Articles 1, 14, 15 and 16 of Ordinance No. 74/1) could be effective without first divesting existing customary owners (village chiefs and individuals) of their customary ownership-type rights. The effect of this all-embracing notion of 'national lands' is that a vast majority of Cameroonians (including individuals and communities), who held land under the customary tenure system and without any state-recognised document of title, found their lands absorbed into the category of national lands. It has been argued that the effect of this notion of 'national lands' is to divest all customary rights holders of their customary ownership-type rights[53] but not necessarily other rights (such as the right to harvest timber products from forest on such lands).

However, it seems clear that this is not actually the case. Everybody still acts as though customary property rights still exist,[54] and subsequent legislation such

[53] Ngwasiri and Nje, *Advocacy for Separate Land Legislation for the Rural Areas of Cameroon*, pp. 3–15; Ngwasiri, 'The Impacts of the Present Land Tenure Reforms in Cameroon', 75–76; Njoh, 'The Political Economy of Urban Land Reforms in a Post-Colonial State', 411.

[54] If there is conflict between the laws, there are certain grounds such as the maintenance of 'public order' or 'public policy' on which written law will prevail over customary law. In other words, the courts

as the 1994 Forestry Law is also drafted on the basis that customary ownership rights still exist.[55] According to Assembe-Mvondo and others[56] this coexistence between written law and customary law is down to what they term the 'spirit of the Cameroonian legal system'; a system that has variously been described as a 'dual legal system where customary and informal practices are legalised or accepted by State authorities'[57] and as a '"hybrid land tenure regime", which mixes informal and legal practices'.[58] For example, although there is no mention in the land legislation of the land control interests of a community chief and/or family head, according to Article 17 of Ordinance No. 74/1 a customary community can at any time apply for the registration of land in the name of a community and/or its members as long as the community and/or its members can show proof of effective occupation or exploitation of the land on the basis of the traditions and customs of the community.[59] Provided that the land is thus registered, this mechanism should guarantee the continuous exercise of any customary communal property rights over the land. Acceptance that the Cameroonian system is a mixture of informal and formal rules is supported by the decision of Cameroon's Supreme Court in the case of *JIMS André v Madame Effa Faustine*,[60] in which the judges rejected as unfounded a petition based on a claim to ownership on the basis that the 'customary

are enjoined to apply only the customary law that is not contrary to the law and public policy or public order. This position was affirmed by the Cameroon Supreme Court decision in the case of *Bessala Awona v Bidzogo Geneviève*, [1962] Cor. A No. 445 of 3 April 1962. For more on the meaning and application of 'public policy' and 'public order', see N. Enonchong, 'Public Policy and Ordre Public: The Exclusion of Customary Law in Cameroon', *African Journal of International and Comparative Law*, 5 (1993), 503–524.

[55] For example the 1994 Forestry Law, section 8(1) recognises the 'customary right' of the local communities in all the different types of forests. This means 'the right which is recognised as being that of the local population to harvest all forest, wildlife and fish products freely for their personal use except the protected species'. Similarly, Law No. 96/12 of 5 August 1996 relating to Environmental Management in Cameroon recognises the exercise of local customary practices as applicable if they offer more efficient environmental management (section 9(f)). The exercise of customary norms is, however, limited to where there is no written law on environmental protection.

[56] S. Assembe-Mvondo and others, 'Review of the Legal Ownership Status of National Lands in Cameroon: A More Nuanced View', *Development Studies Research*, 1 (2014), 148–160 at 153–155.

[57] A. Teyssier, 'La régulation foncière au Cameroun, entre régimes communautaires et aspirations citoyennes', in P. Duguée and Ph. Jouve (eds), *Organisation spatiale et gestion des ressources et des territoires ruraux* (Montpellier, CIRAD/CNEARC, 2003), pp. 1–10.

[58] E. Le Roy, La réforme du droit de la terre dans certains pays d'Afrique francophone (Etude Législative, Rome, FAO, 1987), p. 115.

[59] In principle, landowners who could prove that they were in effective occupation of the land before 5 August 1974 were given a ten-year period within which they could register the land under the provisions of Article 13(2) of Decree No. 76/165 of 27 April 1976 (see Fisiy, *Power and Privilege in the Administration of Law*, pp. 42–47). In practice, though, communities can still apply for the registration of title even after the ten-year period has passed: Assembe-Mvondo and others, 'Review of the Legal Ownership Status of National Lands in Cameroon', 154.

[60] *JIMS André v Madame Effa Faustine*, [2002] Arrêt No 99/CC (Supreme Court of Cameroon) of 4 April 2002, *Juridis Périodique* No. 52, 29–45.

owner' did not hold a land certificate, thereby explicitly recognising the customary ownership of land based on historical facts.[61] It may well be the case that the acceptance of such a compromise on land tenure is an opportunity for the laws to be updated to reflect the reality of the land claims by local people.[62]

The use of formal and informal rules in the Cameroonian legal system means that it is possible to protect some customary communal property rights, but not others. For example, for some communities such as indigenous Pygmy populations, even if they could afford the cost of applying for the registration of land, proving that they have been in effective occupation or exploitation of the land on the basis of the traditions and customs of the community is very difficult considering their traditional hunter-gatherer lifestyles. This is further worsened by the difficulty in finding out what local community land and forest resource rights are in customary law, except by asking people, and the difficulties of verifying what people say in these contexts. Nevertheless, to recommend the grant of a land certificate, the Consultative Board[63] concerned has to first satisfy itself that the applicant was either in occupation or exploitation of the land at issue prior to 5 August 1974. It therefore follows that no registration of land can be accepted in respect of land which is in the possession of another without first revoking the right of the original occupier.[64] As argued above, there is a perception amongst non-hunter-gatherers that hunting and gathering does not confer rights over land. This makes it easy for the government and other outside groups to be able to appropriate Pygmy land, because the Pygmies are not perceived as original occupiers with rights that need to be revoked before registration is granted.

For other communities, though, whose land use practices such as agriculture are accepted as effective use and occupation, the occupation or exploitation of such land at a given time must necessarily be derived from customary law. The implication of this argument is that customary owners are still holding land under the customary land tenure system because at the time of the coming into force of the 1974 Land Ordinances, a vast majority of the citizens were without any state-recognised document of title. Although the Ordinances do not elaborate on the practicality of a community applying for a land certificate, in principle, any application will be in the name of the community head who is considered to hold the land in the name of his people. Judicial support for this view can be found in the observation of Ekema, CJ in the case of *Presbyterian Church Moderator*

[61] Assembe-Mvondo and others, 'Review of the Legal Ownership Status of National Lands in Cameroon', 154.

[62] E. Schlager and E. Ostrom. 'Property Rights Regimes and Natural Resources: A Conceptual Analysis', *Land Economics*, 68 (1992), 249–262; Assembe-Mvondo and others, 'Review of the Legal Ownership Status of National Lands in Cameroon', 157.

[63] Each Administrative Division in the country has at least one Consultative Board.

[64] See the case of *Chief Molinge & 3 others v Chief Musenja & 8 others*, [2000] 2 CCLR 1. See also *Adje Robert Acho v Rev. Ngwane Ediage Thomas*, [1998] 4 CCLR 109.

v D.C. Johnny.[65] After rejecting the contention of the Fon (chief) of Mankon that the land in dispute and all land in Mankon belonged to him,[66] the learned judge observed that, 'The chief holds the land of Mankon not in his own name but in the name of the people of Mankon.'[67]

As suggested above, this is a view that runs deep in African customary land tenure and was applied in Cameroon even before the coming into force of the 1974 Land Ordinances; a view that the community chief is a mere trustee holding the land for the common benefit of the members of the community and is accountable to members of the community to whom the land belongs. The chief is in no way the owner of the land which belongs to the community unless a piece of land belongs to him in this capacity.[68] This view contrasts with the present political dispensation in which, according to Pemunta, 'lineage and family heads own family land, while the chief is the *de facto* owner of all land in the village and the state claims ownership over all parcels of land'.[69] While Pemunta's view explains why some chiefs may now see themselves as 'owners' of land which should belong to members of the community, it has also been argued that the current perception does not depart from the concept of communal ownership. As Mamdani puts it, the reason is that 'corporate and individual land rights co-exist, explaining why the colonial notion of "private property rights" was only a unilineal reductionism of community rights based on the universal European concept of legal tenure'.[70]

For unoccupied land, no registration could take place under Decree No. 76/165, even if the land was claimed by individuals or customary communities. The only rights available to individuals and customary communities on unoccupied lands were hunting and fruit picking rights according to Article 17(3) of Ordinance No. 74/1:

> Subject to the regulations in force, hunting and fruit picking rights shall further be granted to them on lands in category 2 as defined in Article 15, until such a time as the State has assigned the lands for specific purposes.

According to this provision, contrary to customary rules which recognise communal holding of such lands, a customary community and/or its representative

[65] [1974] unreported (Bamenda Court of Appeal).

[66] Although not clearly stated, this erroneous claim was certainly based on the fact that in Cameroon, chiefs and other traditional rulers are officially considered as auxiliaries of the administration of the state and they therefore see themselves to some extent as quasi-public authority.

[67] *Presbyterian Church Moderator v D.C. Johnny*, [1974] unreported (Bamenda Court of Appeal).

[68] See also the case of *Chief Lobe Njembele v Benedict Nsombai*, [1980] unreported (Buea Court of Appeal). This is a case where a chief entered land possessed by another and collected his felled trees. The High Court had ruled in favour of Nsombai but the chief appealed the decision, an appeal that was rejected.

[69] Pemunta, 'The Governance of Nature as Development and the Erasure of the Pygmies of Cameroon', 363.

[70] Mamdani, *Citizen and Subject*, pp. 139–146.

cannot apply for a land certificate for such land either because the law does not recognise the specific form of land and resource use as conferring any land rights, or they cannot claim or prove to have been in use or occupation of the land because the land is truly unoccupied. Such land reverts to the common pool of 'national lands' and the state has a free hand in how such lands are designated and used as per Article 16 of Ordinance No. 74/1.

Public property rights

Under the 1974 Land Ordinances, there are two categories of state lands: the public and the private property of the state, public and parastatal bodies.[71] The public property of the state consists of all personal and real property which, by its very nature (e.g. coastlands; waterways; subsoil; and air space) or intended purpose (e.g. roads), is set aside either for the direct use of the public or for public services.[72] Such lands are inalienable, imprescriptible, and under no circumstances should be subject to any private appropriation.[73] Significantly the public property of the state also includes 'concession of traditional chiefdoms and property relating to it, including where the concession of chiefdoms is considered as the joint property of the community'.[74] In this case, the chief retains a right of enjoyment, but not the community, while the state is the owner. The nature of this category of property suggests that customary communal property rights have always been exercised over much of what is now the public property of the state, but depending on the purpose for which the land has been set aside, such rights may now be limited if their exercise will be contrary to the purpose for which it is set aside.

The private property of the state is acquired from the category of 'national lands' or from private ownership through expropriation on the grounds provided for in Article 18 of Ordinance No. 74/1, as amended by Ordinance No. 77/1 of 10 January 1977:

> The State may classify portions of national lands under the public property of the State or incorporate such lands in the private property of the State or in that of other public bodies for purposes of public, economic and social utility.

This provision suggests that the public and private property of the state are both acquired from national lands, and the main difference between these two categories of state lands lies in the purpose for which they have been classified. In practice, though, the distinction between the two is slim. For example, given that the

[71] Ordinance No. 74/2 of 6 July 1974 to establish rules governing state lands, article 1.
[72] Ordinance No. 74/2 of 6 July 1974, articles 2, 3 and 4.
[73] Ordinance No. 74/2 of 6 July 1974, article 2(2).
[74] Ordinance No. 74/2 of 6 July 1974, article 4(l).

instruments that govern land tenure and determine the status of forest land are the 1974 Land Ordinances, it is possible to establish categories of forest that are equivalent to the legal status of the land on which the forest is found.[75] From this perspective, the land base of state forests should be the public and private lands of the state. However the categorisation of forests makes no reference to state forests being the public property of the state. Instead, all state forests which are made up of the permanent forest estate (forest concessions and protected areas) are classified as part of the private property of the state.[76]

Being included in the category of 'national lands', land which belonged to the community can easily be acquired as the public or private property of the state if it is in the public interest. However, the rights of bona fide owners and occupants held over state lands prior to the entry into force of the Ordinance were protected except where it was in the public interest to dispossess them and subject to the payment of adequate compensation.[77]

Thus where customary communal property rights are exercised over the public or private property of the state, the customary communities or individuals are legally or in practice assumed to be entitled to the protection given by this provision. For example, within state forests, shifting cultivation is strictly forbidden and local use of forest resources is restricted, with the customary logging rights of the local population preserved, but only if they are not contrary to the objectives of such forests.[78] While some activities such as shifting cultivation or public access to state forests may be regulated or forbidden,[79] the local population is entitled to compensation only if the customary logging rights that are contrary to the purpose of the forest are limited.[80] While this provision is laudable, its application is also likely to leave out a large proportion of lands that are, in the eyes of the law, viewed as 'unoccupied' lands and have therefore been subsumed under the category of national lands. As will be seen in the following section, this provision has been given a very wide interpretation by the State, even where there is clear evidence of use or occupation.

[75] Assembe-Mvondo and others, 'Review of the Legal Ownership Status of National Lands in Cameroon', 155.

[76] 1994 Forestry Law, section 25(1). See also FAO, *State of the World's Forests 2011* (Rome, FAO, 2011), p. 179.

[77] Ordinance No. 74/2 of 4 July 1974, article 7.

[78] 1994 Forestry Law, section 26(1) and (2).

[79] 1994 Forestry Law, section 26(3). See also section 30(2).

[80] 1994 Forestry Law, section 26(2).

Expropriation

In Cameroon, land expropriation is carried out under Land Ordinance No. 74/3.[81] Article 1(1) provides that:

> Expropriation for a public purpose shall be pronounced by decree on completion of the procedure defined by the present Ordinance. By the said decree, existing titles over the land in question shall be extinguished and the land thus declared free shall be registered in the name of the State.

Although it is not clear from this provision if, by existing titles, the Ordinance intends to include those still holding land under customary law, it nevertheless gives the state the right to revoke any right of occupancy (existing title) for the overriding public interest. Article 2, however, qualifies the meaning of existing titles to affect only private property. It states that 'Expropriation for a public purpose shall only affect private property as defined in Article 2 [of Ordinance No. 74/1].' This provision seems to mean that only private rights are extinguished, and not customary rights, especially as any land held by virtue of customary tenure under which a land certificate has not been issued is automatically absorbed into the category of national lands. In broad terms, Ordinance No. 74/3 stipulates that any public body, state agency, parastatal, or local council can apply to have land expropriated for public use. The implication of this procedure for existing customary communal property rights is that, depending on the purpose for which the land is being expropriated, these rights can be restricted or even extinguished.

Appropriation

In addition to the expropriation procedure explained above, evidence suggests that Article 1(1) of Ordinance No. 74/3 has been extended to justify the provision of private land reserves for the state which could be redistributed if and when the need arose. This is known as appropriation, and by this notion the state could delineate and claim property from 'unoccupied' lands. As argued above, 'unoccupied' lands include land in respect of which a customary community and/or its representative cannot apply for a land certificate, because the law does not recognise the specific form of land and resource use as conferring any land rights. Such lands were then registered as the private property of the state. This procedure is still widely applied because it does not require the payment of compensation. Once property has been registered as the private property of the state, one of three things can be done to it: (1) the state can sell it or lease it to private individuals or communities in the

[81] Ordinance No. 74/3 of 6 July 1974 concerning the procedure governing expropriation for a public purpose and the terms and conditions of compensation.

same manner as if it were national lands;[82] (2) land can be exchanged between the state and its citizens under the conditions laid down by an empowering degree (no empowering decree has been published and no such situation has yet been recorded under the present law); and (3) the state can give the landed property to a council or public body following the expropriation procedure outlined above.[83] The justification for such appropriation has never been expressly stated in writing, and highlights another dimension of just how state power is used in divesting certain groups of people of their property and reallocating it to others without the 'public interest' justification or payment of compensation. For example, under the 1994 Forestry Law, the council forests (which along with state forests make up the permanent forest estate) are categorised as the private land of the council, but with no equivalent of section 26(1) to protect the customary logging rights of the local population.[84] However, the development of forestry in Cameroon has also seen some form of re-allocation of appropriated land to communities in the form of community forests.

Community forests (and some other forests)[85] are unclassified forests which are on non-permanent forest land. The non-permanent forest estate consists of forest-land that may be allocated for uses other than forestry.[86] The land base of such forests is national land because they are carved out of the national lands category.[87] Although community forests are re-allocated to communities, the exercise of communal property rights over them must be in accordance with a simple management plan. A simple management plan is part of the agreement for the management of a community forest and determines the activities to be carried out. This agreement is 'a contract by virtue of which the service in charge of forestry allots to a community, a portion of national forest, which the community manages, preserves and exploits in its own interest'.[88]

Once the agreement has been signed, section 37(5) of the 1994 Forestry Law provides that, 'Forest products of all kinds resulting from the management of community forests shall belong to the village communities concerned.' This is

[82] Decree No. 76/167 of 27 April 1976 to establish the terms and conditions of management of the private property of the state, articles 6 and 7.

[83] In Cameroon, the local councils remain very much part of the centralised state even though decentralisation as stipulated by the 1996 amendment of the 1972 Constitution of the Republic of Cameroon is gradually being implemented.

[84] 1994 Forestry Law, sections 30–33.

[85] This includes for example communal forests and forests belonging to private individuals; see 1994 Forestry Law, sections 37–39.

[86] For an account of the concept of community forestry in Cameroon, see E. S. Egbe, 'The Concept of Community Forestry under Cameroonian Law', *Journal of African Law*, 45 (2001), 25–50.

[87] A. Karsenty, *Large-Scale Acquisition of Rights on Forest Lands in Africa* (Washington, DC, RRI, 2010).

[88] Decree No. 95-531-PM of 23 August 1995 to determine the conditions of implementation of the forestry regulations (hereinafter, 1995 Decree of Implementation), article 3(16).

significant because it guarantees the rights of communities to own everything from the forests (including timber)[89] and allows them a 'free hand' in determining what is contained in an agreement.[90] Crucially, these management agreements must specify the beneficiaries, boundaries of the forest allocated to the communities, and special instructions on the management of areas of woodland and/or wildlife, formulated at the behest of the communities.[91] This suggests that the communities can specify and exercise their customary communal property rights within such forests. However the process of determining the land use practices that confer land rights, which leaves out hunter-gatherer-type rights, means that some groups such as the Pygmy populations, who also inhabit these forests, are likely to be discriminated against in their management and in the share of benefits.[92]

Furthermore, although section 37(1) of the 1994 Forestry Law requires the services in charge of forests to provide free technical assistance to the local communities, the technicalities involved and the process and cost of setting up a corporate body mean that simple management plans are cumbersome, expensive to put together and difficult to follow for local village communities. This may in turn limit the manner in which the community is able to exercise their customary communal property rights as the state may still allocate the forests for large-scale industrial logging.[93] While the community forestry option has been seen as a positive in terms of encouraging community participation, it is worth noting that the decentralisation of forest management was a 'supply' put forward by the central state, rather than a 'demand' from below.[94] Thus, state authority over natural resources such as forests was validated while at the same time weakening any customary communal property rights the local communities might have had in the past, with the main political argument being that the state wants to regulate forest

[89] This right is further strengthened by the provision of section 37(7) of the 1994 Forestry Law which provides that, 'Village communities shall have the right to preemption in the event of the alienation of products found in their [community] forests.' Despite the apparent guarantee of the right to everything from the forests, including timber, based on the current zoning system approved in 1995 (Decree No. 95-678-PM of 18 December 1995 to institute an indicative land use framework for the southern forested area of Cameroon), it is highly unlikely that the exploitation for commercial purposes of a valuable resource such as timber would ever be permitted in community forests under the terms of a management agreement, or that such high-value forests would ever fall under the community forestry category.

[90] 1995 Decree of Implementation, article 95(2) provides that, 'Each community shall determine the conditions under which forest exploitation acts shall be granted.'

[91] 1994 Forestry Law, section 38(1).

[92] See Pemunta, 'The Governance of Nature as Development and the Erasure of the Pygmies of Cameroon', 359–362.

[93] A. Pénelon, *Community Forestry: It May Indeed Be a New Management Tool, But Is It Accessible? Two Case Studies in Eastern Cameroon* (Forestry Participation Series, London, IIED, 1997), pp. 10–11.

[94] P. R. Oyono, J. C. Ribot and A. M. Larson, *Green and Black Gold in Rural Cameroon: Natural Resources for Local Governance, Justice and Sustainability* (Environmental Governance in Africa Working Paper Series, Washington, DC, WRI, 2006), p. 9.

exploitation in order to ensure rational allocation.[95] The effect is an even weaker or no protection for the customary communal property rights of some communities, such as the Pygmy populations. The failure to recognise the full range of customary communal property rights for the different categories of forest and especially for community forests is one of the main weaknesses of the Forestry Law.[96]

Implications for customary communal property rights in Cameroon

With regard to the pre-existing customary land tenure regime, the important question arising from the above discussion is this: who now owns land (including land that belongs to the community under customary law) in Cameroon? The 1974 Land Ordinances have divested individuals and communities of their customary property rights over land and any natural resources such as forests that it holds, without transferring it to anyone, save that the state is made trustee of it.[97] For land which was customarily owned and for which no land certificate has been issued, it is difficult to know where ownership now lies or whether there is now any kind of ownership of land still existing, especially as there is no mention in the land legislation of the land control interests of chiefs and lineage heads. Nevertheless, there seems to be a consensus that customary landowners have lost their pre-existing rights by the enactment of the Land Ordinances and that the state is now the sole proprietor of these lands and the state alone can allocate the lands in question or deal with them in any other manner.[98] In other words, the guardianship that the state claims over land (Article 1(2) of Ordinance No. 74/1) is not just benign

[95] This was the same argument advanced to justify state claims over ownership of land under the 1974 Land Ordinances. For more on the gap created by the law between the state and local communities, see further, A. Labrousse and F.-X. Verschave, *Les pillards de la forêt: exploitations criminelles en Afrique*, vol. 17 (Marseille, Editions Agone, 2002), pp. 4–7; M. Zoa, 'Community Forests: Reconciling Customary and Legal Concepts', in M. C. Diaw, T. Aseh and R. Prabhu (eds), *In Search of a Common Ground: Adaptive Collaborative Management in Cameroon* (Bogor, CIFOR, 2009), pp. 116–138; and P. R. Oyono, 'The Social and Organisational Roots of Ecological Uncertainties in Cameroon's Forest Management Decentralisation Model', *European Journal of Development Research*, 16 (2004), 174–191 at 174.

[96] See, for example, E. Beauchamp and V. Ingram, 'Impacts of Community Forests on Livelihoods in Cameroon: Lessons from Two Case Studies', *International Forestry Review*, 13 (2011), 389–403 at 399.

[97] Ngwasiri and Nje, *Advocacy for Separate Land Legislation for the Rural Areas of Cameroon*, pp. 3–15; Ngwasiri, 'The Impacts of the Present Land Tenure Reforms in Cameroon', 75–76; and Njoh, 'The Political Economy of Urban Land Reforms in a Post-Colonial State', 411.

[98] Ngwasiri has argued that, 'The present land legislation in the country . . . appears to have reduced all customary land rights to mere . . . limited rights of user with only as much security of tenure as the state is willing to allow': Ngwasiri, 'The Impacts of the Present Land Tenure Reforms in Cameroon', 75–76. This view is supported by Fisiy who has also observed that, 'the corporate nature of customary land rights cannot be legally enforced under the 1974 land law reforms': Fisiy, *Power and Privilege in the Administration of Law*, p. 52.

protection, as it seems; it is ownership with the power to alienate, as demonstrated by the far-reaching powers not only to expropriate land from people, but also to control properties through considerable executive and administrative powers.[99] This view is not only shared by several authors;[100] it is also common for government officials in Cameroon's Ministry in charge of forestry to declare that forest land belongs to the state.[101]

Despite the overwhelming arguments in favour of this view, it has, nevertheless, been suggested that the land and resources that the state holds belong to the Cameroonian nation, and so the guardianship that the state claims over un-allocated lands is only legal custodianship with supervisory powers.[102] In spite of this lack of full recognition of customary property rights (except in cases where a land certificate has been issued), customary communities and individuals have continued to occupy and exploit land (including land that has been re-allocated) as though customary rights still exist. In relation to forestry, for example, the lack of security in tenure puts communities in a precarious situation where they are faced with two options: refusing to allow logging companies access to their forests, or negotiating a high price for allowing the companies access to the site.[103] However, the overriding state power in the management and control of forests means that, in the end, the choice is limited and communities are left with trying to secure as much as possible from the forests even if it is contrary to the law.

There are judicial decisions which go contrary to Ekema, CJ's observation in the case of *Presbyterian Church Moderator v D.C. Johnny*,[104] that the community chief is a mere trustee holding the land for the common benefit of members of

[99] Njoh, 'The Political Economy of Urban Land Reforms in a Post-Colonial State', 411.

[100] See, for example, W. D. Sunderlin, J. Hatcher and M. Liddle, *From Exclusion to Ownership? Challenges and Opportunities in Advancing Forest Tenure Reform* (Washington, DC, RRI, 2008), p. 64; L. Cotula and J. Mayers, *Tenure in REDD – Start-Point or Afterthought?* (Natural Resource Issues No. 15, London, IIED, 2009), p. 67; J. Hatcher and L. Bailey, *Tropical Forest Tenure Assessment: Trends, Challenges and Opportunities* (Technical Series No. 37, Yokohama, ITTO, 2011), p. 48; L. Alden Wily, *Whose Land Is It? The Status of Customary Land Tenure in Cameroon* (Yaoundé, CED/FERN/Rainforest Foundation, 2011), p. 189; L. Alden Wily, 'The Law Is to Blame: The Vulnerable Status of Common Property Rights in Sub-Saharan Africa', *Development and Change*, 42 (2011), 733–757; FAO, *Reforming Forest Tenure: Issues, Principles and Process* (FAO Forestry Paper No. 165, Rome, FAO, 2011), p. 116.

[101] Assembe-Mvondo and others, 'Review of the Legal Ownership Status of National Lands in Cameroon', 155; S. Ongolo and A. Karsenty, 'The Politics of Forestland Use in a Cunning Government: Lessons for Contemporary Forest Governance Reforms', *International Forestry Review*, 17 (2015), 195–209.

[102] Assembe-Mvondo and others, 'Review of the Legal Ownership Status of National Lands in Cameroon', 155.

[103] Pénelon, *Community Forestry: It May Indeed Be a New Management Tool, But Is It Accessible?*, pp. 10–11; Beauchamp and Ingram, 'Impacts of Community Forests on Livelihoods in Cameroon: Lessons from Two Case Studies', 397–399.

[104] *Presbyterian Church Moderator v D.C. Johnny*, [1974] unreported (Bamenda Court of Appeal).

the community, and instead emphasise the view that the state (through its various arms) is now the new 'owner' of land. For example, in *Chief Molinge & 3 others v Chief Musenja & 8* others,[105] the court, in allowing an appeal, made the following observation on the effect of Part III of the Ordinance on customary land tenure in relation to land traditionally occupied by two communities but formally held by the Cameroon Development Corporation (CDC):

> A tenant cannot give what he does not have '*nemo dat quod non habet*'. The law is that, if a tenant like CDC[106] no longer needs the land for [the] purpose for which it was initially assigned, the said land reverts to the state. In particular, Article 13(2) of Ordinance 74/2 of 6 July 1974 in relation to private property of the state renders void any attempt to alienate property of the state without prior approval of the Minister in charge of Lands.[107]

The court found that since the issue was about 'title to land . . . disputed by two communities, and . . . seen as an inter-communal boundary dispute or as a claim over unregistered land', the lower court had no jurisdiction on the matter.[108]

In reaching its decision, the court went further to observe that:

> [A]ccording to Article 17 of Ordinance 74/2 to establish rules governing land tenure, national lands are allocated by grant, lease or assignment. In the event of such land no longer serving the purpose for which it was initially allocated, it becomes automatically incorporated *as of right* in the national lands.[109]

Accordingly, the question was not which of these two communities 'owned' the land. The land in question was formally CDC land and if the CDC no longer used it, the land reverted to the common pool of national land. The interests of the communities were irrelevant.

The position of the court in this case and the other cases mentioned above has something rather curious in it. In addition to emphasising the notion of national lands, the above statement by the court reflects generally the trends the courts have mainly followed since the enactment of the 1974 Land Ordinances, i.e. attempting to read the law as it is without attempting to consider the legality of the customary land tenure rules which are nevertheless still applicable. This is perhaps due to the ambiguity in the jurisdictions of the courts of law and the Consultative Board over unregistered land,[110] but this apparent lack of jurisdiction by the courts over

[105] *Chief Molinge & 3 others v Chief Musenja & 8 others*, [2000] 2 CCLR 1.
[106] A state corporation.
[107] *Chief Molinge & 3 others v Chief Musenja & 8 others*, [15], p. 2.
[108] *Chief Molinge & 3 others v Chief Musenja & 8 others*, [5], p. 7 and [5], p. 8.
[109] *Chief Molinge & 3 others v Chief Musenja & 8 others*, [35], p. 7 (emphasis added).
[110] Ordinance No. 74/1, article 5(3). See also Ngwasiri, 'The Impacts of the Present Land Tenure Reforms in Cameroon', 84; and N. Enonchong, 'Jurisdiction over Disputes Relating to "National Lands" in Cameroon', *African Journal of International and Comparative Law*, 11 (1999), 100–127.

land matters concerning customary law is one of the fundamental weaknesses of the land law.[111]

Notwithstanding, it appears from the current law that the rules of tenure, so far as unregistered land is concerned, are necessarily the rules of customary land tenure even if all land has been 'nationalised'.

The provisions of the Land Ordinances and procedures have made no secret of the intention and purpose of the law. It declared land (occupied and unoccupied, held by individuals and communities under customary law) as national land, except where a land certificate has been issued. There is a bias in favour of private property, and communal property is encouraged only when it is administered by the state as 'national lands'. This has made it difficult to enforce collective customary communal property rights, thereby rendering illegal, for instance, any sale or alienation of unregistered land by a community or individual holding customary rights. At the same time, the state is also unable to completely alienate all land in practice because it is just not possible for communities and individuals to register all lands over which they have traditionally exercised customary communal property rights. In the end, because customary practices remain the de facto dominant tenure type, especially in rural areas,[112] the Cameroonian authorities are forced to tolerate certain practices. For example, in practice, a seller (private individual) of a parcel of 'national land' has to sign a document known as a 'Certificate of Abandonment of Customary Rights', which is certified by the authorities and accepted by the Consultative Board (responsible for investigating developments on a specific plot of national land before a land certificate is issued). So, here the authorities can be seen as implicitly recognising customary ownership of the land.[113]

Nevertheless it now seems obvious that the 1974 Land Ordinances have created a situation where the law cannot be effectively applied without reverting to action for which there is no legal basis. That is, it relies on the very features of the customary tenure systems that it refuses to acknowledge to determine who could be granted title in communally held lands that had been incorporated into national lands.[114] These features include the absolute ownership of land by the community and the community chief or family head's right of management and control, which are the hallmarks of customary land tenure systems. As one scholar has argued:

[111] This view is shared by Ngwasiri, 'The Impacts of the Present Land Tenure Reforms in Cameroon', 73–85; and Enonchong, 'Jurisdiction over Disputes Relating to "National Lands" in Cameroon', 100–127.

[112] J. W. Bruce (ed.), *Country Profiles of Land Tenure: Africa, 1996* (Land Tenure Center Research Paper No. 130, Madison, WI, Land Tenure Center, 1998).

[113] N. A. Tientcheu, *Droits réels et domaine national au Cameroun* (Yaoundé, Presses Universitaires d'Afrique, 2005), p. 486; Assembe-Mvondo and others, 'Review of the Legal Ownership Status of National Lands in Cameroon', 154.

[114] Ordinance No. 74/1 of 6 July 1974, article 17.

> By refusing to acknowledge the existence of local landlords (at least not as owners of land) [but as holders in possession or occupation], the 1974 Land Ordinances have elevated the State to the status of the paramount landlord, claiming, expropriating, and selling land as it deems appropriate. Nobody, not even the [customary] holder of a land certificate can claim to be free from State encroachment.[115]

Conclusion

It could be said that customary landowners have lost their title to land by nationalisation, except where they have applied and obtained a land certificate under the conditions laid down by the 1974 Land Ordinances. Land reform is skewed in favour of private property at the expense of communal property, which is encouraged only when it is administered by the state as 'national lands'. Where there is some recognition of the role of the community to administer communal property, such as in the case of community forests, the exercise of communal property rights is often limited to the extent that the different range of customary communal property rights that have traditionally been exercised is not recognised.

While the 1974 Land Ordinances have 'elevated the State to the status of the paramount landlord, claiming, expropriating, and selling land as it deems appropriate', the state is unable to completely alienate all land, with certain customary practices legalised and tolerated by the Cameroonian authorities. As a consequence, a majority of citizens have continued to live and use land and resources such as forests on an individual and communal customary law basis as if the written laws do not exist. This situation raises questions not just about the legality of such use and occupation, but also about the legitimacy of state power to dispossess communities of their customary property rights, especially in relation to communal property interests. This is compounded by the fact that the effective application of the provisions of the Land Ordinances relies on the very features of the customary tenure systems that it refuses to acknowledge, and the situation is made worse by the fact that some community land use practices are not recognised as conferring land rights of any kind. In the end, reconciling the law with customary ideas on communal property remains a problem. This situation has serious implications for the wider rule of law in society, raising fundamental questions about the sources of legality, illegalities and legitimacy in land ownership.

[115] Fisiy, *Power and Privilege in the Administration of Law*, p. 52 (emphasis added).

7

Customary Law and Communal Property in South Africa

Challenges and Opportunities

JUANITA M. PIENAAR

Introduction

The tapestry of diversity encountered in South Africa exhibits a variety of multicoloured, vibrant threads interwoven and embroidered into a unique, rich fabric. The cloth is both strong and fragile. Different strands represent cultural variety, rich in tradition, representing a broad spectrum: from ancient African culture to more recent Western influences embodying Roman-Dutch and English law, coupled with unique South African law-strands. While not all of these threads are equal in their impact or have contributed evenly to the overall tapestry, the result is striking: colourful, diverse and dynamic. Some threads, for example colonial and apartheid strands, very prominent at one time, have been formally removed from the tapestry. Their removal has scarred the fabric and some remnants remain, albeit less prominent than a decade or so ago. Since joining the international community when a new constitutional dispensation commenced in 1994,[1] foreign and international law influences have also found their way into the fabric.

Framing the tapestry is the South African Constitution,[2] securing the fabric and ultimately holding everything together. While the tapestry is secure, the threads are not permanently fixed. Instead, individual strands can be unpicked, carefully and precisely, and manipulated and rewoven. However, when one strand is

[1] The first democratic election occurred on 27 April 1994. See further I. Currie and J. de Waal, *The Bill of Rights Handbook* (Claremont, Juta, 2014), pp. 2–6; D. L. Carey Miller and A. Pope, *Land Title in South Africa* (Kenwyn, Juta, 2000), pp. 3–44.

[2] The interim Constitution (commencement 27 April 1994) was replaced by the final and current Constitution in 1996. See *Certification of the Amended Text of the Constitution of the Republic of South Africa, 1996 (Second Certification Judgment)*, 1997 (2) SA 97 (CC).

loosened, it reverberates throughout the tapestry, requiring further adjustment and re-alignment. While the strands are all separate and unique, by inter-connecting, the tapestry is formed – one strand supporting the other.

Customary law is one such strand interwoven into the South African tapestry. Undergirding that thread is a right to culture[3] and to be part of a particular cultural community.[4] Inevitably this also includes having and exercising a variety of rights, including rights identified and listed in the Bill of Rights.[5] A dual legal system furthermore emerges representing two legal paradigms: customary law and Western (common) law. Within each paradigm, legal sources, traditions and approaches exist, often in parallel, but also interceding and connecting at different points and axes.[6]

Part and parcel of South African customary law is traditional communal property, in land in particular.[7] It is communal because the land 'belongs' to the community as a whole on the basis of membership.[8] Despite being categorised as communal, it is important to note that different role players emerge at different levels in relation to the allocation, administration, regulation and protection of land rights,[9] as explored in more detail below.[10]

Apart from the inherent complexity, the aftermath of South Africa's history of dispossession is still lingering, compounding complexity.[11] While this is the case with regard to land generally, it is markedly so concerning the former Bantustan areas. This is the case because these areas, evolving from 'Black Spots',[12] to reserves and finally Bantustan areas, continue to accommodate communities that live in accordance with customary law, usually under traditional forms of governance, for example, traditional leaders. These areas are generally referred

[3] Section 30 of the Constitution of the Republic of South Africa

[4] Section 31 of the Constitution of the Republic of South Africa.

[5] Chapter 2 of the Constitution of the Republic of South Africa, encompassing sections 7–41.

[6] See for more detail C. Rautenbach and J. C. Bekker (eds), *Introduction to Legal Pluralism* (Durban, LexisNexis, 2014), pp. 5–16.

[7] See generally T. W. Bennett, *Customary Law in South Africa* (Cape Town, Juta, 2004), pp. 371–410; Rautenbach and Bekker, *Legal Pluralism*, pp. 121–142, J. M. Pienaar, *Land Reform* (Cape Town, Juta, 2014), pp. 464–481.

[8] Editors' note: For the relationship between communal property and community membership, see also Xu and Gong in this volume.

[9] A. Claassens, 'Contested Power in Apartheid Tribal Boundaries: The Implications of "Living Customary Law" for Indigenous Accountability Mechanisms', in H. Mostert and T. Bennett (eds), *Pluralism and Development* (Cape Town, Juta, 2011), pp. 174–211; A. Claassens and B. Cousins (eds), *Land, Power and Custom* (Cape Town, UCT Press, 2008).

[10] See 'Communal property, with a focus on land'.

[11] See for background Pienaar, *Land Reform*, pp. 142–172, D. van der Merwe, 'Land Tenure in South Africa: A Brief History and Some Reform Proposals', *TSAR* (1989), 663–692; T. W. Bennett, 'African Land – A History of Dispossession', in R. Zimmermann and D. Visser (eds), *Southern Cross* (Cape Town, Juta, 1996), p. 66.

[12] Pienaar, *Land Reform*, pp. 82–84.

to as 'communal areas' or 'traditional areas' and form the focus of this chapter. Conceptual clarification of communal property and land is therefore inherently complex and inter-connected in light of the above.

While exploration is necessary at a theoretical level concerning terminology and conceptual clarification, it is equally necessary for practical reasons. Customary law is a very real, everyday, lived experience for approximately 17–18 million South Africans.[13] While it is important for legal scholars to untangle and unpack concepts and definitions, their practical implications for citizens are profound. A range of questions emerge: who decides what customary law is, what the particular rules are, which rights are relevant and exercised and which rights are protected, when, how and by whom? Answers to these questions are furthermore informed by traditional forms of governance, the law-making process itself and the administration of justice.

The current situation in these areas,[14] coupled with recent legislative and other developments, necessitates an urgent, in-depth analysis of all customary property law-related matters. Ideally, this would include analyses of access to natural resources, environmental matters, land use planning, township establishment, housing, infrastructure planning, development, and sustainability in general. Such an ambitious endeavour would extend the boundaries of this chapter. However much that enquiry is needed, the scope of this chapter is limited to the inter-connectedness of customary law and communal property in land and the challenges and opportunities for South Africa.

To this end this chapter consists of five sections, in addition to this introduction. The first section deals with contextualisation of the two main components in this exploration, namely customary law and communal property in land; while the second section sets out and deals with the inter-connectedness of these integral elements. The various role players are identified and discussed, in general but also in light of recent case law, policy and legislative developments. In light of the discussion in the second section, the third section highlights the challenges South Africa is faced with in this context. The fourth section advances some opportunities, while the last section embodies the conclusion.

[13] Claassens, 'Contested Power', pp. 174–211.

[14] In this chapter the phrases 'communal areas', 'traditional areas', former Bantustan or homeland areas, refer to the same geographical space.

Contextualisation: customary law and communal property

Backdrop: a complexity of land control systems

In pursuit of a racially-based land control system, a grid of discriminatory measures was developed over a period spanning several decades, impacting on access to land, tenure security and land ownership patterns. This history, embedded in apartheid, is well known and well documented.[15] While overarching spatial racial segregation was endorsed by way of separate development initiatives,[16] particular racial and cultural backgrounds of individuals and communities provided the necessary points of departure. Linked to spatial racial segregation was the 'homeland' initiative embodying different (separate) homelands or territorial areas for distinctive racial and cultural groups. Gradually and inevitably, this process of separate development resulted in a geographical space consisting of four provinces,[17] four national states[18] and six self-governing territories,[19] generally referred to as 'traditional areas' or Bantustans.[20] The overarching goal of racial segregation was supplemented and supported by the 'three pillars of *apartheid*'.[21] They were, first, provisions dealing with access to and control over land, constituting influx control;[22] second, draconian enforcement of unlawful occupation (squatting)

[15] T. Keegan, *Colonial South Africa and the Origins of the Racial Order* (Cape Town, David Philip Publishers, 1996), pp. 170–208; and see generally S. Dubow, *Apartheid 1948–1994* (Oxford, Oxford University Press, 2014); and S. Friedman, *Race, Class and Power* (Pietermaritzburg, University of KZN Press, 2015).

[16] A. Sparks, *The Mind of South Africa* (Cape Town, Jonathan Ball, 2007), p. 180; L. Evans, 'South Africa's Bantustans and the Dynamics of "Decolonization": Reflections on Writing Histories of the Homelands', *SA Historical Journal*, 64(1) (2012), 117.

[17] Transvaal, Orange Free State, Cape and Natal provinces.

[18] National states, namely Transkei, Ciskei, Bophuthatswana and Venda, were located within the boundaries of South Africa, but were independent with their own legal systems and national symbols. See G. E. Devenish, 'The Development of Administrative and Political Control over Rural Blacks', in A. J. Rycroft, L. J. Boulle, M. K. Robertson and P. R. Spiller (eds), *Race and the Law in South Africa* (Cape Town, Juta, 1987), pp. 31–32; A. Manson and B. Mbenga, *Land, Chiefs, Mining* (Johannesburg, Wits University Press, 2014), pp. 124–141 with regard to Buphuthatswana.

[19] These territories were not yet independent, but were in the process of becoming independent states: Lebowa, KwaNdebele, KaNgwane, Gazankulu, Qwaqwa and KwaZulu.

[20] W. Beinart, *Twentieth Century South Africa* (New York, Oxford University Press, 2001), p. 217. 'Bantustan' means 'Bantu state' and is linked to the 'stans' created following the partition of India in 1947.

[21] Pienaar, *Land Reform*, pp. 105–112.

[22] J. J. McCarthy, 'African Land Tenure as a Popular Issue and Power Relations in South African Urban and Peri-Urban Areas', in C. Cross and R. Haines (eds), *Towards Freehold* (Cape Town, Juta, 1988), pp. 122–127.

measures;[23] and third, group areas legislation.[24] Aligned with objectives of racial segregation and separate development, all land-related matters, including land use planning, survey, deeds and registries, followed suit. Inevitably, the Grand Plan of *Apartheid* resulted in a complex, diverse legal framework, embodying different sets of measures, impacting on different areas in South Africa, aligned with race and culture. Overarching the complex, diverse land control system, a dual legal system furthermore operated, comprising customary law, embodying African elements; and national law, essentially embodying Western elements. Coupled with the dual property law system, the end result reflected a complex, multi-layered legal system in general, but specifically with regard to property rights and property-related concepts.[25]

It was within this complex grid of measures that an all-encompassing land reform programme, consisting of three separate, but inter-connected, sub-programmes, was embarked on post-1994. While all of the sub-programmes, constituting land redistribution,[26] tenure reform[27] and restitution[28] respectively, impact on the former Bantustan areas, in this chapter the focus is on tenure reform only. This is necessary as tenure reform deals specifically with amending the manner in which control is exercised over property, and this chapter highlights the opportunities and challenges embodied in this process in relation to communal property in land. Where the former Bantustan areas are concerned, some measure of progress had been achieved by introducing a new statutory form of ownership, namely a communal property association (or CPA), elaborated on in more detail below.[29] An attempt to formalise communal land rights by way of the Communal Land Rights Act 11 of 2004 was unsuccessful when the Act was found to be unconstitutional.[30] Despite the overarching land reform programme being in operation for more than two decades, the combination of traditional communal land and legislative

[23] J. M. Pienaar, '"Unlawful Occupier" in Perspective: History, Legislation and Case Law', in H. Mostert and M. J. de Waal (eds), *Essays in Honour of CG van der Merwe* (Durban, LexisNexis, 2011), pp. 309–330.

[24] M. K. Robertson, 'Black Land Tenure: Disabilities and Some Rights', in Rycroft et al., *Race and the Law in South Africa*, pp. 119–139, 125–126; H. Schoombee, 'Group Areas Legislation – The Political Control of Ownership and of Occupation of Land', *Acta Juridica*, 1985, 77; and J. Platzky and C. Walker, *The Surplus People: Forced Removals in South Africa* (Johannesburg, Ravan Press, 1985).

[25] Pienaar, *Land Reform*, pp. 142–153.

[26] Section 25(5) of the Constitution enjoins the state to take reasonable steps to broaden access to land for the vulnerable and the landless.

[27] Section 25(6) of the Constitution, read with section 25(9), is aimed at making insecure rights more secure.

[28] Section 25(7) of the Constitution aims to restore lost land or rights of land, due to racially discriminatory laws and practices of the past.

[29] See 'Other property constructs or managerial bodies'.

[30] See also 'The state and the Ministry of Rural Development and Land Reform' below. *Tongoane and Others v Minister of Agriculture and Land Affairs and Others*, 2010 (6) SA 214 (CC); Claassens and Cousins, *Land, Power and Custom.*

adjustments thereof[31] has largely prevailed. Therefore, insecure tenure, often linked to inequitable access to land, especially where women are concerned, continues in Bantustan areas.[32] These conditions, coupled with new developments impacting on traditional governance structures and the administration of justice, explored in detail below,[33] highlight the urgent need for intervention.

Legal pluralism and the Constitution

The tapestry that is South Africa reflects a melting pot of different cultural communities and culturally-based and religion-based legal systems. Legal pluralism, dealing with more than one legal system within a jurisdictional area, immediately becomes relevant.[34] While national law, culturally-based and religion-based legal systems all apply in principle, the exact scope and the extent of particular legal rules and customs are determined by the particular approach to legal pluralism.[35] Two approaches emerge. A broad approach to legal pluralism, constituting deep legal pluralism, recognises all rules as adhered to at grassroots level, irrespective of whether these rules enjoy recognition by the state.[36] On the other hand, a 'narrow' approach to legal pluralism, constituting state law legal pluralism, takes note only of officially-recognised rules.[37]

Historically, South Africa has accommodated both deep and state law legal pluralism, depending on particular colonial needs and objectives.[38] While deep legal pluralism emerged from the outset following colonial occupation, to some extent,[39] state law legal pluralism became more prominent after the second British annexation in 1806.[40] Deep legal pluralism gained momentum when colonial authorities increasingly became unable to enforce foreign official law on indigenous communities. Although unofficial customary law was applied as settlement increased inland, no uniformity existed within the different regions of South Africa.[41] That remained the case until the Black Administration Act 38 of 1927 commenced on

[31] Pienaar, *Land Reform*, pp. 142–151.

[32] Mostert and Bennett, *Pluralism and Development*, pp. 1–22; Pienaar, *Land Reform*, pp. 505–508; W. du Plessis and J. M. Pienaar, 'The More Things Change, the More They Stay the Same: The Story of Communal Land Tenure in South Africa', *Fundamina Editio Specialis* (2010), 73–89.

[33] See 'Recent developments relating to traditional leadership'.

[34] Rautenbach and Bekker, *Legal Pluralism*, p. 5; Bennett, *Customary Law*, p. 410.

[35] Not all religion-based legal systems are recognised, e.g. Jewish, Hindu and Muslim law.

[36] Also referred to as strong, unofficial or non-state legal pluralism.

[37] Rautenbach and Bekker, *Legal Pluralism*, p. 5.

[38] Rautenbach and Bekker, *Legal Pluralism*, pp. 9–10.

[39] Rautenbach and Bekker, *Legal Pluralism*, p. 9.

[40] Rautenbach and Bekker, *Legal Pluralism*, p. 7.

[41] For example, the Cape High Court only applied customary law to the extent that it had been statutorily recognised. See Rautenbach and Bekker, *Legal Pluralism*, p. 9.

1 January 1929. The Act achieved uniformity and, in turn, entrenched state law legal pluralism.

Since the dawning of the constitutional era, customary law has been on a par with South African common law and intrinsically part of South African law.[42] Section 211(3) of the Constitution specifically provides that customary law has to be applied, when applicable, albeit subject to the Constitution and constitutional principles. The application of customary law is furthermore bolstered by the right to culture, specifically provided for in section 30 of the Constitution, as well as the right to affiliate with cultural communities of one's choice under section 31. Given that customary law has inherent links with indigenous culture, the right to culture under the Constitution furthermore enjoins the adherence to customary law.[43]

Customary law

Given the complexity of land rights, historically as well as under the constitutional dispensation, coupled with the operation of legal pluralism and the identification of culture as enabling the application of customary law, it is necessary to explore what the concept of customary law entails.[44] In relevant legislation, customary law is defined as: '[T]he customs and usages traditionally observed among indigenous African peoples of South Africa and which form part of the culture of those peoples'.[45]

Essentially the definition embodies three components, namely, first, the particular relevant norms and customs that are being adhered to; second, the indigenous African peoples of South Africa; and third, the relevant culture. While all of these components are integral in understanding the concept, an in-depth analysis cannot take place here.[46] Suffice it to say that a variety of indigenous communities exist in South Africa.[47] Furthermore, each community endorses particular norms, customs and traditions which are socially embedded and attuned to everyday life. Because customs change, customary law is especially dynamic, fluid and adaptable. This is where 'formal' (or 'official customary law') and 'living' (or 'unofficial customary law') enter into the picture. While formal customary law is easily ascertained, living customary law is more difficult to pin down. Despite difficulties, the concept of 'living customary law' has been employed very effectively in post-constitutional

[42] *Alexkor Ltd v Richtersveld Community*, 2004 (5) SA 460 (CC) para. [53].

[43] Customary law is often defined in line with indigenous culture. See Bennett, *Customary Law*, pp. 76–88.

[44] Editors' note: For further discussion of the definition of customary law, see also Nsoh in this volume.

[45] Section 1 of Act 120 of 1998; section 1 of Act 9 of 2009.

[46] See for a detailed analysis Rautenbach and Bekker, *Legal Pluralism*, pp. 20–24.

[47] Four main ethnic groups are identified: Nguni (with Zulu, Xhosa, Swasi and Ndebele); Tsonga group (Shangaan), Sotho group (Pedi, Sotho and Tswana) and the Venda group.

litigation, resulting in a nuanced and balanced body of jurisprudence.[48] Where living customary law is concerned, there is always scope for change and adaptation. Official customary law, however, is cast in a particular format and remains rigid and unchanged, except by formal adjustment. Codified customary law is contained in legislation[49] or in court judgments[50] under the *stare decisis* rule, where lower courts are bound by judgments handed down by higher courts, as well as amendments to these sources.[51] While official customary law is readily ascertainable, is easy to find and is clear, it is often outdated, not always a true reflection of reality and rarely serves the interests of the community.[52]

Irrespective of whether the law is officially recognised or living, it must comply with the Constitution and must be developed to be in line with constitutional imperatives.[53]

Communal property, with a focus on land

A right to culture enables persons living in South Africa to choose to live in accordance with customary law. In this domain, customary law rules and norms apply, including customary property law, whether codified and formal or living and unofficial.

As explained, racial spatial planning resulted in various geographical spaces within South African boundaries. In the former Bantustan areas, traditional customary law tenure relating to land prevailed, despite the various statutory land control forms that developed under the apartheid regime.[54] These areas are mainly in present-day Eastern Cape, KwaZulu-Natal, Limpopo, North-West and Mpumalanga provinces and encapsulate vast tracts of land, some of which are still

[48] For example, *Bhe v Magistrate, Khayelitsha*, 2005 (10) SA 580 (CC), regarding living customary law of succession that acknowledges female heirs to inherit, as opposed to formal customary law that confirms male primogeniture; *Shilubane v Nwamitwa*, 2009 (2) SA 66 (CC), regarding the appointment of female traditional leaders as opposed to formal customary law that confirms male appointments.

[49] For example, the Black Administration Act 38 of 1927 regulated status of individuals, legal capacity, marriages and succession.

[50] Under the parallel court system, judgments handed down by the (now abolished) Native Appeal Courts provided a massive body of case law.

[51] For example, *Yako v Beyi*, 1944 (NAC) 72; a decision of the Native Appeal Court set out principles relating to the recognition of customary law which were adhered to by all lower courts.

[52] Codifications often tend to reflect the interests of traditional leaders and the elite and not the community as a whole. See further S. Weeks, 'Securing Women's Property Inheritance in the Context of Plurality: Negotiations of Law and Authority in Mbuzini Customary Courts and Beyond', in Mostert and Bennett, *Pluralism and Development*, pp. 140–173.

[53] Section 39(2) of the Constitution. Under section 9 of the Constitution unfair discrimination is prohibited, leading to developments that enable female heirs to inherit.

[54] Pienaar, *Land Reform*, pp. 142–146.

registered in the name of the state.[55] As customary communal tenure is prevalent, overarching traditional leadership constructs emerge here which include traditional leaders and traditional councils, elaborated on in more detail below.[56] Despite the use of words like 'property' and 'rights', where communal land is concerned, the relational interests that underpin customary land ownership are of critical importance. The warning of Cousins[57] that the language of 'ownership' is not universal is pertinent here. Accordingly, individuals and communities relate to each other, as well as to land and resources. In this light, the 'communal property' concept does not resemble 'ownership' or 'freehold', similar to Western-style constructs. Rather, it resembles a set of reciprocal rights and obligations that bind parties and land together.[58]

Access to land is usually gained via membership of a particular community.[59] This involves active participation and production, as reflected in a variety of rights and interests that may vest and be exercised at various levels. Management and control are elements of the community's power and are also located at different levels. The day-to-day management and administration of land rights is usually at grassroots or household level, under the auspices of the local ward head. Access to and control over land therefore cannot be equated to common law ownership, as land rights embody a balance of access, use rights, control and management.[60] Tenure security is thus context-sensitive and prevails where rights are asserted within a set-up that is accountable. Accountability entails households, families and neighbourhoods all being involved in ensuring that rights are exercised sustainably and that transgressions are dealt with effectively and expediently, usually at local level. Such accountability also involves negotiating and re-negotiating land rights, where necessary. Only where conflicts cannot be resolved by way of negotiation and consensus at local level, are conflicts referred to the courts.

Even though the word 'communal' is pertinent, customary tenure is not restricted to a communal dimension only. Instead, individual and communal dimensions

[55] There is no consistency where registration is concerned as the actual entry in the deeds registry differs from area to area. In some instances the land is registered in the name of the relevant Ministry (the Department of Rural Development and Land Reform) or the provincial government. Where the entry is in the name of the Minister, it is deemed that he or she acts as custodian or holds the land in trust for the relevant community.
[56] See 'Traditional leadership and governance forms'.
[57] B. Cousins, 'Characterising "Communal Tenure": Nested Systems and Flexible Boundaries', in Claassens and Cousins, *Land, Power and Custom*, pp. 109–110.
[58] H. W. O. Okoth-Ogendo, 'The Nature of Land Rights under Indigenous Law in Africa', in Claassens and Cousins, *Land, Power and Custom*, p. 102.
[59] Usually by way of birth, affiliation to a specific social community, allegiance or transactions. See G. J. Pienaar, 'The Inclusivity of Communal Land Tenure: A Redefinition of Ownership in Canada and South Africa', *Stellenbosch Law Review* (2008), 259–277.
[60] Okoth-Ogendo, 'Nature of Land Rights', pp. 95–109.

emerge, as follows.[61] In principle a large area of land 'belongs' to the community, even though it may be registered as state land. Land is allocated by the ward head or local chief to families or households who are members of the community. Usually two parcels are allocated, for residential and agricultural purposes respectively. This allocation embodies a strong sense of individual autonomy. The remainder of the land that is not allocated to households constitutes the commonage, thereby involving a communal dimension. Although the rules may differ from community to community, community members generally have access to the commonage and can use its natural resources, including water, grazing, firewood, mud, sand, clay, wild fruit, as well as herbs and plants for medicinal and ritual purposes.[62]

Because communities do not all have identical customs and rules pertaining to land and because the apartheid government promulgated a variety of legislative measures for the various former Bantustan areas, not all identical, the actual grid of measures operating in the areas is extremely complex.[63] This means that addressing tenure matters in these areas is also complex and may require a variety of role players. It is within this context that the relevant role players are identified and discussed further.

Inter-connectedness: customary law and communal property

A broad spectrum of role players and mechanisms

In light of the complexity and the need to comply with constitutional imperatives, a broad spectrum of role players are integrally involved in communal areas. These role players include the state and relevant ministries, traditional communities themselves, traditional authorities and sometimes also 'non-traditional' bodies or institutions. With regard to each role player the relevant contribution is set out briefly, with reference also to mechanisms employed.

The state and the Ministry of Rural Development and Land Reform

The state has a vested interest in land, in two respects specifically: as registered title holder as explained above,[64] and as a matter of government policy. In this light the Green Paper on Land Reform stated as point of departure that land is a national asset and that it may be employed as government sees fit.[65] In practice, the state,

[61] Rautenbach and Bekker, *Legal Pluralism*, p. 134, Bennett, *Customary Law*, p. 390.
[62] Rautenbach and Bekker, *Legal Pluralism*, pp. 133–136, Bennett, *Customary Law*, pp. 374–399.
[63] R. Haines and C. Cross, 'An Historical Overview of Land Policy and Tenure in South Africa's Black Areas', in Cross and Haines, *Towards Freehold*, pp. 73–92; Pienaar, *Land Reform*, pp. 142–153.
[64] See note 55 above.
[65] *Green Paper on Land Reform* (Pretoria, Department of Rural Development and Land Reform, 2011), p. 3.

as a major role player, is usually represented by the Ministry of Rural Development and Land Reform. This department spearheads the all-encompassing land reform programme consisting of, as mentioned, three separate, but inter-connected sub-programmes, constituting redistribution, tenure reform and restitution. It therefore has an obligation to continue land reform and tenure endeavours, as required under section 25(6)[66] and (9)[67] of the Constitution. While land reform is embedded in the Constitution, in section 25, it is undergirded by various policy documents[68] and implemented by way of a detailed legislative framework. In turn, these legislative measures operate within a land administration system, encompassing survey, deeds and registries. The state and its relevant departments are involved in all of these spheres.

As the focus of this chapter is on tenure reform, the particular role of the state in this context needs further elaboration. The tenure reform programme is aimed at streamlining tenure forms to be more effective against interference and aligned with constitutional imperatives such as equality and dignity.[69] As a major role player, the state has employed legislation as the mechanism to achieve tenure reform objectives. This is done, either by employing legislation as a holding measure, for example by way of the Interim Protection of Informal Land Rights Act 31 of 1996, or by overhauling tenure markedly, for example by way of the Communal Property Associations Act 28 of 1996 or the Communal Land Rights Act 11 of 2004. The Interim Protection of Informal Land Rights Act was promulgated to conserve informal land rights for the duration of the tenure reform programme only. Section 1(1)(iii) of the Act provides that an 'informal right' includes the use of, occupation of or access to land in terms of any tribal, customary or indigenous law or practice of a tribe; the custom, usage or administrative practice in a particular area or community and beneficial occupation of land for a continuous period of no less than five years prior to 31 December 1997. Under this overarching measure, informal rights, including rights in communal areas, are thus protected against loss and deprivation. Although the idea was to employ the Act for an interim period only, it has been re-activated annually since 1996.

Measures aimed at overhauling tenure more drastically include, as mentioned, the Communal Property Associations Act and the Communal Land Rights Act (CLARA). The Communal Property Associations Act introduced a new statutory property construct in the form of a communal property association (CPA), elaborated on in more detail below.[70] The importance of the Act as a whole was

[66] Providing for the tenure reform programme.

[67] It provides that the state has to promulgate legislation that provides for more secure tenure.

[68] For a detailed analysis of the policy dimension of land reform, see Pienaar, *Land Reform*, pp. 192–271.

[69] Pienaar, *Land Reform*, pp. 378–381.

[70] See 'Other property constructs or managerial bodies' below.

recently underlined by the Constitutional Court in *Bakgatla-Ba-Kgafela Communal Property Association v Bakgatla-Ba-Kgafela Tribal Authority*,[71] where it was hailed to be a 'visionary piece of legislation' as it:

> [s]afeguard[s] the interests of members of traditional communities and empower[s] them to participate in the management of a communal property [association]. The creation of an association introduces participatory democracy in the affairs of traditional communities. All members of the community are afforded an equal voice in matters of the association and the property it holds on behalf of the community.[72]

Less successful, however, was the CLARA, which was aimed at formalising communal land rights and substituting 'old order' rights with 'new order' rights. Under section 1 of the Act, an 'old order right' included a tenure or other right in or to communal land which was formal or informal; registered or unregistered; which derived from or was recognised by law, including customary law, practice or usage, and which existed immediately prior to the determination by the Minister under section 18 of the Act. A 'new order right' was not defined, although the underlying idea was that these rights would be more secure and would be conferred, converted or validated by the Minister under section 18 of the Act. While various substantive criticisms were raised by academics,[73] revolving around continued insecurity of especially women's land rights and increased power for traditional leaders, the CLARA was finally struck down and found unconstitutional on a procedural ground only. *Tongoane v Minister of Agriculture and Land Affairs*[74] found that the Act was tagged incorrectly and therefore the passage through Parliament was unconstitutional.[75] Substantive matters, however, were not adjudicated on at all.

Following the unconstitutionality finding of the CLARA, the Interim Protection of Informal Land Rights Act is the only statutory measure that protects unregistered, informal land rights that are exercised by communities and individuals.

Traditional communities

Apart from the state and its relevant departments, traditional communities themselves are also crucial role players in communal areas. Traditional communities comprise families, households and individuals actually living on the land in question, exercising and upholding land rights and thereby effectively participating in making and adjusting the law relating to land. Although traditional communities are part-and-parcel of communal land, defining communities and ascertaining their

[71] 2015 (6) SA 32 (CC).
[72] *Bakgatla-Ba-Kgafela* case, para. [30].
[73] For example, H. Mostert and J. M. Pienaar, 'Formalisation of South African Communal Land Title and Its Impact on Development', in E. Cooke (ed.), *Modern Studies in Property Law* (Oxford, Hart Publishing, 2005), pp. 332–344.
[74] 2010 (6) SA 214 (CC).
[75] *Tongoane* case, paras [45]–[97].

membership is not simple, mainly for two reasons. First, communities are defined differently in different legislative measures; and second, communities are not static and cast in stone. Communities evolve and membership changes over time. For example, for purposes of the Restitution of Land Rights Act 22 of 1994, communities are defined as: '[a]ny group of persons whose rights in land are derived from shared rules determining access to land held in common by such group, and includes part of any such group'.[76]

In *Department of Land Affairs, Popela Community v Goedgelegen Tropical Fruits (Pty) Ltd*,[77] Judge Moseneke expanded the definition by formulating a two-pronged test in order to determine whether a community claim was involved by, first, establishing whether the community retained much of their identity and cohesion as part of the original group; and second, establishing whether they derived their possession of the land in question from shared rules.

Section 2 of the Traditional Leadership and Governance Framework Act 41 of 2003 provides for the recognition of traditional communities when a community is subject to a system of traditional leadership of that particular community's customs[78] and if the community observes a system of customary law. Therefore, when customary law is adhered to and when communities live subject to traditional leadership constructs,[79] a formal application may be lodged to acquire formal recognition for the community, which will thereby become a 'traditional community'. When that process is completed, the community has *locus standi* and is able to participate in official litigation.[80]

Individual members and households are furthermore integrally involved in the utilisation and enforcement of land rights, at various levels.[81] For example, while one household has land rights in relation to a particular parcel of land, female members of that household have access to wetlands and land for cultivation, while, simultaneously, other households exercise rights to draw water and collect wood for fuel from the commonage. These rights are cumulatively exercised at different levels, at different times. Accordingly, where disputes emerge, they are invariably resolved at various levels as well, although local level – household or neighbourhood

[76] Section 1.

[77] 2007 (6) SA 199 (CC).

[78] All traditional communities do not have identical customs regarding leadership roles; some communities have kings and queens and others have paramount chiefs only.

[79] The actual traditional leadership construct would depend on the particular community's customs. For example, out of the 7,970 traditional leaders in South Africa, 11 are kings or queens, 3 are principal traditional leaders, 829 are senior traditional leaders, and 7,127 are headmen or headwomen.

[80] For example, lodging applications for mining and prospecting under the Mineral and Petroleum Resources Development Act 28 of 2002.

[81] W. Wicomb, 'Securing Women's Customary Rights in Land: The Fallacy of Institutional Recognition', in A. Claassens and D. Smythe (eds), *Marriage, Land and Custom* (Cape Town, Juta, 2013), pp. 49–72; D. Budlender, 'Women, Marriage and Land: Findings from a Three-Site Survey', in Claassens and Smythe, *Marriage, Land and Custom*, pp. 28–48.

level – would usually be the most effective. In the process of exercising, upholding and enforcing land rights, social relations are paramount and negotiations take place.[82] This is where living land law is formed and practised. In the absence, very often, of official tools and mechanisms, the major contribution of communities in this context is the actual making of and contributing particular rules to customary land law.

Traditional leadership and governance forms

Traditional leadership as an overarching term entails the various customary institutions or structures, or customary systems or procedures of governance, which are recognised, utilised or practised by traditional communities.[83] Although different traditional communities have different customs where leadership and governance constructs are concerned, it is normal to have various categories and levels of traditional leaders. For example, in a hierarchical pyramid, the king or queen would occupy the top spot, followed by principal traditional leaders and subsequently followed by senior traditional leaders.[84] Connected to these positions of authority are equivalent traditional councils,[85] provincial Houses of Traditional Leaders, and finally, a National House of Traditional Leaders.[86] Presently, the recognition of these institutions and forms of governance, as well as the composition of relevant councils, the appointment of members, and the functions and responsibilities of each, are all set out in the Traditional Leadership and Governance Framework Act 41 of 2003.

Under the apartheid regime, traditional authorities were appointed under the Bantu Authorities Act 68 of 1951 with respect to specific geographical areas. In that era the identification and appointment of a particular traditional leader was also aligned with the overarching goal of separate development.[87] Traditional leaders were thus employed by government, thereby effectively resulting in 'indirect rule'.[88] It is argued that in this process much of authentic customary law ascribing particular duties and responsibilities to positions of power and authority fell by the wayside.[89]

[82] Weeks, 'Securing Women's Property', pp. 140–173.
[83] Section 1 of the Traditional Leadership and Governance Framework Act 41 of 2000. See also Rautenbach and Bekker, *Legal Pluralism*, pp. 199–222; Bennett, *Customary Law*, pp. 101–130.
[84] Rautenbach and Bekker, *Legal Pluralism*, pp. 206–208.
[85] For example, a principal traditional leader would be levelled with a principal traditional council, and so forth.
[86] The National House of Traditional Leaders is a statutory body established under the National House of Traditional Leaders Act 22 of 2009 and is composed of delegates of the Provincial Houses which represent the interests of traditional leaders.
[87] Manson and Mbenga, *Land, Chiefs, Mining*, pp. 89–108; Claassens, 'Contested Power', p. 174.
[88] Bennett, *Customary Law*, p. 106; Claassens, 'Contested Power', p. 174.
[89] Manson and Mbenga, *Land, Chiefs, Mining*, p. 64; Bennett, *Customary Law*, pp. 106–110.

The dawning of a new constitutional dispensation did not necessarily sweep the slate clean. That is the case because section 28 of the Traditional Leadership Framework Act provides specifically for the continuation of pre-constitutional institutions and, broadly, for the same geographical areas as those set out under the 1951 Act. Accordingly, to some extent, the adjusted – distorted – institution of the traditional leadership construct continues. This has major implications for communities, for the making of customary law, including land rights and the protection thereof. The situation is exacerbated when recent developments relating to access to justice, and the administration thereof, are also considered, as explained below in more detail.[90]

Other property constructs or managerial bodies

Other role players integral in communal areas, apart from those set out above, comprise 'non-traditional' mechanisms, and are usually facilitated in legislation or the South African common law, which is Roman-Dutch-based. A new statutory property construct, a CPA, resulting from the Communal Property Associations Act, has already been referred to above. Because CPA members draft their own constitutions, can decide their own membership and endorse equal access to and control over communal property, CPAs are more democratic than communities under traditional leaders. That is the case because CPAs have to be aligned with constitutional imperatives,[91] whereas under traditional authorities access to and control over property is gender-based, in favour of men.[92] Establishing a CPA, however, is a complex and time-consuming process, consisting of two phases.[93] Starting from a provisional CPA it develops into a fully-fledged association once particular conditions have been met. *Bakgatla-Ba-Kgafela Communal Property Association v Bakgatla-Ba-Kgafela Tribal Authority*[94] has provided much needed guidance regarding the state's duties in this regard, as well as warning traditional authorities not to interfere when the community has decided democratically to establish a CPA.[95]

In KwaZulu-Natal a unique situation is encountered as communal land amounting to about 2.8 million hectares vests in the Ingonyama Trust and is administered by it under the KwaZulu-Natal Ingonyama Trust Act 3 KZ of 1994.[96] The Trust

[90] See 'Recent developments relating to traditional leadership' below.
[91] For example, fairness, equity and dignity.
[92] *Bakgatla-Ba-Kgafela* case, para. [30].
[93] A Communal Property Associations Amendment Bill was published for comment on 22 April 2016 in *GG* 39943 but has not been finalised yet. The Bill discards the two-phased approach.
[94] 2015 (6) SA 32 (CC).
[95] See J. M. Pienaar, 'Land Reform', *Electronic Juta Quarterly Review*, 3 (2015), for a discussion of the judgment.
[96] This land had been incorporated in the data relating to state-owned land: www.pmg.org.za/report/20130227-drdlr-report-survey-registration-all-state-land-well-creation-comprehen.

was established immediately prior to the first general election in April 1994 following an agreement by the then governing party, the National Party, and the Inkatha Freedom Party in KwaZulu-Natal, to preserve land for the 'Zulu nation'.[97] The Ingonyama, King Zwelithini, acts as trustee on behalf of the Zulu nation. The Act was amended in 1997 to alleviate the administrative burden that fell on the Zulu king by making provision for the Ingonyama Trust Board to administer the land in accordance with Zulu custom, as well as affairs linked therewith.[98]

In principle a further trust option is available, but under the South African common law. This entails the holding of trust property in common on behalf of the trust beneficiaries, by the trustee entrusted with the regulation of the property.[99] While this common law option is also available as it constitutes a form of 'collective ownership' in the sense that beneficiaries can be a group of persons or even a whole community, it does not optimise or incorporate the concept of communally held property at its best for purposes of traditional communities.[100] That is the case because trustees have a lot of independence and need not consult or negotiate with beneficiaries to the same extent that negotiations take place in traditional communities. In this light this option is not very popular among traditional communities, although it is sometimes preferred by traditional leaders, precisely because of the measure of independence the trustee has.[101]

Recent developments relating to traditional leadership

As explained, the Traditional Leadership and Governance Framework Act regulates the recognition of various forms of traditional leadership constructs, in a hierarchical fashion. Linked to these constructs are traditional councils[102] that generally have the duty to assist and support traditional leaders, to participate in and develop policy and legislation; and to perform the duties conferred on them under customary law.[103] With regard to the roles and functioning of traditional leadership, Chapter 5 of the Act, section 20, provides specifically for the roles of leaders with regard to a list of items, which include land administration, administration of

[97] See Pienaar, *Land Reform*, pp. 477–481, for more background on the Ingonyama Trust.
[98] Section 2(4) of the Act.
[99] See in general C. G. van der Merwe, J. M. Pienaar and M. J. De Waal, *International Encyclopaedia of Laws: Property and Trust Law – South Africa* (Alphen, Netherlands, Wolters Kluwer, 2015).
[100] See also Cousins, 'Characterising "Communal Tenure"', pp. 109–137.
[101] For example, in the *Bakgatla-Ba-Kgafela* case the traditional leader, Kgosi Pilane, opted for a trust and was strongly opposed to a CPA. As trustee he would, for example, have had more control over mineral rights and their exploitation.
[102] Regulated under section 3 (traditional council) and section 3B (principal traditional council), respectively.
[103] Section 4(1)(b), (f) and (l).

justice and the management of natural resources.[104] Therefore, holistically, traditional leaders and traditional councils are intrinsically involved in land administration and the administration of justice.

The administration of justice is linked to the court system. Because judicial matters within traditional courts were still being dealt with under the repealed Black Administration Act 38 of 1927, except for remaining sections 12 (dealing with civil matters) and 20 (dealing with criminal matters), new measures for traditional courts were necessary. Finally, after various attempts, the Traditional Courts Bill was published at the end of 2011.[105]

The aim of the Traditional Courts Bill is to affirm the values of traditional justice systems and to affirm the institution of traditional leadership in enhancing access to justice.[106] The promotion and preservation of customary law norms and values are emphasised, coupled with the clear designation of traditional leaders as presiding officers.[107] The unique nature of traditional courts is highlighted, *inter alia* that these courts are not identical to 'formal' courts;[108] and that the process and procedure followed in these courts are in accordance with customary law specifically.[109] Although this means that the courts function subject to the Bill of Rights and in conjunction with the rules of natural justice, it is provided specifically that no legal representation is allowed.[110] However, a party may be represented by a person of choice 'in terms of customary law and custom'.[111] This has important implications for women wanting to claim new or enforce existing land rights, elaborated on in more detail below.[112]

The Traditional Leadership and Governance Framework Act, read together with the Traditional Courts Bill, essentially places 'law making' in the hands of traditional authorities, alongside traditional councils. However, as explained above, traditional communities and their members are intrinsically involved in applying law, at grassroots level, and adjusting it where relevant, by way of negotiating and enforcing, at different levels and at different points in time.

The latest set of legislative measures negates this inter-connectedness of living in accordance with customary law, and adjusting and enforcing it. As traditional authorities make the law, adjudicate on it and administer it, negotiating at different levels falls by the wayside. Whereas women would have had access to wetlands, for example, and would have been able to negotiate additional land and adjust

[104] Section 4(1)(b), (f) and (l).
[105] GN 901 of 2001, in *GG* 34850 on 13 December 2011.
[106] Clause 2.
[107] Clause 4.
[108] Clause 7.
[109] Clause 9.
[110] Clause 9(3)(a).
[111] Clause 9(3)(b).
[112] See 'Reflection' below.

boundaries, if necessary, stating the content of law – including land rights – would now be the prerogative of traditional leaders only. Interaction among households and neighbourhoods regarding the management of commonages and access thereto would likewise fall away and, instead, fall within the scope of the relevant traditional leader and his council. While various concerns may be raised in relation to the Traditional Courts Bill,[113] the negation of the *participatory role of community members* and the removing of negotiation possibilities are especially disconcerting. Removing this flexible approach to dispute resolution and, more importantly, cutting out the potential to interpret and sculpt specific land rights in light of particular needs, has major implications for living customary land law.

The Traditional Courts Bill furthermore has geographical application. The area of relevance is the same area that forms part of the former Bantustan areas. It is thus striking that the geographical boundaries introduced in the apartheid era under the Bantu Authorities Act have effectively survived the constitutional watershed. The application of the Bill is furthermore non-negotiable. In other words: all communities living in these areas are subject to it, by force and not by choice. There is thus no 'opting out' mechanism available.

Women's rights are especially vulnerable if the Bill is implemented in its present form, for mainly two reasons. First, participatory resolution is more attuned to women's needs and demands and therefore more likely to find solutions that accommodate a broader spectrum of rights;[114] and second, as women are generally not allowed to state a case in person, but have to choose a person 'in line with customary law and custom', a woman may be forced to have a male (husband or relative) state her case on her behalf. This is extremely problematic if that person is the same person encroaching on her land and property rights.[115]

Recent developments relating to communal land

Since the unconstitutionality finding of the CLARA in 2010 in the *Tongoane* judgment, various policy documents have been published that impact on land in the former Bantustan areas, including the Green Paper on Land Reform in 2011 and the Communal Land Tenure Policy in 2014. In the Green Paper on Land Reform, a 'single four tier tenure system' was provided for, in which communally owned land constituted the fourth tier embodying communal tenure 'with institutionalised use rights'.[116] What these rights entailed was not clear.

[113] Also see the discussion under 'Challenges' below.

[114] Wicomb, 'Securing Women's Customary Rights', pp. 49–72; Budlender, 'Women, Marriage and Land', p. 48; Weeks, 'Securing Women's Property', pp. 140–173.

[115] Claassens, 'Contested Power', p. 174.

[116] *Green Paper on Land Reform*, p. 6.

The underlying aim of the Communal Land Tenure Policy of 2014 is to 'both secure land rights for those living in communal areas as well as engender the transformation of land governance institutions to embrace the principles of democracy and equity'.[117] Linked to the above is the transfer of ownership of land from the Minister of Rural Development and Land Reform, to traditional councils. Overall, distinctions are drawn between land located inside and outside of former Bantustan areas. For purposes of the Policy, land located outside former Bantustan areas is 'communal land' because the land was transferred to a community under the redistribution or restitution programmes, usually by way of a CPA. These communities do not necessarily live under traditional leaders and could have constituted their own membership in line with the objectives of the Communal Property Associations Act, as explained. It is interesting that the Policy still employs apartheid geospatial terminology by drawing distinctions between land in and outside former Bantustan areas. Another interesting aspect is that, despite the principled idea to transfer land in ownership from the Minister, in whose name it is still registered, to councils, the Policy continues to endorse the state's 'ultimate power to make decisions about land rights and land use in communal areas'. This theme resonates throughout the Policy. It is reiterated with regard to municipal responsibilities at local government level,[118] and again under the section dealing with 'envisioned outcomes'[119] where the Policy foresees 'clear, effective and democratic land governance in which the State (local government) holds authority over land rights and land use'. Exactly how that is to occur once land has in fact been transferred in ownership, is unclear.

The Policy employs two 'wagon wheel figures' to depict the vesting of title and the concomitant rights and duties for relevant role players within communal areas. The two figures are distinctive in that one figure relates to 'conventional traditional communal areas that observe customary laws' relating to land located within the boundaries of former Bantustan areas, whereas the other figure is designed for 'non-traditional communal areas', essentially dealing with land located outside former Bantustan areas. The first category is the focus of this chapter. The second category, the 'non-traditional areas', are the areas alluded to above where land was transferred to communities via the redistribution or restitution programmes. In each instance the outer boundary of the relevant communal area will be demarcated and corresponding title will be vested in a particular governance structure. With respect to former Bantustan areas, traditional councils will be the governance structure, whereas CPAs or trusts will fulfil this role in areas outside former Bantustan areas, in other words, relating to post-1994 restitution or redistribution land. In former Bantustan areas traditional councils or traditional authorities will

[117] *Communal Land Tenure Policy* (Pretoria, Department of Rural Development and Land Reform, 2014), p. 27.

[118] *Communal Land Tenure Policy*, p. 14.

[119] *Communal Land Tenure Policy*, p. 17.

thus be vested with the responsibility of administering the land and land-related resources on behalf of households.[120]

Reflection

From the exposition above it is striking that recent developments relating to traditional courts and communal land by way of the Traditional Courts Bill and the Communal Land Tenure Policy centre law-making capacity in traditional leaders and traditional councils only. The Communal Land Tenure Policy underlines that 'customary law exists only under the control of chiefs'.[121] This approach does not account for the inter-connectedness of culture, customary law and land rights as reflected in the discussion above. Where land is concerned, the community as a whole is involved in its utilisation, exploitation and management. If necessary, household members can negotiate with neighbours to extend land rights and adjust boundaries. Where conflicts emerge, particular needs and demands are taken into account and re-negotiation takes place, usually at grassroots level, aimed at reaching consensus. The new developments are moving away from an approach where the community as a whole is intrinsically involved in the utilisation and management of land, in favour of an approach where the content of customary law, including property and land rights, is to be decided by traditional leaders or chiefs only. In this way, authentic and living customary law rules that operate more equitably and respond to the particular interests of the community as a whole, in particular to the rights of women, may deteriorate systematically or be substituted as a whole. If land rights are to be crafted by traditional leaders and councils only, there is a real risk that control and management of communal property could vest in the elite only or in individuals or families with influence or strong ties with the leadership constructs. This totally negates Moore's concept of 'law as process', alluded to by Claassens and Smythe, where all relevant role players are involved.[122] Furthermore, because the Traditional Courts Bill applies to particular geographical areas, essentially comprising the former Bantustan areas, people living in these areas have no other option but to be subjected to this form of adjudication and law-making. It is thus not so much the *fact* that customary law is applicable, but the particular format of customary law as *stated and interpreted* by traditional leaders only, that is problematic.

The definite distinction between communal areas located within and outside former Bantustan areas is disconcerting – not only because of the continued use

[120] *Communal Land Tenure Policy*, p. 20.

[121] *Communal Land Tenure Policy*, pp. 12, 21.

[122] A. Claassens and D. Smythe, 'Marriage, Land and Custom: What's Law Got to Do with It?', in Claassens and Smythe, *Marriage, Law and Custom*, pp. 1–27 at p. 23.

of apartheid boundaries, but because of the clear stance of government to prevent CPAs from being established in former Bantustan areas: CPAs in these areas are to be 'carefully considered and principally discouraged'.[123]

Where traditional councils act as governance structures, as encouraged by the Policy, constitutionality is furthermore at risk, for two main reasons. First, as the constitutional dispensation operates within a three-tier governance system operating in local, provincial and national spheres, a fourth tier would be unconstitutional; and second, this form of government is not democratically elected and as such does not meet a basic tenet of a constitutional democracy.[124]

Challenges

Operating within a legal pluralistic society is challenging from the outset as different approaches to and forms of legal pluralism determine, ultimately, the extent of legal recognition and application of particular norms and rules. Finding the right balance is therefore difficult in principle, but the difficulty is compounded when the shadow of repression of particular cultural rights and values lingers. It lingers in the sense that apartheid-style geographic boundaries remain relevant, coupled with the bolstering of traditional leaders' powers, reminiscent of 'indirect rule' under the apartheid era. Where customs and values remain resilient and viable, despite repression, the recognition and application of living customary law makes a lot of sense. However, ascertaining the exact content of living customary law and how it is adhered to in practice is difficult and time-consuming. While being challenging, nuanced Constitutional Court jurisprudence relating to the customary law of succession indicated that it is not only possible, but necessary.[125]

Property concepts and governance constructs are increasingly being conflated, especially by way of legislative and policy measures. The Communal Land Tenure Policy envisages the transfer of ownership of communal land to the relevant traditional council. The end result combines a form of property and governance structure: owning land and administrating and governing all elements thereof. In light of this conflation the actual scope of traditional leaders' authority is very difficult to determine and may lead to exploitation and contestations. As explained above, the trend to expand chiefly powers and bolster their authority continues.

How to deal with boundaries and different geospatial areas, also referred to as

[123] *Communal Land Tenure Policy*, pp. 28, 32.

[124] Rautenbach and Bekker, *Legal Pluralism*, p. 229.

[125] *Bhe v Magistrate, Khayelitsha*, 2005 (10) SA 580 (CC) – living customary law confirmed a female heir; *Shilubane v Nwamitwa*, 2009 (2) SA 66 (CC) – confirmed a female appointment as a traditional leader.

'patchwork democracy'[126] is another urgent issue. Resolving this matter has implications for the jurisdiction of traditional courts, for citizens residing in these areas and for the perception that apartheid-style boundaries are being perpetuated under a democratic government. Linked to this is the concept of 'second-rate citizens' where different paradigms exist for citizenry residing within these boundaries, compared to citizens outside these areas.[127] The administration of justice and the compulsory jurisdiction of traditional courts were mentioned above. Seemingly, democratic forms of governance are preserved for citizens outside of these areas, as the discouragement of establishing CPAs demonstrates.

Government has been active in publishing a variety of land reform-related policy documents and legislation. However, on closer scrutiny it is clear that major disconnects exist between policies, legislation and case law, not all of them relevant for purposes of this discussion.[128] Where communal land is concerned, a recent disconnect emerged when the Constitutional Court handed down the judgment of *Bakgatla-Ba-Kgafela Communal Property Association v Bakgatla-Ba-Kgafela Tribal Authority.*[129] The Court supported the formation of CPAs in traditional communal areas on the grounds that redressing the remnants of apartheid necessitated more secure forms of tenure; that the fruits of democracy must be enjoyed equally; and that customary law had to be aligned with the Constitution. These considerations are clearly in conflict with recent overarching governmental initiatives, for example, the Comprehensive Rural Development Plan of 2009[130] and the Communal Land Tenure Policy, set out above. The Rural Development Plan requires rural and agrarian transformation, especially concerning systems and patterns of ownership and control. The Communal Land Tenure Policy, also impacting on rural land, proposes that new CPAs be permitted only in areas where no traditional authorities exist, as explained. This means that CPAs would be limited to areas outside the former Bantustans. If that is indeed the case, the transformation called for in the 2009 policy *would not be realised* in the areas where it is needed the most. It is therefore striking that the judgment handed down in August 2015 is directly contrary to what government intends to do with CPAs generally and with communal land in particular.

[126] B. Oomen, *Chiefs in South Africa: Law, Power and Culture in the Post-Apartheid Era* (Pietermaritzburg, University of KZN Press, 2005), p. 81.

[127] Claassens and Smythe warn against a segregated 'customary law ghetto'. See 'Marriage, Land and Custom', p. 23.

[128] For an exposition of dichotomies and disconnects, see J. M. Pienaar, 'Reflections on the South African Land Reform Programme: Characteristics, Dichotomies and Tensions Part 2', 4, *TSAR* (2014), 689–705.

[129] 2015 (6) SA 32 (CC).

[130] The plan was introduced as part of an overarching economic and rural regeneration project by President Zuma in his second term of office. See further W. du Plessis, J. M. Pienaar and N. J. J. Olivier, 'Land Matters and Rural Development', *SAPL/PR*, 24(2) (2009), 608–610.

Despite the operation of an all-encompassing land reform programme and despite the fact that the dual system of law is recognised and intended to operate *on par*,[131] the system of land administration in the form of survey, deeds and registries in South Africa has remained and continues to be geared primarily towards the recording of private, individual, Western-style title.[132] Therefore, although some attempts have been made, for example, within the (now repealed) CLARA, and although some research and analysis have occurred at a theoretical level,[133] the system is intrinsically biased against customary law rights. Essentially, the disconnect between how rights are actually exercised, enforced and protected in customary law, at various levels and intersections, has to be addressed by way of suitable land administration tools. Ultimately a gap between the different property law paradigms remains. Pope proposes the continuation of two paradigms with different and varied recording systems.[134] Gerrit Pienaar has made valuable suggestions with regard to communal land in particular.[135] His point of departure is that a reliable land information system may be more valuable here as it would provide the necessary basis for an efficient, comprehensive land administration system. This means that less emphasis may be placed on formal registration as such. In the process of developing such an affordable, accessible register of communal land rights in rural areas specifically, various principles have to be adhered to, including that the register should reflect persons, households and families and the rights exercised by each of them within a cadastrally defined or surveyed piece of land.[136] Because overlapping of rights is possible, a system has to be developed to enable such overlapping to be reflected effectively.

Opportunities

Interestingly, the space where challenges emerge is often also the space that provides room for opportunities. For example, the legislative imperative to transform and adapt customary law in line with the Constitution results in extreme tension between consolidating power bases and spontaneously developing rules to address particular needs. But it is exactly within these tensions and fluctuations that development and adaptations can occur. Budlender,[137] considering three particular areas

[131] See especially A. Pope, 'Indigenous-Law Rights: Constitutional Imperatives and Proprietary Paradoxes', in Mostert and Bennett, *Pluralism and Development*, pp. 308–333.
[132] Pienaar, *Land Reform*, p. 844.
[133] G. J. Pienaar, 'Land Information as a Tool for Effective Land Administration and Development', in Mostert and Bennett, *Pluralism and Development*, pp. 238–272.
[134] Pope, 'Indigenous-Law Rights', p. 332.
[135] See especially Pienaar, 'Land Information', pp. 267–268.
[136] For the full list of principles, see Pienaar, 'Land Information', pp. 267–268.
[137] Budlender, 'Women, Marriage and Land', pp. 28–48.

in South Africa, KwaZulu-Natal, the Eastern Cape and the North-West,[138] has shown convincingly that land rights reform has occurred spontaneously, outside any statutory measures. Women have gained greater access to land and more secure tenure by relying purely on the Constitution itself and not on any of the land reform measures. These 'spontaneous' legal reforms, initiated by the Constitution and its basic ethos, have impacted on specific communities, thereby also exhibiting potential to change communities at large and general approaches to and concepts of property and land. Accordingly, in spaces of negotiation, at various intersections and levels, actual land rights were 'created'. Linked to this, is Weeks' suggestion that room for negotiation where customary law and culture intercede needs to be explored and expanded further.[139] Spaces of tension and negotiation can thus be utilised even more effectively.

Because customary law tenure forms are so flexible, responsive and ultimately persistent, it is increasingly pursued as a viable, effective form of secure tenure, but in a somewhat different context. The context is thus not necessarily that of a Western-style format of private ownership, but a system that provides security in its social-embeddedness. In this way Cousins suggests that tenure reform should not be approached from the point of departure of a legal right or basis, but from the *opposite vantage point* instead.[140] This entails that, only where socially secure rights and interests *already* operate effectively, is legal notice taken thereof. Legal recognition thus comes into play almost as an afterthought, as the right or interest is already socially secure and viable. This may open up other avenues with regard to recording and land administration in general.[141]

A contextual approach to interpretation of rights, already utilised quite successfully in Constitutional Court judgments dealing with customary law of succession matters, provides ample opportunity to deal with problematic aspects effectively. As courts hand down more of these kinds of judgments, more certainty overall and predictability will enter into the picture. Claassens refers to this phenomenon as the court's 'real-world contextual approach'.[142] A real-world contextual approach, coupled with creative utilisation of tension and space for negotiating rights, would open up new possibilities – not only for creating new land rights, but also for enforcing and protecting them.

Finally, reconsidering the multitude of demands and challenges may also require a reconsideration of existing legislative measures. The Interim Protection of Informal Land Rights Act, presently employed as a holding measure, could be

[138] Msinga in KwaZulu-Natal: Zulu community, Keiskamahoek in the Eastern Cape: Xhosa community, and Ramatlabana in the North-West: Tswana community.

[139] Weeks, 'Securing Women's Property', pp. 140–173.

[140] B. Cousins, 'Potential and Pitfalls of "Communal" Land Tenure Reform: Experience in Africa and Implications for South Africa' (Cape Town, PLAAS, 2009), pp. 16–17.

[141] Cousins, 'Potential and Pitfalls', pp. 16–17.

[142] Claassens, 'Contested Power', p. 204.

reconceptualised and reshaped for better utilisation. The Act needs to be made permanent and the word 'Interim' deleted from its title. Existing rights and how they operate in practice in relation to the broader communal area as well as to the commonage specifically can be defined and linked to basic spatial delineations, in line with the suggestions of Gerrit Pienaar above.

Conclusion

Though vibrant and beautiful to look at, the tapestry involving a multitude of strands and threads is challenging to maintain and to take care of. Given the inter-dependency and inter-connectedness of culture, customary law and communal property in a country where Western law also applies, different options to organise the various strands may be explored. Pope maintains that South Africa cannot have a unitary system of land rights, because the basic points of departure are just too different.[143] She argues Western law is intrinsically too individual, compared to customary law. Claassens and Smythe urge that customary law should not be isolated.[144] It is integral in daily life and therefore prone to influence and adaptation. Neither can it be isolated within a geographical space as would be the case if customary law is crafted and implemented as suggested in recent draft statutory measures.

It is within the spaces of intersection,[145] where common law and customary law intercede and where custom and legislation intercede, that Weeks[146] identifies room to manoeuvre. This also enables cross-pollination and lending and borrowing between legal systems. Constitutional Court judgments applying real-world contextualisation have shown the way in developing the customary law of succession. Nothing prevents the same phenomenon from occurring in relation to communal property and land.

Communal property within a socially embedded customary law system has many benefits: it provides access to and a safety net for members; the management and control thereof are located within the community, at various levels; and the customs and norms regulating it are flexible and can be adjusted in light of changing needs and demands. For these reasons this kind of property and corresponding system of law has to be protected. But protection has to be aligned with constitutional imperatives. Only by complying with the Constitution, with it acting as the frame holding the different strands together, will the tapestry remain strong and resilient.

[143] Pope, 'Indigenous-Law Rights', p. 332.

[144] Claassens and Smythe, 'Marriage, Land and Custom', pp. 1–27.

[145] Wicomb, 'Securing Women's Customary Rights', pp. 49–72; Budlender, 'Women, Marriage and Land', pp. 28–48.

[146] Weeks, 'Securing Women's Property', pp. 140–173.

8

Understanding Collective Property in the Chinese Context through the Lens of Community

TING XU AND WEI GONG*

Introduction: difficulties in defining the concept of collective property

'Communal property' can be understood as resources owned, used and governed by a group of people defined by reference to some common characteristics. This definition of communal property refers to a resource over which a community and its members together have overall control and the way a resource is managed and regulated by a community for its collective purposes. There is a mix of private property interests and communal property interests in such a resource. Communal property is an important mechanism for allocating natural resources and regulating their use – whether for economic exploitation, recreational use or the promotion of biodiversity and nature conservation.

The importance of communal property, transcending the public/private divide in property rights, is increasingly apparent globally. In England and Wales, the importance of communal land rights has been brought back into sharp focus by a number of developments which have revived interest in communal land and resource rights amongst academics, policy makers and social commentators. The Commons Registration Act 1965 and Commons Act 2006 guarantee the continued survival of traditional agricultural and recreational commons in England and Wales and open up the potential for recognition of newly emerging commons.

The importance of communal property highlights the need to undertake theoretical work in this area with case studies of communal property regimes in jurisdictions such as China, where communal property plays a crucial role in the allocation and regulation of resources. Although the history and present structure

* We would like to thank Alison Clarke and the anonymous reviewer for helpful comments.

of land rights in various regions such as the UK and China are very different, communal property nevertheless emerges in both regions as a key component in the management of resources, notably in four related areas: agriculture; environmental protection; rural and urban development; and housing.

In the case of the People's Republic of China (PRC), understanding communal property requires us to ask the difficult question: what is collective property? We could find a brief answer to this question in Article 10 of the 2004 PRC Constitution, which provides: 'Land in the rural and suburban areas is owned by collectives except for those portions which belong to the state in accordance with the law; residential plots and private plots of cropland and hilly land are also owned by collectives.'[1] However, in explaining in detail the meaning of collective property and exploring the extent to which this kind of collective/communal property[2] in the PRC resembles communal property as understood in England and Wales, we immediately encounter three major difficulties.

The first difficulty is that there is no consensus concerning the definition of 'commons' or 'communal property'. The term 'commons' may be defined as 'a diversity of resources or facilities as well as property institutions that involve some aspects of joint ownership or access',[3] encapsulating 'the emerging conception of access, conservation, and use . . . [as well as] many different grassroots movements'.[4] Various linked concepts, including 'common-pool resources', 'common property' and 'public goods', are often used interchangeably.

A 'common-pool resource' refers to 'a natural or man-made resource system that is sufficiently large as to make it costly (but not impossible) to exclude potential beneficiaries from obtaining benefits from its use' (partially non-excludable).[5] A common-pool resource is rivalrous, as one person's use diminishes another's use.[6] 'A public good' is 'something to which everyone has access, but . . . one person's use of the resource does not necessarily diminish the potential for use by another' (non-rivalrous and non-excludable).[7] The term 'common property' implies 'a kind of management arrangement created by humans rather than a

[1] Article 9 of the Land Administration Law (2004) defines collective ownership in the same way as Article 10 of the 2004 Constitution.

[2] In this chapter, we use these two terms interchangeably. As the relevant Chinese laws use the term 'collective property', we will use the term 'collective property' when referring to communal property defined in Chinese law.

[3] T. Dietz, N. Dolšak, E. Ostrom and P. C. Stern, 'The Drama of the Commons', in E. Ostrom T. Dietz, N. Dolšak, P. C. Stern, S. Stonich and E. U. Weber (eds), *The Drama of the Commons* (Washington, DC, National Academy Press, 2002), pp. 3–36 at p. 18.

[4] J. B. Holder and T. Flessas, 'Emerging Commons', *Social and Legal Studies*, 17 (2008), 299–310 at 300.

[5] E. Ostrom, *Governing the Commons: The Evolution of Institutions for Collective Action* (Cambridge, Cambridge University Press, 1990), p. 30.

[6] C. Hess and E. Ostrom (eds), *Understanding Knowledge as a Commons: From Theory to Practice* (Cambridge, MA, MIT Press, 2009), p. 9.

[7] Dietz et al., 'The Drama of the Commons', pp. 4–5.

characteristic of the resource itself'.[8] Whereas 'common-pool resource' and 'public good' refer only to the physical resource itself, 'common property' refers to the management arrangement adopted by a community to regulate its communal use of a resource. This definition of common property comes closest to the concept of communal property that we focus on in this chapter.

The second difficulty lies in deciphering the meaning of collective property in the Chinese context. The relevant laws provide a sketch of its meaning and the ways in which collective property rights can be exercised. Article 58 of the Property Law (2007) delineates the categories of things that can be owned collectively.[9] Article 59 of the Property Law (2007) outlines the owners of collective property: 'the immovables and movables collectively owned by the farmers belong to the members of the collective'.[10] Article 10 of the Land Administration Law (2004) and Article 60 of the Property Law (2007) set out the ways in which collectively owned land should be managed and administered by the collective economic organisations belonging to a village, a villagers' group or a town; the villagers' committees; or villagers' groups themselves.[11] The above provisions indicate that the collective encompasses multi-layered communities with varied scales. As the meaning of the collective is poorly defined in law, in order to comprehend its meaning we need

[8] Dietz et al., 'The Drama of the Commons', p. 17.

[9] The immovables and movables owned by the collective include the following:

(1) the land, forests, mountains, grasslands, wasteland and tidal flats that belong to the collective, as is provided for by law;
(2) buildings, production equipment, and water conservancy facilities of farmland;
(3) the educational, scientific, cultural, public health and sports facilities; and
(4) other immovables and movables.

[10] The following matters shall be subject to decision by the members of a given collective in accordance with the statutory procedure:

(1) plans for the contracting of land, and the subcontracting of land to other units or to individuals other than those belonging to the collective;
(2) adjustment to be made to the contracted land by the individual persons among themselves who have the contractual management right;
(3) methods for the use and distribution of such fees as compensations paid for land;
(4) such matters as change in ownership of the enterprises invested by the collective; and
(5) other matters as provided for by law.

[11] Article 60 of Property Law (2007) provides: with respect to the land, forests, mountains, grasslands, wasteland, tidal flats, etc. owned by the collective, the right of their ownership shall be exercised in accordance with the following provisions:

(1) For those owned by the collective of farmers of a village, the collective economic organization of the village or the villagers' committee shall exercise the right of ownership on behalf of the collective;
(2) For those respectively owned by two or more collectives of farmers within a village, the collective economic organizations or villagers' groups concerned within the village shall exercise the right of ownership on behalf of the collectives; and
(3) For those owned by the collective of farmers of a town or township, the collective economic organization of the town or township shall exercise the right of ownership on behalf of the collective.

to probe the nature of those communities and the relationship between those communities and their members.

The third difficulty concerns how best to translate the meaning of collective property as it is specifically defined in the Chinese context and to link it with the general study of communal property. One of the particularly challenging tasks is to identify the boundaries of a community: where do the boundaries of a community lie? What is the relationship between collective economic organisations and administrative governance entities, in particular the villagers' committee? Due to the present chapter's space limitations, we focus on providing an explanation of the historical process whereby different layers of the collective have been formed, rather than proceeding to recommend possible reforms remedying this institutional ambiguity.[12]

Further, since 1978, private property rights have been selectively granted to farmers, in the form of 'contractual management rights', through the dismantling of rural communes and the introduction of the household responsibility system. For farmers, once they have discharged their duty to meet the grain quota imposed by the state, they can sell the grain produced over and above the required quota and retain the profits. A market system has been slowly re-emerging where farmers began to pursue their independent economic goals.

Since the initial allocation of rural land rights in the 1980s, contractual management rights have been granted to farmers, in the form of contracts, for the possession and use of rural land for farming purposes. Therefore, these rights may be translated into 'the right to possession and use of rural land for farming purposes', or, in a much simpler form, the right to farm, which is a private property interest. Farmers' private property interests are enforceable against the community, outsiders and the state. The collective economic organisation or the villagers' committee issues contracts to the household, which has responsibility for the management of farming an area of land called 'responsibility land'.[13] Here it should be noted that the household is neither a formal tier of the collective nor a legal entity; rather it functions as a 'close-knit' community[14] that organises agricultural production, forming a kind of collective involvement in the larger communal group. The 'responsibility land' is therefore subject to the farmer's private property interest and layers of communal property interest including the household's interest and the collective economic organisation's interest. The collective economic organisation also directly owns a tiny amount of rural land called

[12] For institutional ambiguity, see for example P. Ho, 'Who Owns China's Land? Policies, Property Rights and Deliberate Institutional Ambiguity', *The China Quarterly*, 166 (2001), 394–421.

[13] Article 3 of the 'Law of the PRC on Land Contract in Rural Areas' (2002) provides: 'Land contract in rural areas shall take the form of household contract within the collective economic organizations in the countryside . . .'

[14] For example, R. Ellickson, 'Property in Land', *Yale Law Journal*, 102 (1993), 1315–1400.

'reserved land' (*jidong di*) for the benefit of present and future members.[15] The 'reserved land' can be used to adjust the rights land allocated to the household when the household has new members.[16]

The second round of the allocation of rural land rights began in 1998. The duration of the contracts increased from 15 years granted in the initial allocation of rural land rights to 30 years under Article 14 of the Land Administration Law (1998). Now, under the Property Law (2007), when the contracts expire, they may be renewed.[17] In fact, responsibility land serves as one kind of basic social security for farmers, enabling them to make a living from farming.

The creation of the right to farm within the collective property system has added another layer of complexity to the ownership system of rural land: it creates a hybrid property regime where private land rights have been selectively readmitted and integrated into collective land rights.[18] This mixed system has been confirmed in Article 8 of the 2004 Constitution,[19] but poses more questions in probing the boundaries of the collective and collective property.

It is argued in this chapter that examining community, in particular its boundaries, is the key to understanding and defining the concept of collective property in the Chinese context. Here, the term 'community' is invoked as both an abstraction and an empirical description. In our following discussion, we use the single form of community when referring to the abstraction of its meaning and the plural form when referring to empirical examples of communities. Blomley argues that 'the boundary, precisely because it is simultaneously a legal and spatial construct, is one useful place to think through these dialectic geographies of law'.[20] The boundary of community we examine is not only a legal and spatial construct but also a construct that is being shaped and reshaped by ideologies, values, interests and political power

[15] Article 63 of the 'Law of the PRC on Land Contract in Rural Areas' (2002) provides:

> Where, before the implementation of this Law, land has already been reserved, the area of such reserved land may not exceed five percent of the total area of the arable land of the collective economic organization concerned. If the area is less than five percent, the area of the reserved land may not be increased.
>
> Where, before implementation of this Law, no land is reserved, no land may be reserved after the implementation of this Law.

[16] See 'The collective, membership of the collective and land rights in the post-commune era'.

[17] Property Law (2007), Article 126.

[18] See, for example, A. Clarke, 'Integrating Private and Collective Land Rights: Lessons from China', *Journal of Comparative Law*, 7 (2013), 177–193.

[19] The provisions of this Article include: 'The rural collective economic organizations apply the dual operation system characterized by the combination of centralized operation with decentralized operation on the basis of operation by households under a contract . . . working people who are members of rural economic collectives have the right, within the limits prescribed by law, to farm plots of cropland and hilly land allotted for their private use, engage in household sideline production and raise privately owned livestock.'

[20] N. Blomley, 'The Boundaries of Property: Lessons from Beatrix Potter', *The Canadian Geographer*, 48 (2004), 91–100 at 93.

in profound social, political and economic transformations. Moreover, community differs from either the aggregations of individuals or the state. Therefore, the examination of the boundaries of community poses important questions concerning the interplay between individuals, communities and the state, and between state law and community norms.[21] Such an examination has significant implications for the probing of the concept of communal property, and in particular the origin of communal property, the identity of rights holders of communal property, the extent of 'dominion' and the configuration of communal assets.[22]

Methodology: invoking the lens of community

In invoking the lens of community,[23] three steps are taken. The first step (the section on 'Community and property') lays out the theoretical framework, exploring the relationship between community and property and examining the legal concept of communal property from a sociological perspective.[24] Community and property are mutually constitutive; our focus in this chapter falls in the community direction, that is, community plays a constitutive role in the definition and understanding of property.

[21] Here the scope of community differs from many other studies of community which do not draw the distinction between community and the state. See, for example, G. S. Alexander and E. M. Peñalver, 'Properties of Community', *Theoretical Inquiries in Law*, 10 (2009), 127–160 (their conception of communities includes the state).

[22] See A. Bell and G. Parchomovsky, 'The Evolution of Private and Open Access Property', *Theoretical Inquiries in Law*, 10 (2009), 77–102 (arguing that the evolution of property is shaped by the interplay of three dimensions, namely, 'number of owners, extent of dominion and asset configuration').

[23] On invoking the lens of community in exploring Chinese property law, see T. Xu, 'Global Legal Transplants through the Lens of Community: Lessons for and from Chinese Property Law', in A. Perry-Kessaris (ed.), *Socio-Legal Approaches to International Economic Law: Text, Context and Subtext* (London, Routledge, 2013), pp. 167–180; T. Xu and W. Gong, 'Taking as Giving, Appropriation as Access: Transfers of Land Development Rights and China's Recent Experiments', *Northern Ireland Legal Quarterly*, 64 (2013), 411–424.

[24] See, for example, R. Cotterrell, *Law's Community: Legal Theory in Sociological Perspective* (Oxford, Oxford University Press, 1995), preface (arguing that 'legal ideas cannot be adequately analysed without study of their social origins, social conditions of existence, and social consequences'); R. Cotterrell, 'A Legal Concept of Community', *Canadian Journal of Law and Society*, 12 (1997), 75–91. For studies of the relationship between community and property, see, for example, Ellickson, 'Property in Land', 1397 (arguing that 'a close-knit group tends to create, through custom and law, a cost-minimizing land regime that adaptively responds to changes in risk, technology, demand, and other economic conditions'); G. Pienaar, 'The Meaning of the Concept Community in South Africa Land Tenure Legislation', *Stellenbosch Law Review*, 16 (2005), 60–76; Special Issue, *Theoretical Inquiries in Law*, 10 (2009); L. A. Fennell, 'Scaling Property with Professor Ellickson', *William & Mary Bill of Rights Journal*, 18 (2009), 173–181 (arguing that the scale of property matters); Clarke, 'Integrating Private and Collective Land Rights'; A. Lehavi, *The Construction of Property: Norms, Institutions, Challenges* (Cambridge, Cambridge University Press, 2014), in particular ch. 4, 'How Property Can Create, Maintain, or Destroy Community', pp. 153–178.

The second step deciphers the meaning of community and provides a socio-legal interpretation of the origin of collective property in the Chinese context. For this purpose, we have conducted a substantial survey of large volumes of laws, regulations and policy documents which concern the meaning of the collective, and that have been promulgated since 1949, the founding date of the PRC. We have surveyed the 'Compendium of the Laws of the PRC (1954–2004)'.[25] However, prior to 1978 very few laws concerning property were made by the Standing Committee of the National People's Congress, and the governance of China primarily relied on policies and documents issued by the Chinese Communist Party (CCP) Central Party Committee (hereinafter the Central Committee). Therefore, we have moved on to examine various collections of documents edited by the Central Committee, including: the 'Selected Important Documents since the Founding of the PRC';[26] the 'Selected Important Documents since the Third Plenary Session of the 11th Central Committee of the CCP';[27] the 'Selected Important Documents since the 12th National Congress of the CCP';[28] and the 'Selected Important Documents since the 13th National Congress of the CCP'.[29] We have examined where and when the concept of the collective appeared in those policy documents, and linked the content of the relevant provisions with the profound political events that occurred before or after the publication of those documents. The result of the survey maps the trajectory of the formation of the collective and the establishment of collective ownership in the collectivisation period (1958–1982), and is presented below in the section on 'The formation and transformation of the collective in the period 1949–1982' and briefly summarised in Table 8.1.

[25] The Legislative Affairs Committee of the Standing Committee of the National People's Congress (ed.), *Compendium of the Laws of the PRC (1954–2004) (Zhonghua renmin gonghe guo falü huibian (1954–2004))* (Beijing, Renmin chubanshe, 2004).

[26] Party Documents Research Office of the CCP Central Committee (ed.), *Selected Important Documents since the Founding of the PRC (Jianguo yilai zhongyao wenxian xuanbian)* (Beijing, Zhongyang wenxian chubanshe, 1992–1998). The series of publications consists of 20 volumes, covering important documents issued between September 1949 and December 1965.

[27] Party Documents Research Office of the CCP Central Committee (ed.), *Selected Important Documents since the Third Plenary Session of the 11th Central Committee of the CCP (Sanzhong quanhui yilai zhongyao wenxian xuanbian)* (Beijing, Renmin chubanshe, 1982). This collection consists of two volumes of 104 papers, including documents issued by the Central Committee, as well as party leaders' speeches and articles published during the period 1978–1982.

[28] Party Documents Research Office of the CCP Central Committee (ed.), *Selected Important Documents since the 12th National Congress of the CCP (Shi'er da yilai zhongyao wenxian xuanbian)* (Beijing, Renmin chubanshe, 1986–1988). This collection consists of three volumes and covers 128 papers including documents issued by the Central Committee and the State Council, as well as party leaders' speeches and articles published during the period 1982–1987.

[29] Party Documents Research Office of the CCP Central Committee (ed.), *Selected Important Documents since the 13th National Congress of the CCP (Shisan da yilai zhongyao wenxian xuanbian)* (Beijing, Renmin chubanshe, 1991–1993). This collection consists of three volumes and covers 186 papers including documents issued by the CCP Central Committee and the State Council, as well as party leaders' speeches and articles published during the period 1987–1992.

The third step examines the transformation of the boundaries of the collective (as shown in Table 8.2) and collective property in the context of a hybrid property system in the post-commune era (the section on 'The collective, membership of the collective and land rights in the post-commune era'). In addition to continuing to draw upon the survey listed above, we have undertaken an analysis of cases concerning disputes over the right to farm. In viewing these cases through the lens of community, we have examined the relationship between the collective, membership of the collective and the right to farm.

We have chosen to focus on disputes occurring in Henan province, and there are a number of reasons for our sampling strategy. First, Henan is located in the central part of China and has the largest population of all the provinces in China.[30] If we use the geographical dividing line, the Huai River-Qin Mountains Line, as the dividing line between northern and southern China, Henan crosses the north–south divide. It therefore embodies the characteristics of both northern and southern China regarding the style of life, means of production and cultural traditions. Second, Henan is regarded as the breadbasket of China and one of the most important producers and processors of food products in China. People's communes appeared first in Henan in 1958.[31] Moreover, since 2009, the Henan People's Court at the High Level has experimented with posting judgments online.[32] Following Henan's initiative, in 2013 the Supreme People's Court requested courts nationwide to put judgments online and then collected these judgments in the Supreme Court's online database.[33]

We have explored the database 'China Judgments Online' launched by the Supreme Court of the PRC in 2013.[34] Searching cases using the keywords 'disputes over the right to farm', 'civil cases', 'disputes occurring in Henan province' and 'cases heard at the local court/the court of first instance',[35] we have found

[30] Henan Statistics Bureau, 'Introduction to Henan Province', www.henan.gov.cn/hngk/system/2006/09/19/010008384.shtml.

[31] P. Luo, *The History of People's Communes in Rural China (Nongcun renmin gongshe shi)* (Fuzhou, Fujian renmin chubanshe, 2002), p. 19.

[32] 'Henan: Comprehensive Implementation of Posting Judgments Online (Henan: quanmian tuixing caipan wenshu shangwang)', 24 November 2013, www.chinacourt.org/article/detail/2013/11/id/1149579.shtml.

[33] 'The Supreme Court: All Legally Effective Judgments Should be Posted Online (Zuigao fa: jinhou shengxiao caipan wenshu yuanze shang quanbu shangwang)', 3 July 2013, http://legal.china.com.cn/2013-07/03/content_29311260.htm.

[34] http://wenshu.court.gov.cn/.

[35] According to Chapter Three of the 2004 Constitution, the structure of governance in China consists of five tiers: the central government, provinces, cities, counties and townships. In correspondence with the first four tiers, the court system in China is divided into four levels: the Supreme Court, the court at the high level, the court at the intermediate level, and the court at the local level. Some courts at the local level have established detached tribunals in townships with large populations. The tribunals function as the constituent of the court at the local level and their judgments constitute the body of judgments of the court at the local level. See Articles 2, 17, 19, 22 and 25 of the Organic Law of the People's Courts (1980, amended 1983, 1986, and 2006).

132 relevant cases tried in the period from 2012 to 2016, which reflect the ways in which the law is implemented to express and support an enduring relationship between the collective and its members with respect to the right to farm.[36]

This study, which is the first step towards analysing the large volume of data only recently made publicly accessible, carries important methodological significance.[37] It is the first to study collective property in China through analysing the Supreme Court's database. The analysis will give non-Chinese speakers important insights into the meaning of collective property in the Chinese context, in the light of decisions made in the Chinese courts.

Community and property

'"Community" is a fluid, often elusive concept.'[38] It may be better understood with reference to some common characteristics or identifiers. Locality is important; people are often bound together via living in a common place. That said, community is not merely a geographical notion, as people may be bound together by a common interest that transcends the territorial boundaries. Community may be formed by a distinctive network of social relations or style of life (for example, the community of farmers, pastoral community, etc.).[39] Community may also be shaped by a strong sense of connection or belonging, for example, many communities such as indigenous communities have members who share a distinctive 'identity'.[40]

In seeking the common characteristics of community, some meaningful taxonomies of community have been developed. Lehavi divides communities into intentional, planned and spontaneous communities.[41] 'An "Intentional Community" may be defined as a group that shares a thick common denominator of ideology, values, or beliefs that are substantially distinctive from those of general society.'[42] The people's commune established in the collectivisation period (1958–1982), to be discussed in the next section, is an example of an intentional community. By contrast, 'planned communities' can only be effectively established with 'the basic

[36] According to Article 20 of the Organic Law of the People's Courts and Article 17 of the Civil Procedure Law (1991, amended 2007 and 2012), cases heard at first instance are under the jurisdiction of the court at the local level.

[37] For discussion on the significance of this methodology, see, for example, B. L. Liebman, 'Leniency in Chinese Criminal Law? Everyday Justice in Henan', *Berkeley Journal of International Law*, 33 (2015), 153–227. Its focus is on criminal cases.

[38] Lehavi, *The Construction of Property*, p. 153.

[39] J. Clarke, 'Community', in D. M. Nonini (ed.), *A Companion to Urban Anthropology* (London, Wiley-Blackwell, 2014), pp. 46–64 at pp. 47–48.

[40] Clarke, 'Community', p. 48

[41] Lehavi, *The Construction of Property*, p. 154.

[42] Lehavi, *The Construction of Property*, p. 160.

structural support of the state legal system'.[43] The collective economic organisation fits within this category of community. 'Spontaneous communities' usually rely on 'relatively fragile modes of cooperation, and even when incorporated as non-profit organizations, they typically do not distinctively hold formal property rights to resources'.[44] The mutual aid teams, to be discussed in the next section, can be included in this category of community.

Another major study that has developed the taxonomies of community has been undertaken by Cotterrell, who sees 'community' as networks of social relations held together by a variety of bonds (for example, a convergence of economic interests,[45] shared custom, common values).[46] Drawing upon Weber's four ideal types of social action (traditional, affectual, instrumentally rational and value-rational),[47] Cotterrell's 'networks of relations of community' encompass four ideal types of community: traditional community, affective community, instrumental community and community of belief. In this approach, one ideal type of community (for example, community of belief) is not to be equated with one empirical manifestation of community (for example, a church); rather it represents a distinctive type of 'collective involvement', and can be combined with other types of community 'in complex ways in actual group life'.[48] Further, social groups can be formed on both a voluntary and involuntary basis. For involuntary groups, individuals are born into the group without necessarily bearing a sense of attachment to the group or other members in the group.[49]

The seeking of the common characteristics of community, or the identification of the bonds that hold community together, helps to develop a meaningful definition of communal property.[50] For example, Clarke defines communal property as 'land and other resources owned and/or used and controlled by a self-interested and self-governing group of people defined by reference to some common characteristics such as kinship, locality, or common interest'.[51] This definition includes at least three important dimensions of communal property: the resource which

[43] Lehavi, *The Construction of Property*, p. 173.
[44] Lehavi, *The Construction of Property*, p. 175.
[45] See also S. R. Munzer, 'Commons, Anticommons, and Community in Biotechnological Assets', *Theoretical Inquiries in Law*, 10 (2009), 271–298 at 273–274 (defining a community as 'a group of people who have shared interests and who work toward shared goals').
[46] R. Cotterrell, *Law, Culture and Society: Legal Ideas in the Mirror of Social Theory* (Aldershot, Ashgate, 2006), p. 74.
[47] M. Weber, *Economy and Society: An Outline of Interpretive Sociology*, trans. E. Fischoff (Berkeley, University of California Press, 1978), pp. 23–26.
[48] Cotterrell, 'A Legal Concept of Community', 81.
[49] Cotterrell, 'A Legal Concept of Community', 85.
[50] See also J. E. Penner, 'Property, Community and Distributive Justice', *Theoretical Inquiries in Law*, 10 (2009), 193–216 at 193 (arguing that 'the topic of property and community normally invokes thoughts about the way in which the concept of property can be extended beyond private property').
[51] Clarke, 'Integrating Private and Collective Land Rights', 181.

is owned/used communally or collectively; the governance of such a resource; and the bonds that hold the community together. Human involvement is the very quintessence of communal property.

Community embodies both inclusivity and exclusivity. For example, a community often embraces its members, but excludes outsiders. Of course, there are also instances where the membership of a community is 'stratified in uncomfortable ways and riddled with practices that seek to reproduce and stabilize certain orderings of authority, power, and knowledge'.[52] For example, in the case of PRC rural society, although the law protects women's property rights in instances of divorce or remarriage, in reality, women's right to farm is often revoked by the village even when they are still its members.[53] Whether women are or are not part of the 'community' has been a crucial issue in China.[54] This point will be further elaborated in the section on 'The collective, membership of the collective and land rights in the post-commune era'.

The observation that communities are both inclusive and exclusive helps explain the co-existence of private property interest and communal property interest within a communal property regime. Indeed, communal property can be seen as a hybrid system:

> Most resource utilising communities, whether or not culturally distinct, use only some of their resources collectively. The rest of their resources may be loosely regarded as community assets but will be allocated to individuals or individual families on a more or less private property basis, perhaps subject only to a prohibition against alienation out of the community.[55]

The absolute homogeneity of community is only 'imagined', as the boundaries of community are often permeable and shifting in the process of social, economic, political and legal transformations.[56] In addition to the increasing mobility of people (for example, migration) and the deconstruction of spatial boundaries (for example, by urbanisation), values, ideologies and interests that used to hold communities together may change, leading to the grouping and regrouping of communities. For voluntary groups, the right to exit enjoyed by members may

[52] Clarke, 'Community', 49.

[53] For example, Article 30 of the 'Law of the PRC on Land Contract in Rural Areas' (2002) provides that marital status changes shall not affect women's right to farm. Editors' note: For discussion of gender discrimination in communal property governance, see also Pienaar and Pieraccini in this volume.

[54] See, for example, J. Stacey, *Patriarchy and Socialist Revolution in China* (Berkeley, University of California Press, 1983).

[55] A. Clarke, 'Property, Human Rights and Communities', in T. Xu and J. Allain (eds), *Property and Human Rights in a Global Context* (Oxford, Hart Publishing, 2015), pp. 19–40 at p. 22. See also C. M. Rose, 'The Comedy of the Commons: Custom, Commerce, and Inherently Public Property', *University of Chicago Law Review*, 53 (1986), 711–781 (arguing that property held by close-knit groups is private property when viewed from the outside).

[56] Clarke, 'Community', 54.

not necessarily lead to the dissolution of the communal group; rather it may strengthen the group. The freedom for members to withdraw also means that their participation in the group is 'more conscious and considered', which helps sustain enduring rather than transient communal relations.[57] If a community is not completely sealed and static, the boundaries of communal property may be fluid and changeable.[58] This point will be discussed in detail in the following sections.

The formation and transformation of the collective in the period 1949–1982

The first-named author has discussed the transformation of communities in China from the historical perspective at length elsewhere,[59] so the description of the role of community in the historical context can be brief here. Throughout Chinese history there have always been tensions between the central government and small communities; the latter refers to self-governing organisations, for example, kinship and grassroots associations. Although lineage-based communities were exclusive, they also linked together and formed larger communities, forming nested communities at varying scales.[60] As the power of kinship grew, the state had to rely on kinships or lineages for local governance. China's traditional adherence to kinship, lineage and community ties, which can be compared to what Cotterrell calls 'traditional community',[61] engendered and affected 'de facto and de jure property holdings'.[62]

Since the founding of the PRC in 1949, the formation of communities has begun to depart from its adherence to traditional community ties, and to be strongly influenced by communist ideology. During the land reform (*tugai*) that occurred in the period 1949–1952, land and other property of landlords (including corporate/

[57] Cotterrell, 'A Legal Concept of Community', 85.

[58] See, for example, H. Dagan and M. Heller, 'The Liberal Commons', *Yale Law Journal*, 110 (2001), 549–624 (arguing that successful commons can exist in a liberal society if participants have appropriate exit rights).

[59] T. Xu, *The Revival of Private Property and Its Limits in Post-Mao China* (London, Wildy, Simmonds and Hill Publishing, 2014).

[60] For nested communities, see, for example, G. W. Skinner, 'Marketing and Social Structure in Rural China, Part I', *The Journal of Asian Studies*, 24 (1964), 3–43; G. W. Skinner, 'Marketing and Social Structure in Rural China, Part II', *The Journal of Asian Studies*, 24 (1965), 195–228; G. W. Skinner, 'Marketing and Social Structure in Rural China, Part III', *The Journal of Asian Studies*, 24 (1965), 363–399; G. W. Skinner, 'Chinese Peasants and the Closed Community: An Open and Shut Case', *Comparative Studies in Society and History*, 13 (1971), 270–281; G. W. Skinner, 'Rural Marketing in China: Repression and Revival', *The China Quarterly*, 103 (1985), 393–413.

[61] See 'Community and property'.

[62] Clarke, 'Integrating Private and Collective Land Rights', 179. See also Xu, *The Revival of Private Property*, ch. 2.

communal landowners such as lineages, temples, and monasteries) was confiscated and equally redistributed so that each household in a rural village could own a piece of land in accordance with the size of the household.[63] Land reform initially allowed every rural household to be allocated an amount of private land, but this allocation proved rather quickly to be a temporary phenomenon.

In 1953, the CCP initiated its first Five Year Plan (1953–1957), aiming for the promotion of 'socialist transformation' and 'industrialisation'. The term 'collective economic organisation' first appeared in the 'Draft Model Charter on Agricultural Producers' Cooperatives', approved by the Standing Committee of the National People's Congress on 9 November 1955.[64] Article 1(1) indicates that the collective economic organisation can be equated with the agricultural producers' cooperative. Article 1(1) provides:

> agricultural producers' cooperatives are working people's collective economic organisations [. . .] These cooperatives make arrangements to use their members' land, livestock and tools collectively, with the aim to transform the ownership of the means of production to public ownership. Cooperatives also organise the members' work so that labour can be shared and income can be distributed in a unified way.

The term 'agricultural producers' cooperative' emerged earlier in the 'Decision on Mutual Aid and Cooperation in Agricultural Production (Draft)', issued by the Central Party Committee on 15 December 1951. Article 4 provides that agricultural production shall be undertaken in three forms of agricultural producers' cooperative: temporary, seasonal mutual aid; long-term mutual aid, which is based on arrangements among several households where labour and the means of production are to be shared; and formal agricultural producers' cooperatives where land is pooled together as shares in the cooperative.[65]

Up until 16 December 1953 when the CCP Central Party Committee formally published its 'Decision on the Development of Agricultural Producers' Cooperatives', more than 47.9 million rural households (43 per cent of rural households nationwide) had participated in the seasonal, long-term mutual aid teams, or agricultural producers' cooperatives; 273,000 rural households, a tiny minority of the 47.9 million rural households, participated in 14,000 formal agricultural producers' cooperatives.[66]

When the Central Party Committee issued its decision on 11 October 1955 to further the development of formal agricultural producers' cooperatives, the number

[63] S. Liu, 'Report on the Issue of Land Reform (Guanyu tudi gaige wenti de baogao)', 14 June 1950.

[64] Party Documents Research Office, *Selected Important Documents since the Founding of the PRC*, vol. 7, pp. 357–395.

[65] Party Documents Research Office, *Selected Important Documents since the Founding of the PRC*, vol. 2, pp. 512–513.

[66] Party Documents Research Office, *Selected Important Documents since the Founding of the PRC*, vol. 4, pp. 662–663.

of such cooperatives had increased dramatically to 650,000 with the participation of more than 16.9 million rural households.[67] Those cooperatives were characterised as being at a primary stage of formation, and were referred to as primary cooperatives (*chuji she*). They were based on a system of apportioning agricultural income in accordance with both the amount of land that the household owned and the labour input of that household. During this period, farmers retained private ownership rights in their own land, while primary cooperatives held use rights over the whole of the land owned by the farmers who were the members of primary cooperatives.

In spring 1956, primary cooperatives were transformed into advanced cooperatives (*gaoji she*), whose establishment had been first proposed in the 'Draft Model Charter on the Agricultural Producers' Cooperatives' in 1955. Compared to primary cooperatives, advanced cooperatives governed a larger territorial area that transcended the traditional boundaries of the 'natural' villages (*ziran cun*) that had been shaped by long-term social interactions of villagers.[68] Farmers were encouraged to join advanced cooperatives as members by handing in their assets, including land and production tools that were distributed to them in the land reform of the early 1950s. Except for a few private plots retained by farmers to grow supplementary foodstuffs, both land ownership and use rights were collectivised and held by advanced cooperatives.[69] Income distribution was implemented through a system of work points (*gongfen*) based on the work done by each person. Farmers still retained the right to exit, that is, to withdraw from advanced cooperatives and take away their properties and receive remuneration for work done.

The nature of the advanced cooperative, as the collective economic organisation, was confirmed in Article 1 of the 'Draft Model Charter on Advanced Agricultural Producers' Cooperatives', issued by the Central Party Committee on 30 June 1956.[70] At that time, the number of rural households which joined advanced cooperatives constituted more than 61 per cent of the number of rural households nationwide.[71] In terms of the scale of cooperatives, on 14 September 1957 the Central Party Committee required that one (administrative) village should

[67] Party Documents Research Office, *Selected Important Documents since the Founding of the PRC*, vol. 7, p. 284.

[68] 'Natural villages' emphasises villages 'in the sense of what is local and long-standing', whilst 'administrative villages' closely resembles 'sub-government institutions'. See S. Feuchtwang, 'What Is a Village?', in E. B. Vermeer, F. N. Pieke and W. L. Chong (eds), *Cooperative and Collective in China's Rural Development: Between State and Private Interests* (New York: M.E. Sharpe, 1998), pp. 46–74 at p. 47. An administrative village may consist of several small natural villages.

[69] Party Documents Research Office, *Selected Important Documents since the Founding of the PRC*, vol. 7, p. 359.

[70] Party Documents Research Office, *Selected Important Documents since the Founding of the PRC*, vol. 8, p. 403.

[71] Party Documents Research Office, *Selected Important Documents since the Founding of the PRC*, vol. 8, p. 359.

have one cooperative and that if the village was small, several small villages could constitute one cooperative. Further, the production team (*shengchan xiaodui*) was to constitute the basic production unit consisting of about 20 households.[72]

Driven by the aim to speed up the process of collectivisation, on 29 August 1958, the Central Party Committee pushed for the expanding of the scale of cooperatives: 'in general, one township should establish one cooperative which should encompass about 2,000 rural households; larger cooperatives should be allowed, each cooperative may consist of 20,000 rural households'.[73] The expansion of cooperatives resulted in the formation of people's communes (*renmin gongshe*) that replaced the cooperatives and the subsequent establishment of collective ownership of rural land in 1958.[74]

Communes directly managed agricultural production and arranged income distribution. As communes consisted of all farmers in a region and membership was compulsory, farmers were deprived of the right to exit. Further, the possible exodus of farmers from villages to cities was prohibited by the household registration system (*hukou*), which was formalised in the process of collectivisation in 1958. Under this system everyone was registered as belonging to a household, which had a registered place of residence; an individual's household registration could not generally be changed.[75] Mobility was severely restricted under this system; rural dwellers were required to remain in their official place of residence in the countryside. Daily necessities, including food and clothing, were allocated through systems of rationing or coupons based on household registration.[76]

The commune was characterised as an organisation which combined political control with economic management.[77] In 1962, rural land ownership was further transformed into three-level agricultural collectives, each headed by a branch of the Party: production teams, production brigades (*shengchan dadui*) and people's communes. Land ownership was formally located at the level of the production team,[78] which functioned as the basic accounting unit, each consisting of 20–30 households.[79]

[72] Party Documents Research Office, *Selected Important Documents since the Founding of the PRC*, vol. 10, p. 552.

[73] Party Documents Research Office, *Selected Important Documents since the Founding of the PRC*, vol. 10, p. 446.

[74] In 1958, even private plots became public property, but private ownership of these plots was soon restored in 1959.

[75] This household registration system is still in operation today.

[76] J. Goldstein, 'Introduction', in M. Y. Dong and J. Goldstein (eds), *Everyday Modernity in China* (Seattle, University of Washington Press, 2006), pp. 3–21 at p. 17.

[77] The nature of communes was confirmed in the 'Principles on the Work of People's Communes (Revised Draft)', issued by the Central Party Committee on 15 June 1961.

[78] Draft Amendment of the Working Regulations of the People's Communes (1962), Article 21.

[79] Party Documents Research Office, *Selected Important Documents since the Founding of the PRC*, vol. 15, pp. 179–186.

Table 8.1 The transformation of the collective economic organisation and the establishment of collective ownership between 1949 and 1982.

Form	Mutual aid teams (*huzhu zu*)	Primary cooperatives (*chuji she*)	Advanced cooperatives (*gaoji she*)	People's communes (*renmin gongshe*)
Period	1950–1953	1951–1955	1956–1958	1958–1982
Nature	The sharing of labour and livestock	Contributing land to cooperatives as shares	Collective ownership of rural land	The integration of political control of the rural community with economic management of the cooperatives

The collective, membership of the collective and land rights in the post-commune era

The transformation in the post-commune era

Following the economic reforms that commenced in 1978, the 'household responsibility system' was first set up in 1978 by a small group of farmers, and was expanded on a nationwide scale between 1980 and 1983.[80] The governance structure of rural China was also transformed. Peng Zhen, the then Vice-Chairman of the Standing Committee of the National People's Congress, delivered a report on the 'Draft Amendment of the Constitution of the PRC' to the National People's Congress on 26 November 1982. He pointed out that:

> it is time to change the system of people's communes where political control and economic management are mixed together. We should establish townships as one tier of the governance structure, and people's communes will only function in the rural collective economy as economic organisations.[81]

This intention was realised in Article 8 of the 1982 Constitution, which confirms that 'various forms of the cooperative economy in rural areas such as producers', supply and marketing, credit and consumers' cooperatives belong to the sector of the socialist economy under collective ownership by the working people'. Townships function at the lowest level of the formal administrative governance

[80] See 'Introduction'.

[81] Party Documents Research Office, *Selected Important Documents since the 12th National Congress of the CCP*, vol. 1, p. 153.

structure,[82] whereas administrative villages serve as an organisational unit at the grassroots level. The boundaries of administrative villages may not correspond to natural villages, which exist spontaneously within rural areas. Villagers' committees function as 'self-governing mass organisations at the grassroots level' (*jiceng qunzhong zizhixing zuzhi*), according to Article 111 of the 1982 Constitution.[83] One villagers' committee may govern several natural villages. However, one big natural village may set up several villagers' committees. The chairman, vice-chairmen and members of each villagers' committee are elected by the villagers.[84]

One villagers' committee may set up several villagers' groups (*cunmin xiaozu*), which may be characterised as equivalent to the production team in the commune system. The villagers' groups do not hold much power. This situation has been shaped by the transformation of rural governance in the post-commune era. In the early 1980s, when communes were dismantled, the production teams at the lowest level of the communes went into decline. After the township replaced the governance function of the commune in the early 1980s, the administrative village took the place of the production brigade, and the villagers' group superseded the production team.[85] Power was concentrated at the administrative village and township levels.

The villagers' committee is responsible to the villagers' assembly, which is convened by the villagers' committee in accordance with the proposal by more than one-tenth of the villagers or more than one-third of the villagers' representatives.[86] The villagers' assembly makes decisions regarding matters including use

[82] Article 30 of the 1982 Constitution provides: 'The administrative division of the PRC is as follows:

(1) The country is divided into provinces, autonomous regions, and municipalities directly under the Central Government;
(2) Provinces and autonomous regions are divided into autonomous prefectures, counties, autonomous counties, and cities; and
(3) Counties and autonomous counties are divided into townships, ethnic townships, and towns . . .'

[83] Article 7(2) of the 'Organic Law of the Villagers' Committee of the PRC (for Trial Implementation)' promulgated on 24 November 1987 provides: 'The Villagers' Committees are established in natural villages: several natural villages may set up one villagers' committee collectively; a big natural village may have several villagers' committees.' Article 15 provides: 'One Villagers' Committee may set up several villagers' groups; each head of the group is elected by the meeting of the villagers' group.' The document is available in the General Office of the State Council of the PRC, Bulletin of the State Council, 1987, no. 27, pp. 885–886.

[84] Article 11 of the 'Organic Law of the Villagers' Committee of the PRC' (1998, amended 2010). Article 6 provides: 'A villagers' committee is composed of three to seven members, including the chairman, the vice-chairman (vice-chairmen) and the members.' Article 11 provides: 'The chairman, vice-chairman (vice-chairmen) and members of a villagers' committee shall be elected directly by the villagers. No organization or individual may designate, appoint or replace any member of a villagers' committee.'

[85] See Ho, 'Who Owns China's Land?', 405.

[86] Article 21 of the 'Organic Law of the Villagers' Committee' (1998, amended 2010).

of the proceeds from the running of the collective economy of the village and plans regarding granting villagers the right to farm in the form of contracts.[87]

The villagers' committee does not have the authority to adjudicate land disputes, because it is one of the authorities that issue land contracts granting the right to farm to rural households.[88] Where a dispute arises over a contract, the parties may settle the dispute though negotiation, or request the villagers' committee or the township government to help settle the dispute though mediation. Where the parties are not willing to have their dispute settled through negotiation or mediation, or neither negotiation nor mediation is successful, they may apply to an arbitral body in charge of rural land contracts for arbitration, or directly bring a suit in the courts.[89]

The blurred boundaries of the collective are manifest in the overlapping functions of the villagers' committee and the collective economic organisation. One cooperative (collective economic organisation) may be founded in an administrative village (equivalent to the brigade in the commune system), or in a natural village (equivalent to the production team in the commune system); as a result, in many localities the collective economic organisation and the villagers' committee are 'the same team with two brands'.[90] The brand 'the villagers' committee' refers to the governance function of the collective, while the brand 'the collective economic organisation' refers to the economic function of the collective.[91] If the villagers' committee and the village collective economic organisation are separate bodies, 'the villagers' committee must respect the power of decision-making of the village collective economic organisation in conducting economic activities according to the law'.[92]

The status of the members of collective economic organisations is not to be equated with that of shareholders. In the early 1950s when collective economic organisations were at the early stage of formation, farmers joined agricultural

[87] Articles 24(2) and 24(4) of the 'Organic Law of the Villagers' Committee' (1998, amended 2010).

[88] Article 12 of the 'Law of the PRC on Land Contract in Rural Areas' (2002): 'Where the land owned collectively by farmers belongs, in accordance with law, to the collectives in a village, contracts shall be given out by the collective economic organization of the village or the villagers committee; where the land is already owned collectively by farmers of more than two rural collective economic organizations in a village, contracts shall be given out respectively by the said organizations or villagers groups in the village. Where contracts are issued by the rural collective economic organizations or villagers committees in a village, the ownership of the land owned collectively by the farmers of the collective economic organizations in the village shall remain unchanged.'

[89] Article 51 of the 'Law of the PRC on Land Contract in Rural Areas' (2002).

[90] Article 3(5) of the 'Notice on Rural Work in 1984', issued by the Central Party Committee on 1 January 1984. See Party Documents Research Office, *Selected Important Documents since the 12th National Congress of the CCP*, vol. 1, p. 428.

[91] Information gathered from fieldwork undertaken by the second-named author at Wuli Village, Wandong Township, Wansheng District, Chongqing province in March 2014.

[92] Article 8 of the 'Organic Law of the Villagers' Committee' (1998, amended 2010).

producers' cooperatives voluntarily by contributing their means of production to the cooperatives and receiving income in accordance with their relevant contributions. At that stage, the status of the members of cooperatives was quite similar to that of shareholders. However, the nature of the membership of cooperatives soon changed when cooperatives were transformed into communes by force. 'Egalitarian allocation' (*yi ping er diao*) of land, livestock and grain harvest prevailed as part of the operation of communes regardless of the members' contribution of land and labour. Free riding continued to plague the running of the communes.[93] Although communes were later dissolved, egalitarianism continues to influence division of land among members of collective economic organisations in the post-commune era. In the initial allocation of rural land rights to the household in the 1980s, the amount of land that a household had the right to farm was based on the equal division of the land among the members of the collective economic organisation, including both children and adults. For example, if a collective economic organisation owned 1,000 *mu* land and had 100 members, each member was entitled to 10 *mu* land. If a household had five people, it could farm 50 *mu* land.[94]

In terms of the relationship between the membership of the collective economic organisation and the membership of the village, prior to the formation of communes, they were different memberships. Although one collective economic organisation was normally established in one village and its members came from the village, the members of the collective economic organisation did not necessarily encompass all the farmers that resided in that village. According to Article 11(1) of the 'Draft Model Charter on Agricultural Producers' Cooperatives' (1955), 'all male and female farmers and other types of workers who can engage in the work of the cooperatives can apply to join in agricultural producers' cooperatives; once approved by the members' assembly, they become members'.[95] After the formation of communes in 1958, and because of the integration of political control and economic management in the commune system and compulsory membership of the commune, the membership of the collective economic organisation began to correspond to the membership of the village. However, in the early 1980s the rigid control of free movement of population, especially between rural and urban areas, began to be loosened. As a result, these two memberships no longer necessarily corresponded to each other. This point will be further examined through an analysis of relevant cases.

[93] For the 'free rider' problem with collective agriculture in China, see, for example, V. Nee, 'The Peasant Household Economy and Decollectivization in China', *Journal of Asian and African Studies*, 21 (1986), 185–203.

[94] 1 hectare =15 *mu*.

[95] Party Documents Research Office, *Selected Important Documents since the Founding of the PRC*, vol. 7, p. 362.

Table 8.2 The relationship between administrative governance entities and collective economic organisations (the entities within the brackets refer to the collective economic organisations)

Traditional administrative divisions	Administrative divisions in the period of cooperatives (1950–1958)	The period of people's communes (1958–1982)	The post-1982 period
Township	Township	Commune 2,000–20,000 households	Township (the agro-industrial-commercial cooperative)
Natural village	Administrative village (In general, one administrative village established one cooperative. The production team, which consisted of around 20 rural households, is the basic accounting unit)	Brigade 200–300 households (equivalent to the advanced cooperative) Encompassed 10 production teams; each team consisted of 20–30 households In some places, a small natural village corresponded to a team	Administrative village (the agricultural producers' cooperative) Consists of villagers' groups (the cooperative in accordance with the size of the villagers' group)

The present system through case analysis

The transformation of the interplay between membership of the collective and land rights in the post-commune era has shaped the present system. Collective ownership is intimately linked with membership of the collective economic organisation, which embodies the close relationship between farmers and the land. A member of the collective economic organisation is automatically entitled to the right to farm. However, if the connection between the farmers and the land discontinues, their membership will be revoked by the collective economic organisation or the villagers' committee.

In the 132 cases we have examined concerning disputes over the right to farm, 28 cases are related to membership of the collective. Among these 28 cases, there are 15 cases where the court has supported the argument that if farmers have lost their membership of the village, they could still retain their membership of the collective economic organisation. These 15 cases are primarily concerned with married or divorced women's membership of the collective economic organisation. It has been decided by the court that if the right to farm has not been granted to farmers in the new village that they have moved into, their membership of the old collective economic organisation should be retained and their right to farm should not be revoked by that collective economic organisation.

However, if farmers have been granted the right to farm in the new village, they will lose membership of the old collective economic organisation and the right to farm previously granted to them will be revoked. In our analysis of the 28 cases, three cases have been decided on this basis. Three other cases are concerned with the issue that the loss of membership of the village may lead to the loss of membership of the collective economic organisation: one case concerns a person who has moved out of a village to work in another place; the other two cases concern the fact that once farmers have died, their membership of the collective economic organisation terminates automatically. That said, the obtaining[96] or retention[97] of membership of the village does not necessarily secure membership of the collective economic organisation. Six cases have been judged on this basis. In terms of women's right to farm, this is often revoked by the village when women are divorced even if they are still members of the village.[98] One case among the 28 cases concerns this type of instance, and the court decided that a divorced woman should retain her membership of the collective economic organisation and continue to enjoy the right to farm.

Several general principles concerning the relationship between membership of the collective economic organisation and the right to farm can be gleaned from our analysis of the 28 cases. Membership can be obtained by birth through the maternal line: if the mother has obtained membership, her children can obtain membership as well.[99] Membership can also be obtained through moving into the collective economic organisation via marriage or adoption. In most instances, this means that the newcomers need to change their household registration and register with the new collective economic organisation. However, there are exceptions to this rule. For example, without any change in the household registration, the newcomers may still obtain membership, if they have lost membership of the old collective economic organisation to which they belonged.[100] Moreover, to become members,

[96] For example, through marriage or purchasing houses.

[97] For example, in instances where a person's household registration is still with the village, but he or she no longer relies on farming to make a living.

[98] Such a practice contravenes Article 30 of the 'Law of the PRC on Land Contract in Rural Areas' (2002), which provides: 'where a divorced woman or a woman who loses her spouse still lives at her original residence or does not live at her original residence but undertakes no contract for land at her new residence, the party giving out the contract may not take back her originally contracted land'.

[99] For example, *Cui Yuqing, Cui Jianlong, Wang Yuyan, and Cui Mou v No. 4 Villagers' Group at Baiqiang Village, Zhaohe Township, Mengzhou City, Wang Weixing, and Wang Tianfa*, People's Court at Mengzhou City, Henan Province, 29 January 2016. Chinese names are cited in their Chinese order: family name comes first, followed by given name.

[100] For example, *Huang Lizheng v Huang Zuhe and Huang Guangchuang*, People's Court at Guangshan County, Henan Province, 15 April 2015; *Wang Guiqin v The Villagers' Committee at Anzhuang Village and An Hongjun, Chiying Township, Xihua County*, People's Court at Shangshui County, Henan

the newcomers need to prove that they will rely on farming and the means of production provided by the new collective economic organisation in order to make a living. Without the required proof, even if they have changed their household registration, they cannot obtain membership.[101] In some cases, both of the requirements, the change of household registration and the reliance on the collective economic organisation to make a living, need to be fulfilled, in order to obtain membership.[102]

The loss of membership of the collective economic organisation is often due to the death of the members.[103] The revocation of membership may also be explained by persons moving into new collective economic organisations through marriage and adoption processes. However, if a person has not been allocated the right to farm in the new collective economic organisation after marriage, he or she will not lose membership of the previous collective economic organisation, no matter whether his or her household registration has been changed or not.[104]

Province, 17 August 2015; *Zhao Fang, Guo Aihong, and Guo Yuling v Wang Shuanzhu*, People's Court at Runan County, Henan Province, 18 August 2015.

[101] For example, *Chen Sihan v The Villagers' Committee and its No. 1 Villagers' Group at Qiaoxie Village, Hongmen Township, Hongqi District, Xinxiang City*, People's Court at Hongqi District, Xinxiang City, Henan Province, 25 April 2015; *Yang Yuxuan v The Villagers' Committee and its No. 1 Villagers' Group at Qiaoxie Village, Hongmen Township, Hongqi District, Xinxiang City*, People's Court at Hongqi District, Xinxiang City, Henan Province, 25 April 2015; *Wang Changfu v The Villagers' Committee and its No. 1 Villagers' Group at Qiaoxie Village, Hongmen Township, Hongqi District, Xinxiang City*, People's Court at Hongqi District, Xinxiang City, Henan Province, 25 April 2015; *Gao Xiangwei and Gao Mingxuan v The Villagers' Committee and its No. 1 Villagers' Group at Qiaoxie Village, Hongmen Township, Hongqi District, Xinxiang City*, People's Court at Hongqi District, Xinxiang City, Henan Province, 25 April 2015. In these four cases, the plaintiffs were not able to provide sufficient evidence to prove that they had formed a stable relationship with the collective economic organisation in terms of production and life, therefore the court did not support their claim for obtaining membership of the collective economic organisation.

[102] *Yan Shude v Ren Daoxing*, People's Court at Huaibin County, Henan Province, 20 June 2012. Although the plaintiff relied on farming to make a living, his household registration had not been moved to the new collective economic organisation, and the court did not support his claim for membership.

[103] *Zhu Xiujiang v The Villagers' Committee and its No. 2 Villagers' Group at Qiaoxie Village, Hongmen Township, Hongqi District, Xinxiang City*, People's Court at Hongqi District, Xinxiang City, Henan Province, 8 April 2015; *Zhang Jixiang v The Villagers' Committee and its No. 2 Villagers' Group at Qiaoxie Village, Hongmen Township, Hongqi District, Xinxiang City, Hongqi District, Xinxiang City*, People's Court at Hongqi District, Xinxiang City, Henan Province, 8 April 2015. In both cases, the plaintiff argued that the compensation for the acquired land should have been allocated to the plaintiff's deceased mother. The court held that because the plaintiff's mother died, she had lost membership of the collective economic organisation, and her children were not entitled to the compensation, which was only to be allocated to the members of the collective economic organisation.

[104] For example, *Peng Chunxiu and Zhang Yangxia v Zhang Jingwei*, People's Court at Tangyin County, Henan Province, 20 June 2014; *Liu Yunfang v Liu Yunkui*, People's Court at Tongbai County, Henan Province, 28 March 2015; *Guan Hua and Niu Yongjian v Niu Li*, People's Court at Yanjin County, Henan Province, 30 March 2015; *Sun Shunling v Sun Haogui*, People's Court at Hua County, Henan Province, 20 April 2015; *Liu Yuhua v The Villagers' Committee at Liu Zhuang Ying Village, Hongmen Township, Hongqi District, Xinxiang City*, People's Court at Hongqi District, Xinxiang City, 25 August 2015; *Wu Fenglian v Wu Mingxun, Meng Xiangling, Wu Linlin, Zhang Dandan*, People's Court at Ningling

If farming is no longer relied upon to make a living, a person will also lose membership.[105]

Further, while the right to farm is held by individual members of the collective economic organisation, the right to farm the contracted land is closely linked to membership of the collective economic organisation, enabling the existence of private land rights in a collective land system. The increase or decrease in the number of people in the household will not affect the amount of the contracted land within the contractual period,[106] an arrangement that is similar to the operation of joint ownership but without the limit to the number of co-owners. Aiming to sustain communal property, this arrangement differs from the initial allocation of the rights to 'responsibility land', which depended on the number of people in the household. As demonstrated in those cases examined, this arrangement that the amount of 'responsibility land'[107] does not increase/decrease if the size of the household increases/decreases has caused problems in practice. To solve some of the problems, especially in instances where the household increases in number, the collective economic organisation may allocate a portion of its 'reserved land'[108] to the household. If the farmer ceases to be a member or no longer relies on farming to make a living, the farmer's right to farm automatically ceases and reverts to the household the farmer belongs to. If the household ceases to exist, the right to farm held by its previous members reverts to the collective economic organisation.

Moreover, the right to farm enjoyed by members of one household can be transferred to another household belonging to a different collective economic organisation within a given contractual period.[109] Transfers shall be subject to the consent by the collective economic organisation.[110] Members of the collective economic organisation to which the transferor belongs have the right of first refusal.[111] Members of the household that has transferred the right to farm do not necessarily lose their membership of the collective economic organisation to which they

County, Henan Province, 6 November 2015; *Zhu Fulian v Hewan Villagers' Group at Gaomiao Village, Yangshan New District, Xinyang City*, People's Court at Pingqiao District, Xinyang City, Henan Province, 26 January 2016; and *Zhao Guihong v The Villagers' Committee at Xinzhuang Village, Juling Township, Linying County*, People's Court at Linying County, Henan Province, 16 February 2016.

[105] For example, *Zhang Shanlin v The Villagers' Committee at Qiaoxie Village, Hongmen Township, Hongqi District, Xinxiang City*, People's Court at Hongqi District, Xinxiang City, Henan Province, 12 June 2015.

[106] The Notice concerning 'the Opinion on Stabilizing and Improving the Land Contract Relationship Issued by the Ministry of Agriculture and Approved and Distributed by the State Council' (guowu yuan pizhuan nongye bu guanyu wending he wanshan tudi chengbao guanxi de yijian), 28 March 1995.

[107] See 'Introduction'.

[108] See 'Introduction'.

[109] For example, Article 32 of the 'Law of the PRC on Land Contract in Rural Areas' (2002) provides: 'The right to land contractual management obtained through household contract may, according to law, be circulated by subcontracting, leasing, exchanging, transferring or other means.'

[110] Article 37 of the 'Law of the PRC on Land Contract in Rural Areas' (2002).

[111] Article 33(5) of the 'Law of the PRC on Land Contract in Rural Areas' (2002).

belong. The criteria used to judge whether those people can retain their membership include whether they still rely on the collective economic organisation to make a living and obtain provision of social welfare.

Conclusion

Through invoking the lens of community, the abstract concept of 'the collective' has been disaggregated into various communities with varying natures that are located at differing levels of the collective. The collectives appeared in the form of relatively small-scale communities such as mutual aid teams and primary cooperatives in the 1950s, but by the late 1950s transformed into large-scale, ideology-driven and politically fabricated communes, which overrode the boundaries of traditional communities. The eventual failure of the communes shows that communal property is more likely to be sustained in close-knit, limited-access communities. The boundaries of community matter not only in terms of demarcating territorial scale, but also in locating political power.

Invoking the lens of community also brings humans to the centre of the analytical framework of the concept of communal property. Communities, such as small-scale cooperatives including the mutual aid teams and primary cooperatives formed in the early 1950s, are neither merely geographical entities nor constructs of political power. They are quintessentially the construct of social relations that are held together by various bonds, creating a sense of identity and belonging and underpinning cooperation between people.[112] These bonds include tradition, interests and values. To sustain communal property, we need to think about these bonds, that is, how to hold people together.

In many cases the boundaries of community have been penetrated by state power, eroding the bonds of community. The replacement of cooperatives with communes is one of the prominent examples. However, bonds such as ideologies that have been imposed by the state to hold communities together may be weakened in profound socio-economic transformations, leading to social regroupings. The regroupings of communities may in turn shape the ways in which property can be obtained, retained or lost. The formation of the hybrid property system in the post-commune era, via the introduction of the household responsibility system and the selective readmission of private property interest in the collective land system, exhibits one of the most important examples of this.

Communities are not completely sealed entities; their boundaries are penetrable (as shown in Table 8.1). The boundaries of community shift; the configuration of communal property changes correspondingly. As such it is difficult to sustain

[112] R. Cotterrell, 'Is There a Logic of Legal Transplants?', in D. Nelken and J. Feest (eds), *Adapting Legal Cultures* (Oxford, Hart Publishing, 2001), pp. 69–98.

a unified, coherent vision of communal property. The cases we have analysed through the lens of community show that the law can be interpreted and applied to strengthen the bonds that hold the community together and sustain communal property.[113] This study has important implications for questioning the nature of the role that the law plays in protecting and developing communal property as a hybrid property system with penetrable boundaries.

[113] See 'The present system through case analysis'.

9

Ownership and Belonging in Urban Green Space

SIMONE ABRAM AND SARAH BLANDY

Introduction

This chapter is concerned with a particular type of communal property: urban green spaces which are used by the general public and are prevalent throughout the UK. 'Urban' refers to spaces within town or city boundaries, and 'green' to areas with vegetation, not paved squares or plazas. In this chapter we have adopted the term 'communal property' to capture the understanding that rights of access, use and enjoyment of these urban green spaces are shared in common by the general public. Urban green spaces transcend the public/private divide and provide natural beauty in urban settings, opportunities for chance encounters, spaces for community development and neighbourhood events; they are 'critical to the social and communal fabric'.[1] Consideration of legal strategies for their development and protection raises many interesting and important issues, particularly relevant at a time of austerity when local authority parks are facing financial cuts, and other sources of funding for urban green spaces are also diminishing.[2]

Green spaces in the UK are strikingly varied in form, governance and ownership arrangements. The traditional fenced or walled park owned by the local authority faces increasing financial pressures. Councils are exploring the practicalities of different forms of management, especially partnership arrangements between public, private and voluntary sector organisations. There are also pocket parks in community management, neighbourhood gardens, and green spaces owned and managed by charitable trusts and private subscription societies, among others.

[1] J. Page, 'Towards an Understanding of Public Property', in N. Hopkins (ed.), *Modern Studies in Property Law*, vol. 7 (Oxford, Hart, 2013), pp. 195–216 at p. 214.

[2] See full discussion of this context in Communities and Local Government Committee, *Public Parks: Seventh Report of Session 2016–17*, House of Commons, HC 45: www.publications.parliament.uk/pa/cm201617/cmselect/cmcomloc/45/45.pdf.

Proceedings of the British Academy, **216**, 177–201.

A number of reasons have been suggested for the changes to urban green spaces since the mid-twentieth century when the majority of UK parks were owned and managed by local authorities. For instance, there has been a resurgence of individual and, particularly, collective ways of engaging with the land;[3] some local authorities have adopted innovative practices to involve residents with their local green spaces; and funding cuts to local authorities since the financial crash in 2008 have prompted the establishment of many partnership arrangements.

The relevant property rights of ownership, management, access and use cannot necessarily be divined through the materiality of the space itself, nor is it always apparent where responsibility lies for a particular space and what kinds of activities are permitted there. This raises the issue of democratic accountability in relation to decision-making over urban green spaces owned and managed both by local authorities and by community groups. As will become apparent, there are difficulties in categorising parks in terms of property law in this jurisdiction, and a bewildering array of possible alternative legal arrangements for the ownership of parks by a range of different organisations. Although these issues are discussed in this chapter, we want to move beyond a single focus on property law to consider the wide range of literature addressing the phenomenon of urban green space.

Urban green spaces have attracted attention from a range of academic disciplines. The interrelationship of this research is used here to illuminate understanding and to contribute to the development of theories of communal property, despite the difficulties caused by similar-sounding terms used in different ways. For example, critical urbanist scholars are concerned with theorising 'public space',[4] and in particular the effects of its commodification and privatisation.[5] Anthropological research highlights the connection between individuals, community and place, closely examining the concepts of belonging and ownership.[6] Recent scholarship on the 'urban commons' describes and theorises the process of claiming space as communal.[7] Similarly, legal geographers use the concept of performativity to

[3] S. Farran, 'Earth under the Nails: The Extraordinary Return to the Land', in N. Hopkins (ed.), *Modern Studies in Property Law*, vol. 7 (Oxford, Hart, 2013), pp. 173–191.

[4] H. Lefebvre, *Writings on Cities*, trans. E. Kofman and E. Lebas (Oxford, Blackwell, 1996; first published in French, 1968).

[5] D. Mitchell, *The Right to the City* (New York, Guilford Press, 2003). See also legal scholarship on this issue: A. Layard, 'Shopping in the Public Realm: A Law of Place', *Journal of Law and Society*, 37 (2010), 412–441.

[6] M. Strathern, *Property Substance and Effect: Anthropological Essays on Persons and Things* (London, Athlone Press, 1999); C. M. Hann (ed.), *Property Relations: Renewing the Anthropological Tradition* (Cambridge, Cambridge University Press, 1998); V. Strang and M. Busse (eds), *Ownership and Appropriation* (Oxford and New York, Berg, 2011).

[7] D. Bollier, *Think Like a Commoner: A Short Introduction to the Life of the Commons* (Gabriola Island, BC, Canada, New Society Publishers, 2014); P. Linebaugh, *The Magna Carta Manifesto: Liberties and Commons for All* (Oakland, University of California Press, 2009); I. Susser and

shed light on ideas of property and possession in land.[8] Landscape researchers have clarified the important distinction between initial acts of place-making and the ongoing process of place-keeping,[9] and have also analysed the partnership arrangements between public, private and third sector organisations, through which many urban green spaces are now owned and managed.[10]

The breadth of the literature referred to above, on which we draw in this chapter, underlines the significance of this type of communal property. A unifying theme is the transformation over time of urban green spaces through human interactions. These collective activities change the look of the land, and drive changes to the legal and practical arrangements for its ownership, management and rights of access and use. This chapter investigates the co-constitutive relationship of people (individuals and communities), place and law in relation to urban green spaces. In contrast to legal scholarship's customary 'sharp boundaries between people and place',[11] we explore feelings and experiences of belonging and ownership, and how community identity coheres around particular spaces.[12] We examine these themes, and not just legality, along a temporal axis.[13]

The rich variation of types of urban green space as communal property, the different disciplinary approaches, and the importance of studying changes over time, all point to the value of detailed contextual research. Analysis of 'practices as well as the spatial, social and legal interaction[s]'[14] at a particular site over time can reveal the mismatch between legal and popular understandings of communal property. This chapter focuses on Heeley People's Park in Sheffield in the UK as a case study, exploring its creation and development over time and the current strategies intended to ensure its future. As trustees of Heeley Development Trust, which holds leasehold title to the park, both authors enjoy 'insider status'[15] giving us access to particular experiences and rich knowledge and information about the

S. Tonnelat, 'Transformative Cities: The Three Urban Commons', *Focaal – Journal of Global and Historical Anthropology*, 66 (2013), 105–132.

[8] N. Blomley, 'Un-Real Estate: Proprietary Space and Public Gardening', *Antipode*, 36 (2004), 614–641.

[9] N. Dempsey and M. Burton, 'Defining Place-Keeping: The Long-Term Management of Public Spaces', *Urban Forestry and Urban Greening*, 11 (2012), 11–21.

[10] C. de Margalhaes and M. Carmona, 'Dimensions and Models of Contemporary Public Space Management in England', *Journal of Environmental Planning and Management*, 52 (2009), 111–129.

[11] A. Layard, 'Public Space: Property, Lines, Interruptions', *Journal of Law, Property, and Society*, 2 (2016): www.alps.syr.ed.u/journal/2016/08/JLPS-2016-08-Lyard.pdf, at p. 47.

[12] D. Cooper, 'Opening up Ownership: Community Belonging, Belongings, and the Productive Life of Property', *Law and Social Inquiry*, 32 (2007), 625–664.

[13] A. Margalit, 'Commons and Legality', in G. S. Alexander and E. M. Penalver (eds), *Property and Community* (Oxford, Oxford University Press, 2010), pp. 141–164.

[14] Layard, 'Public Space', 49.

[15] P. Hodkinson, '"Insider Research" in the Study of Youth Cultures', *Journal of Youth Studies*, 8 (2005), 131–149.

park. Combining socio-legal[16] and anthropological[17] perspectives enables us to explore issues of belonging and community as well as property and ownership. This highlights the tensions and gaps between the reality of owning, managing, funding and using a local park, the various conceptualisations of communal property, and the legal frameworks which are currently available in this jurisdiction.

The chapter is structured as follows. We first set out the case study of Heeley People's Park. Current strategies of acquiring assets and establishing a subscription society to raise funds for the continuing maintenance of the park introduce two other urban green spaces in Sheffield. This enables the succeeding, more theoretical, sections on understanding ownership and belonging, and conceptualising urban green space in property law, to be grounded in real-life examples. An overview of the available legal frameworks for urban green space in this jurisdiction is then provided, paying attention to governance and issues of democratic accountability. The following section explores difficulties in articulating the discourse of communal property, especially in relation to the crucial issue of funding maintenance of urban green space. Conclusions are reached in the final section.

Heeley People's Park, Sheffield

Sheffield is a post-industrial city in the north of England with a population of around 550,000. One of the local authorities in the UK that has been worst affected by austerity measures, Sheffield City Council has seen its revenue grant from central government cut by 50 per cent between 2010 and 2015, and overall spending (excluding health) reduced from £970 million to £829 million,[18] with further cuts to come.[19] But Sheffield certainly has advantages. Branding itself in 2015 as 'the UK's first Outdoor City',[20] Sheffield is 'the greenest city in England' with an estimated 2 million trees and is the only core city to include part of a national park, the Peak District, within its boundaries.[21] Sheffield boasts more than 700 green

[16] See R. Pound, 'Law in Books and Law in Action', *American Law Review*, 44 (1910), 12–36; S. Blandy, 'Socio-Legal Approaches to Property Law Research', in S. Bright and S. Blandy (eds), *Researching Property Law* (London, Palgrave Macmillan, 2015), pp. 24–42.

[17] See Strathern, *Property Substance and Effect*; Hann, *Property Relations*; Strang and Busse, *Ownership and Appropriation*.

[18] *Financial Times*: http://ig.ft.com/sites/2015/local-cuts-checker/#E08000019ZZE08000019.

[19] Local Government Association, *Under Pressure: How Councils Are Planning for Future Cuts* (London, LGA, 2014). Sheffield City Council's budget for 2018/19 is estimated to be approximately £400 million: *2018/19 Revenue Budget Report*, Chief Executive and the Executive Director, Resources, Sheffield City Council (undated).

[20] http://theoutdoorcity.co.uk/.

[21] Sport Industry Research Centre, *Valuing the Contribution of the Outdoor Economy in Sheffield* (Sheffield, Sheffield Hallam University, 2014), p. 4.

spaces, of many different kinds and sizes,[22] more than one for every thousand Sheffield inhabitants.

The People's Park lies just to the south of Sheffield city centre in Heeley, an inner-city community of about 4,500 residents. Heeley's population increased tenfold from 1843 to 1871 during the industrial revolution, then doubled again over the following ten years.[23] The neighbourhood is now characterised by a mixture of industrial buildings dating back to the early nineteenth century, dense Victorian terraced housing, some large detached houses, and social housing stock. Heeley has a diverse, multi-racial population which has long included some 'alternative' middle-class households. Deprivation levels in Heeley are similar to the Sheffield average, except for significantly higher levels of crime and a significantly lower secondary school attendance rate. The population aged between 25 and 44 years is much higher in Heeley (37.0 per cent) than in Sheffield as a whole (27.9 per cent).[24] Notably, Heeley residents have a strong sense of neighbourhood and community.

A large swathe of hillside land in Heeley, to which Sheffield City Council held freehold title, remained derelict after wartime bomb damage and subsequent slum clearance. In the 1970s, plans were published to route a Sheffield South Relief Road across this land, which would have torn the Heeley community in two. Well-organised local residents fiercely and successfully opposed these plans, and the road was never constructed. In 1981 the local authority leased two hectares of the derelict land to establish Heeley City Farm. Like other city farms, Heeley City Farm brings the countryside to the inner city so that adults and children can interact with a range of animals; it remains a popular local resource today.

In 1993 the Millennium Commission was set up, offering National Lottery funding to community projects. This was the catalyst for Heeley residents to organise around developing the remaining unused land into a park, although their first bid was unsuccessful. However, momentum had grown through communal endeavour, organisation and community consultation, and funding was secured in 1996. The council then offered a 125-year lease of the remaining three and a half hectares of the hillside, a 'bramble covered taxi rank which had begun collapsing in on itself, with pockets of wildly overgrown, debris-filled wasteland crumbling inside the remains of post-war terraced cellars'.[25] In order to take leasehold title to this land, then named Heeley Millennium Park, the local activist group adopted a corporate entity: Heeley Development Trust (HDT), which is both a company limited by guarantee and a charity. Community development trusts flourished in

[22] http://theoutdoorcity.co.uk/.

[23] www.oldheeley.supanet.com/oldheeley9.htm.

[24] Sheffield Health and Well-Being Profiles 2012, for Heeley Neighbourhood: www.sheffield.gov.uk/profile.

[25] http://heeleypark.org/history/.

the 1990s–2000s, undertaking asset-based area regeneration and development in deprived areas with devolved funding from central government. HDT is an unusual development trust because its sole initial property was the wasteland destined to become Heeley Park, intended to be accessible and enjoyed by the public. It would first need development with lottery funding, and then continual maintenance as a community park: the antithesis of an income-generating asset.

HDT was incorporated in December 1996, and then registered as a charitable trust in January 1998. Its charitable purposes mirror the aims set out in the company's Memorandum: 'to create and manage Heeley Millennium Park'; to 'promote education, training and learning, particularly in skills relevant to securing employment' in Heeley; and 'to promote other charitable purposes for public benefit'. The HDT company directors took on a dual role as charitable trustees. HDT is subject to top-down regulation from both the Companies Registrar and the Charities Commission, and is accountable to both bodies. However, HDT has no formal duty to make itself accountable to the community it serves. It does not have a membership. Nonetheless the Trust's origins in the local community are clear. The original subscribers to the company were the headteachers of the two local primary schools, a youth worker and a development officer from the local authority, the owner of a local business, and other local residents. Those who witnessed the subscribers' signatures include representatives of the local Youth Centre, Heeley City Farm, and the local Tenants and Residents Association.

Lottery funding made the land safe for public use; then HDT sought the views of 3,000 neighbouring households on how the park should be developed. After numerous public design events, the area was landscaped and planted; traditional play equipment and the first open-access climbing boulder in the city were installed. Over a decade later in 2010, HDT was awarded one of nine national Big Lottery Community Spaces flagship grants to further improve the park and its landscaping. A BMX track, mountain bike and nature trails, a community orchard, a wildflower meadow, a multi-use games area and an amphitheatre were developed. HDT organises music and other festivals in the summer months. In 2016 the park was re-named Heeley People's Park, for reasons which are discussed in the discourse section of the chapter.

Heeley people have seen the park develop over the past 20 years into an exciting and well-run resource. They use and appreciate the facilities, and thousands more enjoy events there. Local residents get involved in planting new trees, shrubs, plants and bulbs. The way the park is landscaped and the facilities it offers constitute an open invitation to public access and use, and make it clear what sort of conduct is expected and acceptable. The impact of HDT is summarised by a resident who has lived in Heeley for over 50 years, who told the local newspaper:

> This [the park] is the best thing that ever happened here. I remember looking at this area from the bus and it was just a load of bricks. I'd never in a month of Sundays think it could look like this. It's unrecognisable compared to what it was, it's a lovely

place to walk in and these lads do a grand job looking after it and improving it every day.[26]

However, HDT quickly realised that owning a park was less of an opportunity than a liability, since parks require maintenance and there was no obvious source of continuing income. Therefore from an early stage HDT aimed to acquire buildings as assets, to fund park maintenance and to provide accommodation for other community activities. In 2001 HDT took a nil-rent 25-year lease of the Heeley Institute, a converted Methodist chapel, which is now used for community facilities, events and educational courses. More recently, the Trust has taken a long lease from the local authority of a former primary school whose Victorian premises adjoin the park. Funding was obtained to convert the largest of the school's three buildings into managed workspaces, named SUM Studios. The renovation won eight prizes at the 2015 Royal Institute of British Architects Yorkshire awards, including the sustainability award.[27] The building is now fully let at commercial rents, to provide an income stream to support the Trust's charitable purposes.

Faced with an increasing financial challenge as funds from charitable sources as well as from local authority contracts diminished, HDT has recently adopted two particular fundraising strategies. Each strategy has resonances with those adopted in other Sheffield parks. Examining these strategies and connections highlights the importance of a contextual and temporal analysis of urban green spaces, and reveals the mismatch between legal structures and a community's sense of belonging and ownership.

In 2015 HDT proposed to solicit funds through establishing a subscription society, realising that park maintenance costs could be met if local households each paid an average of £10 annually. HDT's approach was supported as a nationally-significant innovation by the Rethinking Parks programme run by Nesta.[28] Yet there is a clear, and geographically nearby, precedent which might give HDT pause for thought. The Sheffield Botanical Gardens were established in 1834 on land purchased by a private subscription society. In legal terms an unincorporated association, its members were local residents concerned about the lack of green space in Sheffield. Rather like HDT 150 years later, their intention was to promote both healthy recreation and education. However, the financial difficulties of maintaining urban green space caused the failure of two successive private subscription societies within 50 years. In 1897 the freehold was transferred to a large local charity, the Sheffield Town Trust, which opened the Gardens to the public. In 1951 the Town Trust leased the Gardens, once more rundown, to the local authority

[26] 'Community Turns Slum Clearance to Parkland', *Sheffield Telegraph*, 27 April 2010: www.sheffieldtelegraph.co.uk/what-s-on/community-turns-slum-clearance-to-parkland-1-802431.

[27] www.architecture.com/StirlingPrize/Awards2015/Yorkshire/SumStudios.aspx.

[28] The National Endowment for Science, Technology and the Arts was established in 1998, becoming in 2010 an independent charity, Nesta, funding innovative ideas and practices.

for a peppercorn rent. In 1996, after ten years of closure, the Sheffield Botanical Gardens Trust was formed and applied successfully to the Heritage Lottery Fund, just as HDT did. Sheffield City Council now manages the fully restored Botanical Gardens, in partnership with the Town Trust which still owns the freehold and with the Botanical Gardens Trust and the Friends of the Botanical Gardens group.

HDT's second strategy, adopted in 2016, was driven by its need for increased income from property assets. This coincided with threats to public parks caused by drastic public finance cuts.[29] About half a mile from Heeley Park is Meersbrook Park, a typical local authority-run large park with varied facilities, including a late eighteenth-century Hall. In 1886 the land and buildings were purchased for the benefit of Sheffield residents by the city council, which has owned and managed the park ever since. Meersbrook Hall was occupied first by the Ruskin Museum, and then by the council Parks department. In 2014 the council decided to relocate its Parks team to city centre offices. Fearing that the council's asset management staff would try to sell the vacant Hall for private development, local residents formed the Friends of Meersbrook Hall group and began campaigning for the Hall to remain in public ownership. They initially hoped to transform the Hall into a community venue themselves, but it became apparent that they needed the assistance of HDT, which, as a Building Preservation Trust,[30] was the relevant local community development organisation with experience of this task. HDT saw the opportunity to add the Hall to its asset base, enabling it to continue its community development activities. In 2016 the Friends and HDT joined forces. At the time of writing, the council has issued a licence permitting HDT to occupy the Hall, allowing it to locate its adult education services in the Hall and to host community meetings there while negotiations for a long lease to HDT continue. HDT is seeking funding for the renovation of the Hall, and will then maintain it through part-letting it as commercial office space, offering the rest for community activities including a café.

This contextual account clearly demonstrates how the status and operation of all three parks have changed over time, alongside the use and ownership of the land. It also shows how the history and future of the Heeley People's Park and HDT are bound up in the land itself, since its acquisition engendered the need to acquire rent-producing assets to maintain the park itself. It is not only the pattern of ownership and the materiality of the land, but also its legal status and people's understandings of that status which have changed over time and feed into current practices. The critical events in Heeley occurred in 1979, when the relief road plans

[29] Ninety-two per cent of park managers report that their maintenance budgets have reduced in the past three years, and 95 per cent expect their funding will continue to reduce: Heritage Lottery Fund, *State of UK Public Parks 2016*: www.hlf.org.uk/state-uk-public-parks-2016.

[30] HDT is a member of the Heritage Trust Network: www.heritagetrustnetwork.org.uk/heeley-development-trustHeritageTrustNetwork.

were abandoned; in 1996 when funding was secured and the newly incorporated HDT took the lease of the land; and in 2015 when the subscription society was launched and the park was re-named as Heeley People's Park; and 2016 when Meersbrook Hall was adopted by HDT.

Ownership and belonging

Heeley exemplifies 'the strength of the feeling people have for their local parks and green spaces, and how much parks are valued by individuals, families and communities'.[31] HDT's activities, in particular the development of the park, express the ways in which the park's particular properties reinforce that feeling of belonging, rather than that the park 'belongs to HDT'. There are no by-laws or rules displayed in the park, yet knowledge of acceptable practices seems to be shared as tacit knowledge, and linked to community governance.[32] Residents certainly report feeling a sense of 'ownership':

> I felt really proud afterwards when we walked past, I thought 'I helped plant those!' (Volunteer at Plant Your Park, 2012). I've just moved back to Heeley after a year away to find a new boulder in the park! Well done and thanks to everyone involved, a wonderful contribution to the community. The whole park looks great and has a fantastic atmosphere. It's great to be back in a community with so much energy and creativity! (Heeley Resident, 2013). Really great – kids and adults all enjoying it. Love these events – so important for the local community (Heeley Resident, Big Boulder festival 2012).[33]

How can this sense of belonging and ownership in relation to communal property be reconciled with legal concepts? Although it is correctly stated that '[d]espite what the layman might think, there is no concept of ownership in English law',[34] much property scholarship recognises that each resource belongs to a named individual (or a corporate body) through the 'name/object correlation', which constitutes the essence of ownership.[35] Recent anthropological debate has highlighted the many forms and sentiments of owning that fall outside the legal definition of title, and many means of relating to property that are not encompassed by property rights.[36] Cooper's attention to what property 'does', in the specific context of the experimental Summerhill school, allows her to identify relations of

[31] Noted generally in House of Commons, *Public Parks*, para. 3.
[32] M. Valverde, *Law's Dream of a Common Knowledge* (Princeton, Princeton University Press, 2003).
[33] HDT, Asset of Community Value Nomination Form (2015), on file with authors.
[34] W. Swadling, 'Unjust Delivery', in A. Burrows and A. Rodger (eds), *Mapping the Law: Essays in Memory of Peter Birks* (Oxford, Oxford University Press, 2006), pp. 277–298 at p. 281.
[35] J. Waldron, *The Right to Private Property* (Oxford, Clarendon Press, 1988).
[36] Strang and Busse, *Ownership and Appropriation.*

belonging shaped by personal, civic and boundary dimensions.[37] The difficulties in applying notions of communal property to urban green spaces should be understood as highlighting the limitations of property as a relation between persons and space, while seeing sharing of property as a way to extend the boundaries of a relationship of owning, as articulated through the legal concept of the corporate body and the institution of trust (as a particular relationship) and Trusts (as a legal form in British law).

One way forward may be the understanding, shared by legal anthropologists[38] and by many property law theorists,[39] that property is concerned with relations between people. Yet property title presumes that it is the thing that is owned by the person, and that relations of ownership are bound by this directional logic. However, in the case of land, it is clear that ownership also moves in the opposite direction, since people not only feel ownership of land, but feel that they belong to it: the land 'owns' them. Anthropological discussions of belonging have considered this ambiguity, and the confusion between belonging to a place and belonging to a people.[40]

Much early anthropological and sociological research (in line with its Western colonial context) presumed an equation between ethnicity and place. Since Tönnies' arguments in the nineteenth century that the authenticity of village life was tied to the land, in contrast to the alienation of urban Modernity, many European intellectuals have romanticised the notion of village life as grounded in land and social relations. Hence we still see maps of ethnic groups laid out in terms of territory, which they either 'own' or 'belong in'. This idiom (widespread but not universal)[41] is also recognisable through its own shadow concept in the twinned romanticisation and persecution of nomads who are seen not to 'belong' to a particular permanent place. The bidirectional relation of ownership/possession, of/by place, is rather inadequately addressed in legal terms through property and trespass, not least in assuming that owning implies exclusion. This could, in fact, be seen to be the very conundrum that the idea of communal property seeks to address, along with apparent compromises such as the Right to Roam, which suspends the potential for trespass on what is otherwise private property.[42] In separating ownership

[37] Cooper, 'Opening up Ownership'.
[38] Hann, *Property Relations*.
[39] See, for example, the definition of property as 'a network of jural relationships between individuals in respect of valued resources', in K. Gray and S. F. Gray, *Elements of Land Law*, 5th edn (Oxford, Oxford University Press, 2009), p. 6.
[40] A. Cohen (ed.), *Belonging: Identity and Social Organisation in British Rural Cultures* (Manchester, Manchester University Press, 1982).
[41] It is always worth reminding ourselves that there are societies in which neither material nor land can be conceptualised into a relationship of ownership, where 'property' is an entirely foreign concept. The ethnographic record is rife with accounts of researchers struggling to keep hold of their supplies in the face of people helping themselves.
[42] Countryside and Rights of Way Act 2000.

from use, the possibility is created that people may feel they belong to places that they do not own.

Through her empirical research into concepts and uses of property, Cooper has developed two dimensions of 'belonging'.[43] The first is the classic subject/object of relationship which is materialised through property law, and the second concerns the 'social relation of belonging' which is constitutive of a part/whole relationship between individuals or communities, and property. This second dimension echoes Radin's perception that the 'physical and social characteristics' of a local neighbourhood 'can become bound up over time with the . . . group's existence as a community'.[44] This suggests both that property relationships can engender community identity, and that time is important in this process; both of these elements are present in Heeley People's Park.

The small group of dedicated activists who established Heeley Park in 1996 must have experienced a great sense of belonging and communal ownership when they successfully defeated the plans for the relief road. Their activities at that time and the nascent park could best be described in the (non-legal) term 'urban commons', coined in recent academic literature to encapsulate ideas of common ownership and participative citizenship.[45] Linebaugh uses the verb form 'common*ing*' to express the concept of the urban commons as a continuous process which requires participation, taking place in a particular local space.[46] Commoning is by definition a group activity, for example the creation of social movement centres from unused buildings.[47] Urban commons are often linked to the concept of the right to the city,[48] which encompasses rights not to be expelled from social life, to use urban space and to participate in decision-making. Lefebvre explained these as neither natural nor contractual rights, but a necessary product of the qualities of urban space: convergence, ceremony, recreation, and commerce. For Lefebvre, the urban is 'more or less the *oeuvre* of its citizens',[49] shaped by their continuing actions in using and claiming space for public use. Anthropologists also recognise that property relations, as 'acts of communicating and upholding ownership, are processual rather than static'.[50] The performance of property can be seen in the appropriation of land through guerrilla gardening.[51]

[43] Cooper, 'Opening up Ownership'.

[44] M. J. Radin, 'Time, Possession, and Alienation', *Washington University Law Quarterly*, 64 (1986), 739–758 at 757.

[45] Bollier, *Think Like a Commoner*. Editors' note: For further discussion of 'commoning projects', see also Pieraccini in this volume.

[46] Linebaugh, *The Magna Carta Manifesto*.

[47] S. Hodkinson and P. Chatterton, 'Autonomy in the City? Reflections on the Social Centres Movement in the UK', *City*, 10 (2006), 305–315.

[48] Lefebvre, *Writings on Cities*.

[49] Lefebvre, *Writings on Cities*, p. 117.

[50] Strang and Busse, *Ownership and Appropriation*, p. 4.

[51] Blomley, 'Un-Real Estate'.

New forms of property relations are thus established through everyday practices; the creation of the Heeley park was an example of this. Urban green spaces offer what might be described as a right to be a citizen, a city-dweller with full access to the opportunities that the city offers. Ideally, therefore, parks are places for civic participation, a means for people to exercise the desire to belong, socially and territorially, to something other than their own immediate property. Observations of Heeley Park suggest that a sense of belonging and ownership, in the sense of constituting a part/whole relationship between individuals and community,[52] is influenced by factors such as proximity, frequency of use and the time and effort invested. Those who live beside the park, or walk through it on the way to work or when taking children to school, are likely to feel that sense of belonging. If you give your time to attending meetings, or to planting trees and flowers, you are likely to feel more 'ownership' and pride in the park as 'ours'.

Conceptualising urban green space in property law

Parks are complex and varied places, as illustrated by the different histories and legal frameworks of the three Sheffield parks, Heeley, Meersbrook and the Botanical Gardens. Urban green spaces pose difficulties for the law. Property law in England and Wales does not recognise public (or communal) property as a category. Most of what is usually understood to be 'common land' in England is actually in private ownership; only the rights to access and use that space are held in common.[53] These lesser rights may in certain circumstances be protected by law through registration of that land as a commons, or as a village green, if it has been used by people in the neighbourhood for recreational pastimes for more than 20 years.[54] However, very few urban green spaces, and none of the three examples considered in this chapter, meet the criteria for protection through registration.

If communal property cannot be categorised as public property or as commons, it must be considered as a form of private property. Some private property theorists emphasise the owner's right to selfishly exploit the property they own,[55] whereas others point to the wider responsibility or stewardship approach to ownership.[56] The conventional model of private property is individual and exclusionary. In Honoré's famous 'incidents of ownership' analysis, the owner of land enjoys rights to determine its governance and rules of use, and to exclude all others from

[52] Cooper, 'Opening up Ownership'.
[53] Editors' note: For rights of common and registration of common land in England and Wales, see Rodgers in this volume.
[54] Commons Registration Act 1965; Commons Act 2006, section 15(2).
[55] J. Harris, *Property and Justice* (Oxford, Oxford University Press, 2001).
[56] G. S. Alexander, E. M. Penalver, J. W. Singer and L. S. Underkuffler, 'A Statement of Progressive Property', *Cornell Law Review*, 94 (2009), 743.

it.[57] Most land owned by local or central government can be categorised as private property (albeit owned by a public institution), because rights of access may be withdrawn.[58] In this jurisdiction there is no general legal doctrine that local authorities hold property on public trust, as municipalities do in the US. However, there are statutory provisions which determine the extent of rights that local authorities may exercise over parks, balancing the owners' rights of management and control with the right of access held by the general public. For example, 'any open space' acquired by a local authority for public access must be held and administered 'in trust to allow . . . the enjoyment thereof by the public'.[59] More recently, the Court of Appeal held that 'the council, whether as owner, possessor or occupier of the [in this case, Farnham] park, was a trustee for the general public in the exercise of its powers and duties of management and control'.[60]

Sheffield City Council therefore acts as trustee for the public in the Botanical Gardens (as leaseholder) and in Meersbrook Park (as freeholder). HDT (as leaseholder of Heeley People's Park) is bound by its charitable purposes to act for the public benefit. Both these landowners have only 'quasi-ownership' rights because they lack 'legitimised self-seekingness', the right to selfish exploitation of their property.[61]

Private property's 'impulse to supervise, control and exclude' is at odds with fostering an integrative sense of community.[62] These opposing aims are well illustrated in the 1886 conveyance of the land that became Meersbrook Park. Mutual covenants were included to ensure that the land would be 'used solely for the purpose of a Public Park and Public Walks or Pleasure Grounds' to benefit the people of Sheffield, but also that a 'substantial iron fence' would be built around the new park. Today, Meersbrook Park remains enclosed in accordance with the 1886 covenant but its gates are now permanently open and there is no caretaker on site. The wall built around the new Botanical Gardens enabled admission to be restricted to paid subscribers, creating restricted-access communal property in which property rights are held in common by members of a group that excludes all others.[63] Until 1897 the Gardens only opened to 'the general public on about 4

[57] A. Honoré, 'Ownership', in A. G. Guest (ed.), *Oxford Essays in Jurisprudence* (Oxford, Oxford University Press, 1961), pp. 107–128.

[58] The exception is public highways, over which there are public rights of use: Highways Act 1980, section 130. But see *City of London v Samede*, [2012] EWHC 34 (QB), for the limitations of these rights, and the discussion in Layard, 'Public Space'.

[59] Open Spaces Act 1906, section 10.

[60] *Waverley Borough Council v Fletcher*, [1996] QB 334, per Auld LJ, at p. 349.

[61] Harris, *Property and Justice*, p. 108.

[62] Gray and Gray, *Elements of Land Law*, p. 1335.

[63] A. Clarke, 'Property Law: Re-Establishing Diversity', in M. Freeman (ed.), *Law and Opinion at the End of the Twentieth Century, Current Legal Problems*, vol. 50 (Oxford, Oxford University Press, 1997), pp. 119–154.

Gala days per year',[64] an illustration of the exclusionary power of private property. The public-private partnership which now runs the Botanical Gardens continues to close its gates between dusk and dawn. Further, in common with a growing national trend,[65] parts of the Gardens are sometimes withdrawn from public access for commercial reasons: to accommodate private, paying events such as concerts and theatre performances. HDT as the leaseholder could regulate access to Heeley Park, although there are no enclosing fences at present and no intention to build any. This park constitutes open-access communal property, to which everyone has the right of access.[66]

There is no need or wish to exclude people from most parks (subject to compliance with rules of conduct acceptable to that locality). In fact the reverse is true: parks 'have value precisely because they reinforce the solidarity and fellow-feeling of the whole community; thus the more members of the community who participate . . . the better'.[67]

Page argues that it makes little sense to define rights associated with communal property through the lens of exclusion, because these are 'collective rights, enjoyed by individuals in common with others'.[68] It may therefore be more relevant to analyse property relations in parks through conceptualising the 'rights of property [as] a bundle of powers, capable of being separately enjoyed',[69] rather than accepting the right of exclusion as the defining feature of property.[70]

We suggest that the relevant rights in the 'bundle' of communal property are those of ownership, of management, of access and of use. In all three parks discussed here, property ownership is currently fragmented between freehold and leasehold titles. The significance of these legal constructs is not easily understandable by non-lawyers. Rights of management in the Botanical Gardens and Meersbrook Park are not devolved to Friends groups, which are very involved and committed but do not 'hold any alienable title or property interest in the resource',[71] nor do they have the right to 'regulate access to the resources, control

[64] http://sbg.org.uk/history.asp.

[65] A. Minton, *Ground Control: Fear and Happiness in the Twenty-First-Century City* (Harmondsworth, Penguin, 2012).

[66] Clarke, 'Property Law: Re-Establishing Diversity'.

[67] C. Rose, 'The Comedy of the Commons: Custom, Commerce and Inherently Public Property', *University of Chicago Law Review*, 53 (1986), 711–781 at 720.

[68] Page, 'Towards an Understanding of Public Property', p. 196.

[69] Sir H. S. Maine, *Village-Communities in the East and West: Six Lectures Delivered at Oxford* (London, John Murray, 1881), pp. 133–134. See also C. B. MacPherson (ed.), *Property: Mainstream and Critical Positions* (Toronto, University of Toronto Press, 1978).

[70] See, for example, H. E. Smith, 'Property as the Law of Things', *Harvard Law Review*, 125 (2012), 1691–1726.

[71] S. Foster, 'Collective Action and the Urban Commons', *Notre Dame Law Review*, 87 (2011), 57–133 at 58.

or impose restrictions on individual behavior'.[72] Friends, like members of the general public, have the rights to use and access these parks determined by their respective owners, discussed above. The local authority's right to manage Meersbrook Park and the Botanical Gardens is embodied in the 1966 'Byelaws with respect to Pleasure Grounds' which apply to all the parks in their ownership; the very extensive provisions include the council's right to close parks from dusk to dawn and various prohibitions on conduct.[73] The lack of any similar managerial rules at Heeley People's Park has already been noted.

The bundle of rights analysis has shown a tension between the social, or perhaps moral, understandings of ownership and belonging, and the legally recognised rights in property, whether public, private or communal. We suggest that a similar analytical approach to property in any particular urban green space will highlight similar complexities.

Legal frameworks available for communal property ownership and governance

The previous section has shown how difficult it is to conceptualise urban green space using conventional property law tools. As Layard observes, '[p]ublic space is not property. Or better put, public space is not *just* property',[74] being created and developed through human interactions and community use. We now turn to the legal frameworks which are available in this jurisdiction for owning, managing and using urban green space. These are discussed in the context of the themes already established: belonging and ownership, communal property, governance and democratic accountability. Time is also an important element. The tension between a place that is continually evolving through the work and use of human actors, and its legal structure, is beautifully expressed by Strang and Busse's observation that the wider interactions 'between people and the environment . . . [can only be] temporarily crystallised through legal artefacts'.[75] Yet a property transaction such as the creation of a long lease is 'a scenario of executed obligation: the "deal" has been "done"'.[76] There is limited opportunity as land and community develop over time to change the legal framework, or to bring in new arrangements for the democratic

[72] Foster, 'Collective Action and the Urban Commons', 108–109.
[73] http://sheffielddemocracy.moderngov.co.uk/documents/s18882/Appendix%203%20-%20Bylaws%20in%20Respect%20of%20Pleasure%20Grounds.pdf.
[74] Layard, 'Public Space', p. 43 (original italics).
[75] Strang and Busse, *Ownership and Appropriation*, p. 5.
[76] K. Gray and S. F. Gray, 'The Rhetoric of Realty', in J. Getzler (ed.), *Rationalizing Property, Equity and Trusts: Essays in Honour of Edward Burn* (London: Butterworths, 2003), pp. 204–280 at p. 241.

governance of an urban green space. Therefore legal frameworks tend to reflect only the initial stage of place-making.[77]

Evaluative research into ongoing place-keeping by urban green space partnerships has identified criteria for success.[78] These factors chime with HDT's experiences and include: continued motivation 'beyond the initial, place-making project stage'; the ability to attract funding; commitment (covering a wide range of activities including unpaid time, sharing knowledge, attendance at meetings, and 'signing up' both to formal constitutional documents and to the organisation's aims); establishing a skills base; and effective communication.[79] One of the emerging themes from this study is the importance of establishing a governance structure for an urban green space that is representative of the local community.[80] A flexible legal framework is needed to facilitate and support ongoing place-keeping activities that meet these criteria.

Property law in this jurisdiction prevents activist or community groups from taking on freehold or leasehold title to urban green space, as land cannot legally be transferred to more than four individuals.[81] A corporate identity is needed before a group can acquire ownership, but Strang and Busse raise the question of whether legal and material ownership vested in one body can lead to 'social disownership' by the community, over time.[82] This is an issue of importance both for non-statutory bodies such as HDT and for local authorities as owners of urban green spaces. Legal ownership should go alongside 'soft ownership': '"It feels like it is mine; legally and technically it might not be, but it feels like it may be mine", [which reflects the feelings of local residents who] make the decisions about what that green space is used for and what benefits really come from that green space'.[83] Participation in decision-making is part of the right to the city[84] and should surely be encouraged as part of an appropriate legal framework, despite the practical difficulties involved in ensuring participation and integrating different voices into decision-making about local urban green spaces.[85] However, as Cooper notes, 'governance, importantly, can operate when no

[77] Dempsey and Burton, 'Defining Place-Keeping'.

[78] A. Mathers, N. Dempsey and J. Froik Molin, 'Place-Keeping in Action: Evaluating the Capacity of Green Space Partnerships in England', *Landscape and Urban Planning*, 139 (2015), 126–136.

[79] Mathers et al., 'Place-Keeping in Action', 128.

[80] Mathers et al., 'Place-Keeping in Action', 133.

[81] Law of Property Act 1925, sections 34 and 36, as amended, establish that co-owners must hold the land on trust; Trustee Act 1925, section 34, provides that there can be no more than four legal co-owners of land.

[82] Strang and Busse, *Ownership and Appropriation*, p. 187.

[83] House of Commons, *Public Parks*, para. 107, citing evidence of Alan Carter (the Land Trust).

[84] Lefebvre, *Writings on Cities*.

[85] See S. Low, D. Taplin and S. Scheld, *Rethinking Urban Parks: Public Space and Cultural Diversity* (Austin, University of Texas Press, 2005).

particular or distinctive relationship of belonging with that which is governed exists'.[86]

There is a widely held view that local authorities are 'democratically accountable bodies',[87] based on the argument that they may be challenged under administrative law or at the ballot box. It is debatable whether holding local councillors accountable through elections every few years, or the practical everyday accountability of an incorporated body like HDT, is of greater value to local residents. Although some companies limited by guarantee have established a wide membership to reflect local interests, as we have seen, there is no legal requirement for democratic accountability. HDT staff and trustees would argue that, as a local organisation with open-door offices, providing courses and facilities, it has much closer contact with its community than a local authority; it makes itself accountable on a daily basis. Twenty years on since HDT was founded, some new trustees/directors have been appointed and some founders remain. The trend has been towards a more 'professional' board, although all current directors have strong connections with Heeley, either living or working (or retired from working) in that community. It is surprisingly difficult to discover information about the trustees/directors of HDT, except through searching the records of Companies House or the Charity Commission. Nor does HDT have a membership structure, whereas the Friends of Meersbrook Hall have over 500 members. Thus the Friends group may certainly feel a sense of ownership in the non-legal sense, but the Friends have no property rights in the Hall. This is similar to the position of Park Friends groups in general, whose contribution to a park's management and decision-making is by agreement with the local council which owns it, and which has power to terminate or change the terms of that agreement.

In terms of its legal framework, HDT's founding 'legal artefacts'[88] in 1996 were the trust deed for the charity and the Memorandum and Articles of Association of the company limited by guarantee. Another option would have been to set up HDT as a fully mutual cooperative. This is a long-established form, but cannot be charitable as it must be run for the benefit of the members, thus enabling only restricted-access communal space like the Botanical Gardens.[89] Most community groups have therefore adopted the company limited by guarantee as their legal structure to facilitate ownership and management of urban green spaces. This is a private company controlled not by shareholders but by its members, whose personal liability is limited to the sum guaranteed, usually one pound. It is regulated under the Companies Act 2006, and must register at Companies House and file annual returns. The company must have at least one director, and hold annual

[86] Cooper, 'Opening up Ownership', 629.
[87] House of Commons, *Public Parks*, para. 108.
[88] Strang and Busse, *Ownership and Appropriation*, p. 5.
[89] Co-operative and Community Benefit Societies Act 2014.

and general meetings. Its aims are set out in its Memorandum of Association, aims which in the case of HDT and many similar organisations simply echo their charitable purposes.

For new community organisations currently wishing to incorporate, there are alternative legal structures to the company limited by guarantee. On detailed examination none of these provides a particularly good match with the concept of communal property. Recently there has been a conscious political initiative to shift regulation and management of public resources to the third sector. For example, the community interest company (CIC), limited either by guarantee or by shares, was introduced in 2006 specifically for social enterprises which carry on some trading activities and aim to benefit the community.[90] The CIC Regulator registers CICs and regulates their community benefit objectives, but CICs cannot have charitable status. Further, the term 'company' conveys a corporate image, as discussed in the following section of this chapter.

Community land trusts[91] would seem, on the basis of their name alone, appropriate for community ownership of local urban green spaces. However, the primary purpose of these trusts, which were introduced in 2008, is to develop and manage affordable homes. In 2011 another new legal framework was introduced: the charitable incorporated organisation (CIO).[92] Like a charitable trust, a CIO must have exclusively charitable purposes and is regulated by the Charity Commission. Each CIO is free to determine its degree of democratic accountability, like companies limited by guarantee; decision-making may be limited to the initial company members and directors, or could be opened to a wider membership although this is not a requirement.

Community benefit societies ('bencoms') have been available since 2014.[93] These must operate for the benefit of the community and can have charitable status. Bencom rules may, and often do, include an asset lock on any property that the society owns, limiting its use to purposes for the benefit of the community. Most bencoms have been established to raise finance for purchasing land or property; 'recently, the model has been popular among organisations seeking to galvanise local communities through ownership of community assets, such as pubs'.[94] Membership is open and voluntary, with each member having one vote, which could lead to greater feelings of ownership than in charitable trusts. Enhanced participation and democratic accountability are dependent on the number of members.

[90] Companies (Audit, Investigations and Community Enterprise) Act 2004, as amended by Companies Act 2006, section 6.

[91] Housing and Regeneration Act 2008, section 79.

[92] Charities Act 2011, sections 204–250; *Charities, England and Wales: The Charitable Incorporated Organisations (General) Regulations 2012*, SI No. 3012.

[93] Co-operative and Community Benefit Societies Act 2014.

[94] Co-operatives UK, *Community Benefit Society* (undated): www.uk.coop/the-hive/sites/default/files/uploads/attachments/resource-community-benefit-society.pdf.

However, bencoms operate on a subscription model, thus forming a restricted-access commons. Membership is only achieved by purchasing one or more shares of a specified value which may unfairly exclude poorer people, or make the bencom an inappropriate vehicle for less affluent neighbourhoods.

The legal form of a charitable trust registered with the Charity Commission ensures that purposes are 'for the public benefit',[95] and that a trust's rights and powers are exercised only to further those purposes.[96] Although charitable trusts are subject to top-down regulation, through the trustees' duty to report annually to the Charity Commission on how the trust has carried out its purposes for the public benefit,[97] there is no requirement for democratic accountability such as being answerable to a wider membership. As with HDT, trustees thus clearly retain the power to 'set the agenda' and make decisions about their property.[98] This has led to concerns about the potential for charitable trusts to become 'self-perpetuating oligarchies' exercising control over 'public assets'.[99]

HDT may convert to CIO status when Regulations are brought in to enable this,[100] ending its dual regulation as both charitable trust and company limited by guarantee. Interestingly, HDT made creative use of the law in 2015 when part of Heeley People's Park was threatened by a road-widening scheme. HDT applied for the park to be listed as an Asset of Community Value (ACV).[101] Although this process was not designed for assets already in 'community ownership', Sheffield City Council accepted HDT's application and listed the park for five years. ACVs gain limited protection against sale of the asset by private owners, through giving local groups time to prepare a bid. Also, ACV status constitutes a material consideration in a planning application, meaning it could be used to refuse planning permission for change of use, for example from a park to land for housing development. The legal label, 'an asset of community value', seems a perfect description for Heeley People's Park although it does not affect or reflect either property rights or accountability.

[95] Charities Act 2011, sections 1–4.

[96] *Harries v Church Commissioners for England*, [1993] E All ER 301.

[97] Charities Act 2011, section 162.

[98] L. Katz, 'Exclusion and Exclusivity in Property Law', *University of Toronto Law Journal*, 58 (2008), 275–315.

[99] House of Commons, *Public Parks*, para. 107, citing evidence of Mark Walton (of Shared Assets).

[100] Cabinet Office and The Charity Commission, *Converting to a Charitable Incorporated. Organisation* (London, Cabinet Office, 2016); and *The Charitable Incorporated Organisations (Conversion) Regulations 2017*, No. 1232.

[101] Localism Act 2011, section 8.

Articulating the discourse of communal property

In this section we discuss how the ideas of communal property and belonging can be articulated to the local community, park users, funders and others, given the lack of recognition in property law and mismatch with available legal frameworks. The difficulties that this causes are highlighted by the House of Commons Committee's struggle to define urban parks in its recent report on public parks. It variously described them as 'just one element of our wider green infrastructure networks',[102] 'shared community assets',[103] and 'spaces which are open and available to all'.[104] The Committee concluded that 'local authorities are best placed to make decisions which are appropriate for their local circumstances',[105] and clearly found it difficult to envisage a different model of ownership.

Heeley People's Park, however, is an example of non-local authority ownership and management of urban green space. HDT communicates with neighbourhood residents and disseminates its plans through *Heeley Voice*, the community magazine it publishes and distributes. HDT also makes use of Twitter and Facebook. There is a distinctly pragmatic reason for community use and activities in the park to be recorded in images and reports in *Heeley Voice* and on social media, as potential funders for parks routinely seek evidence of how well the space is used, and by whom, before committing any money. In its grant applications and publicity material, HDT uses the language of community ownership, custodianship, civic responsibility and community stewardship. However, the law remains largely hidden unless and until a deliberate decision is taken to make it visible through a narrative strategically deploying legal terms such as trust, company or charity.

On Facebook, HDT describes itself as 'a small, charitable development trust, founded by local volunteers, business people & residents', delivering 'youth, community, environmental and economic development projects in and around our neighbourhood', with the stated aim of making 'Heeley a great place to live, with a real sense of place, pride and community . . . successful, vibrant and inclusive'. On the Charity Commission website, HDT is described as a 'community-led anchor organisation'. Charitable status is obviously essential for accessing resources from funders which only make grants to charities. However, in terms of strategically communicating the idea of communal ownership, and fitting with community feelings of belonging, a charitable trust has certain drawbacks. Charities have had a bad press recently in the UK because of dubious fundraising activities.[106]

[102] House of Commons, *Public Parks*, para. 265.
[103] House of Commons, *Public Parks*, para. 3.
[104] House of Commons, *Public Parks*, para. 17.
[105] House of Commons, *Public Parks*, para. 265.
[106] The Charity Commission was forced to issue new guidance: *Charity Fundraising: A Guide to Trustee Duties* (London, Charity Commission, 2016).

Similarly, trusts are often seen as vehicles for disguising and ensuring inheritance of wealth.[107]

We now examine the discourses connected with HDT's two recent strategies: the subscription society, and taking on the lease of Meersbrook Hall. Nesta's funding to support HDT with launching the subscription society was partly spent on commissioning a PR campaign from 'one of Sheffield's cooler design and branding companies'[108] (a SUM Studios tenant). Their advice to the HDT trustees at the time was that the Trust itself was seen as an abstract entity with a confusing name and no clear message, so the focus should be on the park, re-branded to 'give people a better sense of connection to a space and a better sense that, "This is my space"'.[109] Heeley Millennium Park was therefore re-named as Heeley People's Park, described as *'Sheffield's first and largest, community owned and managed public green space'*.[110] The PR campaign encouraged people to sign up to the subscription society using the following text:

> This land is ours
>
> Heeley People's Park belongs to the community – paid for and owned by the people and businesses that love it. The more we give, the more we all get – new play equipment, new space, more trees, more events, more to love and play with and relax in. Whatever that park means to you, your help will mean everything to us, and makes the difference between us keeping it, improving it and losing it forever.[111]

This re-branding of Heeley Millennium Park was designed both to encourage people to feel ownership of the park and to contribute towards it if they could. The phrase 'this land is ours' was made famous by the Diggers, who claimed St George's Hill, Surrey, as common land in 1649 during the English Civil War.[112] This sense of ownership is closely tied to the idea of belonging – 'the park is ours, I belong in it' – and contrasts with the fear of trespassing on private land. It is worth remembering that many Sheffield citizens were involved in the mass trespass on Kinder Scout in 1932 that led to the establishment of the National Parks, but also to the imprisonment of five ramblers for walking over private grouse moors in the Peak District;[113] and in the 1990s movement for open access to moorland which paved the way for the Countryside and Rights of Way Act 2000. The notion of

[107] See, for example, FT Adviser, *Using Trusts to Preserve Family Wealth* (2016): www.ftadviser.com/2016/05/05/training/adviser-guides/using-trusts-to-preserve-family-wealth-wNL0QGj1nPfyvuoGCU1IoJ/article.html.

[108] www.nesta.org.uk/blog/peoples-progress.

[109] Oral Evidence of Senior Programme Manager, Nesta, to Communities and Local Government Committee, 23 November 2016: http://data.parliament.uk/writtenevidence/committeeevidence.svc/evidencedocument/communities-and-local-government-committee/public-parks/oral/43789.html.

[110] www.heeleypark.org/.

[111] www.heeleypark.org/.

[112] Editors' note: For further discussion on the Diggers, see Malcolm and Clarke in this volume.

[113] See discussion in Layard, 'Public Space'.

'owning' Heeley Park thus echoes these calls for open access and references the history of socialist politics in the city. However, the use of these terms in relation to Heeley People's Park begs the questions of who really owns the park, in what way it can be described as 'ours', and what it means to say that we have 'paid' for it, when most funding has come from outside sources.

Heeley People's Park subscription society was launched in June 2015. It was intended to generate wider local recognition of HDT's role in maintaining the park, and to demonstrate local 'buy-in' to the park to boost the success rate of future funding bids. Disappointingly few people subscribed online in the following year, although those attending Heeley Festival and other events in the park were happy to make one-off donations by text message and in cash. There may be a range of reasons for this, both practical and conceptual. Nesta's evaluation identified the problem that 'people are mistrusting of digital giving and social media campaigns, they want a form to fill in'.[114] It is also likely that social media fails to reach all Heeley residents, especially those who have 'belonged' there for decades and generations. Additionally, the benefits of membership of the new subscription society are not clear; the park was never intended to become restricted-access communal property, excluding non-members as the Botanical Gardens had originally done.

A more entrenched problem is the difficulty of getting across the message that Heeley People's Park is different from most urban parks in Sheffield, which are owned by the local authority, paid for from council tax receipts, and are therefore 'free'. In a sense, HDT may have become the victim of its own success through providing a well-maintained and apparently well-resourced park for so long. During that time, HDT has moved on from its 'commoning' origins, and some of the people involved at that time have moved on from the Trust. Even so, those origins could be used as a powerful reminder of why the park can properly be described as 'ours'. The invention of the subscription society and the People's Park by HDT can be seen as an attempt to change perceptions of the park among local residents from that of land managed by a distant 'someone else' into a shared space for which subscribers have some degree of responsibility, and over which they could claim a form of (moral, if not legal) ownership.

HDT's plans to take a long lease of Meersbrook Hall depended on being able to reassure the Friends group about HDT's identity and intentions. Some local residents initially saw HDT as a remote corporate body and, rather like the House of Commons Committee, viewed transfer of the Hall to HDT from the local authority as a form of privatisation. It was difficult, for the reasons already discussed, for HDT to articulate the discourse of communal property managed by a community body established for public benefit at a time when Meersbrook residents felt, understandably, that their local 'public' asset was under threat. Although the two

[114] www.nesta.org.uk/blog/peoples-progress.

neighbourhoods adjoin each other, and when HDT was formed in 1996 Heeley was understood to include Meersbrook, the latter has emerged as a separate area over the intervening 20 years. The name and the charitable purposes of HDT, which define its geographical scope as Heeley, were therefore among the problems which had to be resolved in a series of meetings with the Friends group.

Conclusions

This detailed, contextual account of the park in Heeley and the comparisons with the two other Sheffield parks has highlighted that property law in England is unable to deal conceptually with communal property. Nor can it provide an appropriate legal framework for the property interests and rights associated with urban green spaces that align with the general understandings and experiences of community belonging and ownership. This failure puts urban green space at risk in a time of austerity as it makes it difficult to articulate a discourse of communal property to both funders and local residents. We have shown how HDT's narrative of civic responsibility, community stewardship, and custodianship of communal land does not match well with its company and charitable trust status.

Funding problems sharpen the issues raised by this mismatch between legal status, belonging and ownership, and local democratic accountability. The challenge is how best to establish a community of reciprocity and to encourage voluntary contributions of time and money, essential for the maintenance of urban green spaces. It is apparent from our contextual analysis that when legal arrangements may never have matched a particular narrative and aspirations, or over time may have become mismatched, then there may be a search for a new legal status that will better reflect popular understanding and ward off threats, such as the move to have Heeley People's Park declared an asset of community value. It therefore seems that legal frameworks matter. However, rather than any strategic approach, legal arrangements have been pragmatically adopted based on the structures available at a particular time, for a variety of different types of space.

The interdisciplinary approach adopted in this chapter has also emphasised the importance of origins and of changes over time to urban green spaces. Community feelings of belonging and ownership develop alongside and co-constitute changes to the land itself. Knowledge about appropriate conduct in that space becomes common, over time, and may also alter as the land changes. The precise form of belonging often comes into focus at moments of change or crisis. It is therefore important to understand the history of a specific urban green space.[115] For example, the sense of ownership and the sense of belonging of users of the Heeley People's

[115] This point is also made in Mathers et al., 'Place-Keeping in Action'.

Park have changed over time, and are different from those of the original 'commoning' activists, but the legal form was crystallised in 1996 when it was chosen from the available alternatives. For urban green spaces in general, it seems that legal frameworks are managed through various compromises, examples of what Lindblom famously described as a process of 'muddling through'.[116]

In this chapter we have tracked the complex shifts in layered legal status, meanings and understandings over time, through the specific context of Heeley People's Park and its connections with two other Sheffield parks. Their associated property rights have, it seems, always been fragmented and have moved between public and private and 'communal' and back again. In the nineteenth century the Botanical Gardens were created by an affluent group for their own private enjoyment, and Meersbrook Park was created as a public park by a benevolent city council. The much more recent activism which brought Heeley Park to life, and the similar process to save Meersbrook Hall, were born out of specific crises. These case studies demonstrate the limitations of analysis through property law. Ownership and management of the Botanical Gardens has shifted from private to public to partnership, whereas the survival of Meersbrook Hall as publicly accessible, communal property has relied on a partnership between the Friends group, the local authority and HDT. The 1886 covenants between the private vendor and the public authority, designed to ensure the continuing dedication of the park and its buildings for public use, also played a significant role in preventing the sale of the Hall to the private sector well over a century later. The lease of the Hall to HDT, currently under negotiation, will transfer rights in public land to a private corporate entity. It is debatable whether this constitutes privatisation or the creation of communal property.

Recent deliberations about community access to Meersbrook Hall demonstrate that property ownership is less significant than who feels that they 'belong' in that building. Ironically, the nature of Heeley People's Park as communal property has been sustained by a series of private property ownership arrangements (acquisition and conversion of SUM Studios, and now Meersbrook Hall) to raise funding for maintenance of the park.

It is apparent that distinctions between public, private and communal property have become very blurred in relation to urban green space. Any differences between local authority ownership ('public sector') and charitable, third sector or community ownership seem largely irrelevant in terms of property rights, as all these bodies are subject to restrictions on the rights usually associated with legal ownership. Although governance and accountability arrangements are very important in communal property, the current legal frameworks available to community organisations with property rights in urban green space do not encourage or require participative democracy.

[116] C. E. Lindblom, 'The Science of "Muddling Through"', *Public Administration Review*, 19 (1959), 79–88.

We conclude that the legal frameworks for ownership, governance, access and use are poorly understood and do not match the dynamic and constitutive relationships of belonging between people and place. This leads to difficulties in articulating the discourse of communal property, with serious consequences for funding the maintenance of urban green spaces which are so important for community and civic life.

10

Water: A Common Treasury

ROSALIND MALCOLM AND ALISON CLARKE

Part I: Introduction

In this chapter we examine the notion of water as a common treasury, and the implications that this characterisation of water has for property rights in water. We argue that a property rights system centred on neoliberal conceptions of absolute private ownership, allowing private dominion over water and its commodification, is inappropriate for water and subverts its role as a common treasury. To enable water to function effectively as a common treasury, we argue, a more appropriate property model is one that emphasises and facilitates collaboration and cooperation rather than competition – in other words, a property rights system which acknowledges and promotes communal property in the forms we describe below.

Scope of the argument

As we explain in Part II, the physical inter-connectedness of water on our planet is one of the main imperatives for treating water as a common treasury, and also one of the principal reasons why communal property is, as we argue, of central importance in the governance of water. It is of the essence of this physical inter-connectedness of water that inland surface and subterranean waters[1] and all offshore waters are part of the same ecosystem: the water we draw from our bathroom tap probably came from a local river or reservoir, but it may well end up in international waters in the sea and then come back to us, or to someone else on the other side of the planet, as rain. In our conception, therefore, the common treasury of water comprises both inland and offshore waters, including coastal waters under the jurisdiction of nation-states, and the high seas.[2] In this chapter, however, we concentrate our arguments

[1] In this chapter 'inland waters' includes both surface and subterranean water (groundwater).
[2] W. Howarth and S. Jackson, *Wisdom's Law of Watercourses*, 5th edn (London, Sweet & Maxwell, 2011), pp. 19–30.

Proceedings of the British Academy, **216**, 202–229.

on one small part of the overall picture, by putting our central focus on inland waters and their regulation and governance in England. This is partly because of limitations of space, but also because very different legal regimes apply to inland waters and to offshore waters. Also, choices about regulatory and governance regimes for inland waters and about property rights systems tend to be made at national level and to be heavily influenced by the national cultural, geographic and legal environment. For the present, therefore, we merely observe that the case we advance here in favour of collaborative and cooperative legal regimes governing inland waters, and against private ownership and commodification of any part of them, appears to us to be even stronger in relation to offshore national waters, and surely overwhelming in relation to international waters.

Communal property in water

We look more closely at these collaborative and cooperative legal regimes in Part III, but for the moment we need only note that when we refer to communal property in water we mean rights in water which are held by a community consisting of, for example, local users of, or stakeholders in, a particular stretch of water or a particular water resource, who act collectively in their use and management of the water they share.[3] Examples include local farmers who have set up their own communal irrigation system, associations of neighbouring riparian landowners or of individuals holding fishing or abstraction rights, or perhaps water boards set up by all those who have interests in maintaining the health of a particular water resource. These communities share some distinctive features which it may be helpful to draw attention to at this stage. First, they regard themselves as bound by rules regulating their collective use of the resource which generally are self-generated and exclude outsiders. Second, we refer to both their individual and their collective rights as property rights because they are rights in relation to a resource which are enforceable as between themselves and as against outsiders. Finally, their collective rights are generally not alienable. The community's objective is sustainable cooperative use and management of the resource: they do not see it, or their collective interests in it, as a commodity to be bought and sold.

These communal property institutions are, we argue, central to the modern governance and regulation of water, and normatively provide the best fit for its governance and regulation as a common treasury, either on their own or within a framework of other kinds of property interest.

[3] We are not concerned here with open-access communal property rights, such as public rights of navigation, where the community consists of all members of the public: see further the categorisation of communal property rights in A. Clarke, 'Creating New Commons: Recognition of Communal Land Rights in a Private Property Framework', in J. Holder (ed.), *Current Legal Problems* (Oxford, Oxford University Press, 2006), pp. 319–357 at pp. 322–332.

Outline of the argument

This argument, which we develop in Part II and Part III of this chapter, proceeds as follows. In Part II we explain the notion of a common treasury, grounded in Gerrard Winstanley's foundational principle that the resources of the earth are to be used in common by all, and developed by him in 1649 as a challenge to private property, specifically in the context of the enclosure of common land. Adopting Winstanley's characterisation, we argue that water is an archetypal common treasury resource because of its unique physical qualities which make it essential to life and to our physical environment, and because of the consequent public perception of water as a human right and a common resource. We then end Part II by pointing out that this characterisation of water as a common treasury has implications for the choice of property regime for water. Specifically, the guiding principle must be that property rights in water should facilitate and not subvert water's function as a common treasury, and this, we point out, is problematic for private property rights which allow commodification of water itself or of use rights in water.

In Part III we explore these implications. We start by rejecting the no-property option – the argument that property rights in water are neither necessary nor desirable for the governance and management of water as a common treasury – and sketch out the present range and function of property rights in water in England today, dominated by private and regulatory use rights. We go on to explore why it is that absolute private ownership of water and alienable private use rights in water – both historically of little importance, but now brought back into prominence by the promotion of trading in bulk water and in water abstraction licences – are inappropriate for water as a common treasury. We then assess the relative merits of alternative property institutions based on public trust, stewardship and third sector ownership. We finish by arguing that, because water is by its nature a shared resource, a better alternative is provided by the forms of communal property which develop within the frameworks of private use rights and regulation, and argue for the recognition and promotion of communal property as a key component in a property rights system facilitating water's role as a common treasury.

Part II: Water as a common treasury

The idea of a common treasury

Gerrard Winstanley's common treasury

We borrow our notion of 'common treasury' from the writings of Gerrard Winstanley who, in 1649, during the Commonwealth era following the English Civil War, was one of the leaders of a group of people who established themselves on waste land in Surrey, England, known at the time as George Hill. They claimed as a right that it was 'an undeniable equity that the common people ought to dig, plow, plant and dwell upon the Commons without hiring them or paying rent to any'.[4] The leaders of this group were William Everard and Gerrard Winstanley,[5] the former of whom was known as a Leveller, a group who sought to take further the new political order which had been established after the Civil War. It was Winstanley, though, who appears to have been the key author of various leaflets and other texts around this era.[6] The band of people who sought to use the common land in this way called themselves the 'True Levellers' and were popularly known as the 'Diggers'. It is important to note that the expressed objective of this group was not to usurp private property in general but to take land which was common land or waste land and work it for the benefit of the people. Nevertheless, they had a vision of the future where present freeholders of land would ultimately join with their community. Their vision was communistic and egalitarian with notions of private property as antithetical to equality. This offshoot of the Leveller movement is noteworthy for this experiment in self-help of remarkable originality – described by Bernstein as a sketch at a communitarian reconstruction of society.[7]

Winstanley's challenge to private property

Winstanley's challenge to private property is based on the fundamental position that if a person claims property as subject to their own private ownership then that excludes others and asserts that person's authority over them;[8] private property is an institution where one individual can dominate over another. In Winstanley's vision, the right of one individual not to be dominated by another is inalienable. This assertion of authority, in Winstanley's challenge, is contrary to God's laws and the concept of moral equality.[9]

The foundational principle that the Diggers advocated, and which we argue for as a normative description for water, was that the earth was a common treasury – the resources of the earth were to be used in common by all. An important pamphlet of the Diggers sets out their philosophy:[10]

[4] J. Winstanly, 'A LETTER TO The Lord Fairfax, AND His Councell of War, WITH *Divers Questions to the Lawyers, and Ministers*: Proving it an undeniable Equity, That the common People ought to dig, plow, plant and dwell upon the Commons, without hiring them, or paying Rent to any.' *Delivered on Saturday June 9* (London, 1649): www.bilderberg.org/land/letter.htm.

[5] The spelling of Winstanley's name varies.

[6] C. Hill, *The World Turned Upside Down* (London, Maurice Temple Smith Ltd, 1971).

[7] E. Bernstein, *Cromwell and Communism: Socialism and Democracy in the Great English Revolution* (London, Frank Cass & Co, 1930, reprinted 1963), p. 116.

[8] D. Klimchuk, 'Property and Necessity', in J. Penner and H. Smith (eds), *Philosophical Foundations of Property Law* (Oxford, Oxford University Press, 2013), pp. 47–67.

[9] Klimchuk, 'Property and Necessity', p. 49.

[10] J. Winstanley et al., *The True Levellers Standard Advanced: or the State of Community opened, and presented to the Sons of Men* (26 April 1649; reprinted Oxford, Benediction Classics, 2009).

> In the beginning of time the great Creator Reason made the earth to be a common treasury . . . I affirme, (and I challenge you to disprove) that the earth was made to be a common Treasury of livelihood for all, without respect of persons, and was not made to be bought and sold: And that mankind in all his branches, is the lord over the Beasts, Birds, Fishes, and the Earth, and was not made to acknowledge any of his owne kind to be his teacher and ruler, but the spirit of righteousnesse only his Maker, and to walk in his light, and so to live in peace, and this being a truth, as it is, then none ought to be Lords or Landlords over another, but the earth is free for every son and daughter of mankind, to live free upon.

The modern concept of property as something 'bounded, spatially exclusive and individually owned',[11] which we challenge in Part III, emerged in the sixteenth century with land use changes and enclosure.[12] Writing in the seventeenth century, in some regards Winstanley's perspective on property comes to the same point as Hobbes, both holding that property, depending on sovereign power, is the act of that power. While Hobbes' theory of the political state was based on the idea that a sovereign with absolute authority was essential to avoid anarchy,[13] Winstanley saw the power of 'Reason' as dominating human psychology and based his solution on community and cooperation. He challenged the Hobbesian theory of a de facto authority, arguing that if competitive property relations were abolished, the problem of sovereignty would disappear.[14] These powerful debates about the constitution and the institutions of property were of their time – that is, the period starting with the establishment of the Commonwealth in 1649 after the English Civil War up to the compromise of 1660 which saw the restoration of all the trappings of hereditary monarchy and aristocracy.[15] The epitome of this discourse can be found in the Putney debates[16] where, for example, Ireton argued that the communitarian Levellers, who were proposing that liberty and property were ultimately incompatible,[17] were challenging the accepted authority of property owning, suffrage and kinghood.[18] Contextually, the language of these debates and

[11] B. McDonagh and C. J. Griffin, 'Occupy! Historical Geographies of Property, Protest and the Commons, 1500–1850', *Journal of Historical Geography*, 53 (2016), 1–10 at 3.

[12] D. J. Seipp, 'The Concept of Property in the Early Common Law', *Law and History Review*, 12(1) (1994), 29–92.

[13] T. Hobbes, *Leviathan* (Clarendon Edition of the Works of Thomas Hobbes, Oxford, Oxford University Press, 2014).

[14] There is no evidence that Hobbes and Winstanley ever read each other's works. But they overlap temporally. See Hill, *The World Turned Upside Down*, Appendix 1.

[15] P. Baker and E. Vernon (eds), *The Agreements of the People, the Levellers, and the Constitutional Crisis of the English Revolution* (Basingstoke, Palgrave Macmillan, 2012).

[16] P. Baker, *The Levellers: The Putney Debates* (London and New York, Verso, 2007); M. Mendle (ed.), *The Putney Debates of 1647: The Army, the Levellers, and the English State* (Cambridge, Cambridge University Press, 2001).

[17] A. S. P. Woodhouse (ed.), *Puritanism and Liberty: Being the Army Debates 1647–9* (London, Everyman, 1986).

[18] For a full account see C. Firth (ed.), *The Clarke Papers: Selections from the Papers of William Clarke,*

Winstanley's contributions rest upon biblical scriptures but the debate is metaphysical. While Winstanley argues that the institutional structure of private property is an offence to the Creator, nevertheless his argument is fundamentally about moral equality.[19] As Klimchuk argues, Winstanley presents a 'morally neutral challenge to private property', that is that 'private property . . . is morally inconsistent with equality',[20] thus for Winstanley, the right to hold the earth as a common treasury is an inalienable right. It is on this basis of moral neutrality that we argue for water, today, to be treated as a common treasury.

Common treasuries, common-pool resources and public goods

The term 'common treasury', as we use it, describes the nature of the resource, that is, its physical nature and importance to all forms of life.[21] It tells us nothing about the legal nature of any rights anyone might have in relation to the resource (a point we return to later). Moreover, it is a normative description of the resource. By that we mean that, *because* of its physical characteristics and its importance to all, it *ought* to be available to all ('all' to be understood here as encompassing all creatures of the earth today and into the future, and the environment as a whole). In these respects a 'common treasury' differs from a 'common-pool resource' and a 'public good', both of which are purely descriptive of the resource, not normative, and describe only the physical nature of the resource, telling us only the extent to which it is non-excludable (too difficult or too expensive to exclude outsiders from it) and rivalrous (limited in quantity, with the total quantity reduced by each use).[22]

Water as a common treasury

What makes water special

As far as water is concerned what makes it special – what qualifies it as a common treasury – is a combination of water's unique physical characteristics and the consequent public perception of water. Specifically, access to drinking water has been given the status of an international human right, despite the obvious

Secretary to the Council of the Army, 1647–1649, and to General Monck and the Commanders of the Army in Scotland, 1651–1660 (Offices of the Royal Historical Society, 1992).

[19] Klimchuk, 'Property and Necessity', p. 50.

[20] Klimchuk, 'Property and Necessity', p. 50.

[21] A. Clarke and R. Malcolm, 'The Role of Property in Water Regulation: Locating Communal and Regulatory Property Rights on the Property Rights Spectrum', in C. Godt (ed.), *Regulatory Property Rights: The Transforming Notion of Property in Transnational Business Regulation* (Leiden, Brill Nijhoff, 2016), pp. 121–140 at pp. 123–124.

[22] Clarke and Malcolm, 'The Role of Property in Water Regulation', pp. 124–125.

practical difficulties in implementing the right, simply because of its physical importance to human life and to the quality of human existence. Similarly, what appears to be a universal public perception of water as a local, national or global resource is undoubtedly founded on public awareness of water's physical importance to humans and to our immediate local and global environment. We explore these physical characteristics and public perceptions, which together provide the imperative for treating water as a common treasury, in the following paragraphs.

The unique physical qualities of water

The nature of water as a cyclical self-sustaining resource is one of the reasons for its normative treatment as a common treasury. As a resource which is essential as part of the ecosystem on sustainable development principles – for current and future generations – water is a core requirement for human and planetary existence.[23] Water is a natural resource which is finite, recyclable but non-renewable, the very nature of which merits differential treatment. Its nature can be treated in strictly scientific terms. It is a chemical which, in its pure form, is a molecule containing one oxygen and two hydrogen atoms (dihydrogen monoxide), the one formula – H_20 – known to everyone. These are two of the four elements essential to the existence of the earth so it is also one of the essential bases of life: 'life everywhere must be composed of carbon, nitrogen, hydrogen, and oxygen, upon an organic chemistry therefore much as on Earth; and that it can arise only in an atmosphere rich in water'.[24] Water can take different forms: liquid, gaseous and solid as it appears in frost, ice, snow, rain, lakes, waterfalls, clouds. The earth is composed mainly of water – 70 per cent of the surface of the planet is covered by water of which 97 per cent is in the seas and oceans, just under 2 per cent in groundwater, and a similar amount in glaciers and the polar ice caps. A tiny fraction is in vaporised form in clouds and in precipitation. Most of this water is saline, with only 2.5 per cent as freshwater, most of which is in the form of ice or underground as groundwater. Humans, too, are made of water – our bodies overall are 66 per cent water (our brains around 80 per cent). Thus, we can survive some weeks without food but only days without water. It is this sense of water as a source of life to humans, and to the earth (and possibly life elsewhere), together with its peculiar cyclical nature which has caused water to be imbued with metaphysical qualities and to acquire romantic and poetic associations in a way which is exceptional for a chemical: 'Water was the matrix of the world and of all its creatures.'[25] Inevitably

[23] Clarke and Malcolm, 'The Role of Property in Water Regulation', pp. 125–127.

[24] G. Wald, 'The Origins of Life', *Proceedings of the Academy of Natural Sciences*, 52 (1964), 595–611 at 606.

[25] Paracelsus, quoted in P. Ball, *The Devil's Doctor: Paracelsus and the World of Renaissance Magic and Science* (London, Arrow Books, 2007), p. 263.

it is the stuff of creation stories from the Bible to the Qur'an: 'By means of water we give life to everything.'[26]

The nature of water as a self-sustaining resource is central to our argument about its management and governance. Water has a unique life cycle and cannot disappear or be destroyed.[27] There is no new water – the water we drink and use for all purposes is constantly recycled from the same water that has existed on the planet for billions of years; 'all the waters of the Earth are decomposed and recomposed by photosynthesis and respiration every 2,000,000 years'.[28] A dinosaur will have drunk the same water which we are drinking today.[29] This hydrological life cycle works as a closed system transporting water around the earth from solid to liquid to gas and round again – a continuous process of evaporation, transpiration and precipitation akin to a giant plumbing system. This cycle involves water moving from the atmosphere to groundwater stored kilometres below the earth's surface. Water evaporates, changing to vapour; the clouds produce precipitation which mainly falls into the sea with less than a quarter falling on land. Plants lose water through transpiration which varies according to temperature, humidity and wind. When the precipitation reaches land it soaks through until saturated and then percolates into groundwater aquifers.[30] At most temperatures on the surface of the earth, water is a liquid. In this state water is an excellent solvent, and because there is so much of it available on the earth's surface, water is home (oceans, lakes and rivers) to much of life.

This hydrological cycle is one of the most important biogeochemical processes whereby chemical substances move through the different spheres of the earth, and represents a series of changes which always come back to their starting point and which are repeatable. The element is recycled, although during the cycle water may be stored in lakes, oceans and groundwater reservoirs, sometimes for thousands of years. The key principle behind the hydrological cycle is that all phases are interdependent and continuous.[31] This critical principle establishes that water is indestructible and its total quantity cannot be diminished. It is also true that water cannot be increased except through exceptional processes.[32] Other chemicals such as carbon, oxygen, nitrogen, phosphorus, calcium and sulphur also pass through

[26] The Qur'an, Book of the Prophets, 21.30; The Bible, Ecclesiastes 4, 7.

[27] See S. Sitch and F. Drake, 'The Changing Water Cycle', in J. Holden (ed.), *Water Resources: An Integrated Approach* (London, Routledge, 2014), pp. 19–48.

[28] E. I. Rabinowitsch, *Photosynthesis* (New York, Interscience, 1945), vol. 1, pp. 7–10.

[29] P. Ball, *H_2O: A Biography of Water* (London, Phoenix, 1999), ch. 2.

[30] A. N. Charalambous, *Transferable Groundwater Rights: Integrating Hydrogeology, Law and Economics* (Oxford, Routledge, 2013), pp. 3–41.

[31] R. C. Ward and M. Robinson, *Principles of Hydrology*, 4th edn (Maidenhead, McGraw Hill Higher Education, 2000).

[32] S. Foster and D. P. Loucks (eds), *Non-Renewable Groundwater Resources: A Guidebook on Socially Sustainable Management for Water-Policy Makers*, IHP-VI, Series on Groundwater No. 10 (Saint-Denis, UNESCO, 2006).

such biogeochemical cycles and all are critical for life and ecosystems. But it is water which is the lubricant for all the other biogeochemical cycles, making it the single common factor for the chemical operation of the earth.[33] There is much more science to be studied and learned about the detail of the operation of the water cycle.[34] But an understanding of the nature of the water cycle and water's recyclability is essential to the way in which it should be managed and should underpin the governance frameworks for its supply and distribution. The nature of the water cycle is an underlying reason for its normative treatment as a common treasury; that is, a resource which is essential as part of the ecosystem in its broadest meaning, both presently and for the future.

The problem then is not that water can be used up, in the way that fossil fuels can; the exploitation of water will not mean that its overall supply diminishes. So, with all this water in us, around us and under us, where does the problem lie? If we cannot destroy water or use it up like oil, gas or coal, then why is there any concern?

The problem rests in the need for us to have water at hand to drink (or for use in respect of our other needs – agriculture, industry and so on) and for it to be safe to drink.

> The trouble with water – and there is trouble with water – is that they're not making any more of it. They're not making any less, mind, but no more either. There is the same amount of water in the planet now as there was in prehistoric times. People, however, they're making more of – many more, far more than is ecologically sensible – and all those people are utterly dependent on water for their lives (humans consist mostly of water), for their livelihoods, their food, and increasingly, their industry. Humans can live for a month without food but will die in less than a week without water. Humans consume water, discard it, poison it, waste it, and restlessly change the hydrological cycles, indifferent to the consequences: too many people, too little water, water in the wrong places and in the wrong amounts.[35]

So the availability of water when and where it is needed and in adequate and safe supplies is the key problem, which it is necessary to address in terms of adequate measures for its management. This problem is exacerbated by the interconnectedness of water, which makes every human interaction with water liable to result in widespread and not easily predictable externalities.

Water as a human right

At international level, because of the fundamental status of water as the basis of life, it has acquired the anthropocentric status of a human right in international law:

[33] Ball, *H_2O*, p. 27.
[34] For example, J. Evaristo et al., 'Global Separation of Plant Transpiration from Groundwater and Streamflow', *Nature*, 525 (2015), 91–94.
[35] M. de Villiers, *Water: The Fate of Our Most Precious Resource* (New York, Mariner Books, 2001).

'Water is fundamental for life and health. The human right to water is indispensable for leading a healthy life in human dignity. It is a prerequisite to the realization of all other human rights.'[36]

The legal basis for the right to water as a human right has been well rehearsed.[37] The three instruments which together constitute the International Bill of Human Rights – the Universal Declaration of Human Rights; the International Covenant on Civil and Political Rights; and the International Covenant on Economic, Social and Cultural Rights[38] – did not contain any specific and explicit reference to the right to water, although it would not appear that it was deliberately omitted. The effect though of not expressly including it was that it subsequently proved necessary to imply it into other rights.[39]

Then, on 28 July 2010, the UN General Assembly adopted Resolution 64/292 recognising 'that safe, clean drinking water and sanitation were integral to the realization of all human rights'.[40] In 2010, the UN Human Rights Council, in Resolution A/HRC/RES/15/9, affirmed that 'the right to water and sanitation is derived from the right to an adequate standard of living and inextricably related to the right to the highest attainable standard of physical and mental health, and the right to life and human dignity'. This was re-affirmed with further details in 2011.[41]

Further, water is the subject of aims and objectives, formulated now in the Sustainable Development Goals, to ensure the provision of drinking water for all. Goal 6 of the Sustainable Development Goals[42] continues the aims[43] of seeking to ensure availability and sustainable management of water and sanitation for all by 2030 with further specific targets. These goals signify an internationally

[36] The United Nations Committee on Economic, Cultural and Social Rights, 27 November 2002.

[37] P. H. Gleick, 'The Human Right to Water', *Water Policy*, 1 (1998), 487–503; A. Cahill, 'The Human Rights to Water – A Right of Unique Status: The Legal Status and Normative Content of the Rights to Water', *International Journal of Human Rights*, 9 (2005), 389–410 at 391.

[38] Universal Declaration of Human Rights (adopted 10 December 1948), General Assembly Resolution 217 A(III) United Nations Document A/810, 71 (1948) (UDHR); United Nations, International Covenant on Civil and Political Rights, UN General Assembly resolution 2200 A(XXI) of 16 December 1966; United Nations, International Covenant on Economic, Social and Cultural Rights, UN General Assembly resolution 2200 A(XXI) of 16 December 1966.

[39] S. C. McCaffrey, 'A Human Right to Water: Domestic and International Implications', *Georgetown International Environmental Law Review*, 5 (1992), 1–24 at 9; F. Menghistu, 'The Satisfaction of Survival Requirements', in B. G. Ramcharan (ed.), *The Right to Life in International Law* (The Hague, Nijhoff, 1985), pp. 63–83; H. J. Steiner and P. Alston, *International Human Rights in Context: Law, Politics, Morals* (Oxford, Oxford University Press, 2000), p. 734.

[40] 64th General Assembly Plenary, 108th Meeting: www.un.org/News/Press/docs/2010/ga10967.doc.htm.

[41] N. Chowdury et al., *The Human Right to Water and the Responsibilities of Businesses: An Analysis of Legal Issues*, Research Paper No. 03/2011, SOAS School of Law Legal Studies Research Paper Series: http://ssrn.com/abstract=1850782.

[42] United Nations, 'Transforming Our World: The 2030 Agenda for Sustainable Development', United Nations General Assembly Resolution A/RES/70/1, adopted 20 September 2015.

[43] See also the Millennium Development Goals, Goal 7, and UNICEF Water, Sanitation and Hygiene Annual Report 2009 (UNICEF WASH Section Programmes, UNICEF, New York, May 2010).

agreed desire to improve the provision of water (and sanitation) for the world's populations. They also encourage international cooperation and the provision of capacity-building support for developing countries.[44]

It is difficult to envisage such a programme being achieved without attention being paid to the mechanisms for the governance and management of water. To achieve the stated aims and objectives, such mechanisms need to address social needs as a priority, which is hardly compatible with a process driven by commodification or with the generation of private profits. This late acceptance of the right to water as a social and cultural good comes at a time when the discussion of the economic value of water and methods of protecting water through the mechanism of an attributed economic value have become dominant.[45] This represents a clash in the perception of water and its value as a human right and its value as a commodity which can be bought and sold, and it brings into sharp relief the dichotomy between the human right to water, which can be seen as a human right for the water 'have-nots', and traditional private property rights in water which, as we note below, protect embedded pre-existing rights – the rights of the water 'haves'. We return to this point later.[46]

Thus, the status of water as a human right makes a central role for private property in water governance problematic, partly because markets in resource rights cannot accommodate human rights to those resources, but also because of a fundamental incompatibility between secure private rights *in* water and human rights *to* water.

However, treating water as part of a common treasury accommodates its treatment by the international community. The right to have water as the manifestation of a right speaks against its management through commodification, while a normative approach to water as a common treasury would be consistent with the fundamental right. A fundamental human right to access to safe water can sit within the framework of a common treasury.

Public perceptions of water as a common resource

At municipal level, the approach to the management and governance of water passes periodically through different phases.[47] Neoliberal approaches leading to liberalisation policies in the late twentieth century saw programmes advocating the privatisation of water resources management systems, many of which had previously been in some form of public ownership whether at municipal or state

[44] *Charting Our Water Future*, a report of the 2030 Water Resources Group: www.mckinsey.com/client_service/sustainability/latest_thinking/charting_our_water_future.
[45] Water Act 2014.
[46] See Part III – 'The absolute ownership model': 'Incompatibility with human rights'.
[47] D. Hall et al., 'Public Resistance to Privatisation in Water and Energy', *Development in Practice*, 15 (2005), 286–301.

level.[48] A variety of outcomes have resulted from these changes which were apparently intended to improve a range of matters such as the availability of water and environmental protection measures. But from around the start of the twenty-first century, in response to a number of crises[49] surrounding these marketisation approaches, there has been increasing pressure from communities to return to the public ownership of water.[50]

A major campaign led by the European Federation of Public Service Unions in 2014 saw 1.9 million people from 12 EU member states signing a petition arguing for water to be treated as a right rather than a commodity. This campaign was the subject matter of a European Citizens' Initiative (ECI).[51]

> This campaign is a tool to commit the EU and Member States to implement the human right to water and sanitation. It is a tool to change the mind-set in the European Commission from a market-based approach with the focus on competition to a rights-based approach with the focus on public service. It aims to achieve universal (global) access to water and sanitation and to safeguard the limited public water resources for future generations.[52]

The primary argument was that water should be treated as a public good not a commodity, and thus, water supply and the management of water resources should not be subject to 'internal market rules' and should be excluded from liberalisation. This trend can be seen in both the developed and industrialised world as the ECI shows and also in developing countries,[53] so there is no clear bifurcation in this community perception that water is best treated as a public good. A recent report shows 183 high income countries where individual cities or regions remunicipalised water and sanitation services, and 50 like instances in middle to low income countries.[54]

[48] M. Florio, *The Great Divestiture – Evaluating the Welfare Impact of the British Privatizations 1979–1997* (Cambridge, MA, MIT Press, 2004).

[49] House of Commons Committee of Public Accounts, 'Economic Regulation of the Water Sector', Fifteenth Report of Session 2015–16 HC505 (London, The Stationery Office, 2016).

[50] E. Lobina, S. Kishimoto and O. Petitjean, *Here to Stay: Water Remunicipalisation as a Global Trend*, report by PSIRU, Transnational Institute, and the Multinationals Observatory, November: http://psiru/sites/default/files/2014-11-W-HeretoStay.pdf; D. Hall, E. Lobina and P. Terhorst, 'Re-Municipalisation in the Early 21st Century: Water in France and Energy in Germany', *International Review of Applied Economics*, 27 (2013), 193–214; and see also the 'new commons' movement in Italy discussed by M. Pieraccini, 'Taking Stock of Italian Commons: Un-Common Grounds', in this volume.

[51] COM (2014) 177 final. Communication from the Commission on the European Citizens' Initiative 'Water and sanitation are a human right! Water is a public good, not a commodity'; European Parliament 2014–2019, Committee on the Environment, Public Health and Food Safety, 2014/2239(INI), 10 March 2015.

[52] www.right2water.eu.

[53] A. de O. Filho, *Brazil: Struggle Against the Privatization of Water* (2002), report to PSI InterAmerican Water Conference, San Jose, 8–10 July 2002: www.psiru.org/Others/BrasilLuta-ing.doc (English).

[54] S. Kishimoto, E. Robina and O. Petitjean (eds), *Our Public Water Future. The Global Experience with Remunicipalisation* (Amsterdam, Transnational Institute and others, 2015), pp. 18–29: www.tni.org/sites/www.tni.org/files/download/ourpublicwaterfuture-1.pdf.

Implications for property holdings

What we have said so far about the rationale for treating water as a common treasury has some implications for the choice of property regime. The classification of a resource, in this instance water, as a common treasury must form the presumption or starting point for consideration of the way in which the resource is governed and managed. It must also dictate that the governance mechanisms adopted are such as to give first priority to preserving and retaining its critical status as a common treasury, that is, that it is available to all. Where water is treated as a commodity, access to all is not guaranteed since an ability to pay and the vagaries of the market turn citizens into consumers. Then the citizen must look to the state and the intervention of regulation to protect the right and protect the citizen against the private operator whose primary duty is to run a business for profit.

Part III: Property and water

The property rights spectrum

As we said in Part II, it is the nature of water (its physical nature and its importance to life and the environment) that makes it a common treasury. For Winstanley, it was of the essence of a common treasury that it should not be the subject of private property, but rather that it should be open-access communal property: everyone should have the right of access to it in common with all others, to use for their own needs and for the common good. However, in our analysis, the designation of water as a common treasury does not presuppose that it should be governed by an open-access property regime, even if it does rule out regimes which commodify water: open access is not the only alternative to commodification. When considering the role of property in relation to water, it is central to our argument that there is no simple private/public dichotomy in the concept of 'property'. We do not have to make a stark choice between the kind of absolute-dominion exclusionary private ownership that Winstanley categorised as private ownership on the one hand, and his ideal of open access on the other. The reality is that the common law world (as most other jurisdictions) recognises a spectrum of property interests which include these two extremes but also encompass a wide variety of other interests, including proprietary rights to use water in various ways, which have always been of far greater importance than ownership.[55] In particular, holders of property interests in water – whether owners of water or water resources or holders of use rights in

[55] W. Howarth, 'The History of Water Law in the Common Law Tradition', in T. Tvedt, O. McIntyre and T. K. Woldetsadik (eds), *A History of Water, Series III, Volume 2 Sovereignty and International Water Law* (London and New York, I. B. Taurus, 2015), pp. 66–104 at pp. 70–71.

water – need not be private profit-seeking individuals or Leviathans: all kinds of property interests in water can be, and are, also held by individuals and public and quasi-public bodies mandated to use their interests only for public benefit of one kind or another, and, most importantly for present purposes, they can also be held by communities.

The question, then, is which kinds of property interest within this range best allow water to function effectively as a common treasury? There is no obvious simple answer, equally appropriate to all jurisdictions at all times. The most appropriate (in the common treasury sense) property regime in any given state at any given time must depend at least to some extent on the prevailing social, cultural, economic and environmental conditions, and on the nature and historical evolution of its current water institutions. As Heinmiller pointed out,[56] water governance is heavily path-dependent: how you get where you want to be in the future is dependent on where you are now, and how you got where you now are:

> path dependency is not about historical determinism or inevitability, but is instead about 'context-bound rationality': past events and choices establish constraints and incentives that narrow future choice sets . . . [prior events] alter the context of future decision-making, pre-empting some options and making other options more or less attractive. Thus, it matters that [water] apportionment institutions were introduced well before efforts at resource conservation because the pre-existence of these apportionment institutions constrains the decision options available to actors involved in conservation issues.[57]

The no-property option

However, before considering the choices of property regime open to us now in this jurisdiction, a prior question has to be addressed: is property necessary at all for water to function effectively as a common treasury in a complex society such as ours?

At one level, the imposition of a property rights system of some kind seems inevitable. Water cannot be left as an unregulated no-property resource, in which no one has rights but where all are at liberty to take as much as they want, whenever they want, and use it for whatever purpose they want, regardless of the effect on others.[58] This goes without saying in a no-property world in times and places of water scarcity, but even where water is plentiful, unregulated free access would carry what we would now regard as unacceptable risks to the environment. It would

[56] B. T. Heinmiller, 'Path Dependency and Collective Action in Common Pool Resource Governance', *International Journal of the Commons*, 3 (2009), 131–147.

[57] Heinmiller, 'Path Dependency', 134.

[58] Essentially Garrett Hardin's thesis in 'The Tragedy of the Commons', *Science*, 162 (1968), 1243–1248.

also make it impossible to organise reliable water supply and drainage systems (except for the rich and powerful), still less so as to satisfy the human right to water, and it would leave every de facto access to and control over water insecure.

There is less of a free-for-all if no-property in water is combined with private ownership of land, but the result is even less likely to lead to water functioning effectively as a common treasury. We are left with this situation in England as a result of the House of Lords decision in *The Mayor, Aldermen and Burgesses of the Borough of Bradford v Pickles*,[59] where it was held that, unlike the position with surface water and water running in defined channels, no one has any kind of property rights in or to percolating groundwater at common law. On this analysis, Pickles, a private landowner, was held entitled to drain groundwater from his land even though the (predicted) result was to cut off the supply of water to a nearby spring which was used by the municipal water company to supply water to the rapidly expanding industrial city of Bradford. In other words, Pickles had no property rights to abstract the groundwater under his land, but because he (like everyone else in the world) was free to do whatever he wanted with it (because no one else had property rights in it either), he was free to divert it so that it never reached the spring on Bradford Corporation's land; the Corporation had no right to complain because it had no property rights in any groundwater under its land until it appropriated whatever water happened to be there by drawing it from the spring. So, if no-property in water is combined with private ownership of land, two consequences follow. The first is that the private owners of the land lying above groundwater have a de facto monopoly over the water as against the rest of the world: everyone else in the world is in theory free to appropriate it but in practice unable to do so without trespassing on someone else's land. The second is, however, that as between themselves, each private landowner's access to the water is precarious: it all depends on who gets to the water first. This looks very much like the worst possible outcome from all perspectives.[60]

However, it can be argued that, in the case of common treasury goods such as water, the key to avoiding such hazards is not property but regulation, and that some things can be regulated effectively without being propertised. In the case of water, consumer supplies and services could be safeguarded by contract and statutory duty, with domestic, agricultural and industrial users contracting to receive water, drainage, and other water-related services from bodies under a statutory duty to provide them. These bodies need not hold property rights in water, so the argument goes; they could operate under licences from the state allowing them

[59] [1895] AC 587.

[60] The outcome is made even more unsatisfactory by the House of Lords' rejection in the same case of a doctrine of abuse of rights, which means that landowners can exercise their property rights in their land and their liberties to extract water from under their land even if their sole motive is to deprive others of access to water. We return to this point in the section on 'Public trust and stewardship' below.

to acquire water from water sources to use for those limited purposes. Similarly, the state (or other bodies mandated to implement state policy) could design and operate a framework of regulations to achieve environmental and supply goals and the preservation and protection of water resources for whatever purpose it wanted, without vesting property rights in water in itself or in anyone else. Any failure by the state to do the job fairly and effectively, and any lack of power it may have to overcome problems caused by the transboundary and global inter-connectedness of water, could be mitigated by participation in supra-national regional or international bodies, which could devise overarching regulatory frameworks within which member states must operate, and impose obligations on member states to attain and maintain common standards. So, the argument goes, citizens of the state do not need property rights enforceable against the state to ensure that the state makes water serve as a common treasury: they could rely on domestic political pressure and supra-national regulation.

Property and water in England

In many ways, our present legal relationship with water in England strongly resembles this regulatory no-property model. Unlike other jurisdictions, the state does not have underlying (or any other kind of) ownership of water in general,[61] and private ownership of water is not recognised except when, and for so long as, it is in the physical possession of the owner.[62] It is true that landowners have common law property rights and liberties appurtenant to their land ownership to use water from natural and some artificial water sources adjoining, running across or lying under their land: we retain the common law rules noted above confirmed by the House of Lords in *Bradford v Pickles*.[63] Many water users (some farmers, breweries, electricity companies and a few domestic users) do rely on these common law rights and liberties to abstract water directly from source. However, since

[61] Compare, for example, some states in the USA and in Canada: R. K. Craig, 'A Comparative Guide to the Western States' Public Trust Doctrines: Public Values, Private Rights, and the Evolution toward an Ecological Public Trust', *Ecology Law Quarterly*, 37 (2010), 53–197; R. K. Craig, 'A Comparative Guide to the Eastern Public Trust Doctrines: Classification of States, Property Rights, and State Summaries', *Penn State Environmental Law Review*, 16 (2007), 1–113; J. M. Glenn, 'Crown Ownership of Water *in situ* in Common Law Canada: Public Trusts, Classical Trusts and Fiduciary Duties', *Les Cahiers de droit*, 51 (2010), 493–519.

[62] *Moore v British Waterways Board*, [2013] EWCA Civ 73 per Lewison LJ at 54–58; Howarth and Jackson, *Wisdom's Law of Watercourses*, paras 1.28–1.29.

[63] [1895] AC 587. For a comprehensive account see Howarth, 'History of Water Law', pp. 70–96. Other users have proprietary use rights in water derived from rights granted by private Acts of Parliament to the entrepreneurs and municipal authorities who built the foundations of our present water and electricity supply infrastructures in the eighteenth to twentieth centuries. *Bradford v Pickles* itself illustrates the interplay between the private rights and liberties of landowners at common law and the statutory rights of private and municipal water providers in the late nineteenth century.

1963[64] no one has been able to exercise any property rights or liberties to abstract water from anywhere without an abstraction licence issued by the government's Environment Agency. These abstraction licences prescribe in detail how much water can be abstracted by whom, for what purpose, when and from where.[65] So, in the case of water users who abstract water from source, their property rights to do so are of far less importance than their licence rights.

All other water users, including the vast majority of domestic users and many industrial, commercial and agricultural users,[66] do not rely on property rights at all. Their water is provided under contract by one of a small number of privately owned water supply companies which, following privatisation of the water supply industry in 1987, have a statutory monopoly over the public supply of water in England. These water supply bodies are heavily regulated by the state. They are under detailed regulatory control governing the supply, price, and quality of the water they supply, the environmental effects of their activities, and the ways in which they conduct their businesses. These private bodies are mandated to carry out the common treasury objectives of the state, directed and monitored by no fewer than six state agencies.[67]

The government, in its turn, is subject to extensive supra-national control over its water policy and how it is implemented. Our modern national water system is based on and designed to implement the EU Water Framework Directive 2000/60,[68] which provides a framework for pan-EU water management based on river basins. The duties imposed on member states require them to achieve 'good status' (by reference to specified chemical and ecological status for surface water and chemical status and quantity for groundwater) and fixed environmental objectives.[69]

Continuing relevance of property

So, in these respects, water governance in England bears some resemblance to the regulatory no-property model. However, several features of our system make property nevertheless central.

[64] Water Resources Act 1963; currently governed by Ch. II Water Resources Act 1991 as amended.
[65] Section 24(1) Water Resources Act 1991.
[66] See www.gov.uk/government/statistics/water-usage-on-farms-england-201415 and www.gov.uk/government/statistical-data-sets/env15-water-abstraction-tables.
[67] Water Services Regulation Authority; Environment Agency; Drinking Water Inspectorate; Competition and Markets Authority; Department of the Environment, Food and Rural Affairs; and Consumer Council for Water.
[68] Directive 2000/60/EC of the European Parliament and Council [2000] OJ 2 327/01.
[69] See A. Rieu-Clarke, A. Allan and S. Hendry (eds), *Routledge Handbook of Water Law and Policy* (Abingdon, Routledge, 2017).

Continuing influence of historic property rights in water

The first is that, historically, our present water governance system was grafted on to pre-existing proprietary use rights in water: it did not replace them. So, for example, although abstraction licences can now be granted to anyone who demonstrates a mere 'right of access' (not necessarily proprietary) to land from which the water is to be abstracted, many of the current holders of abstraction licences do also have private property abstraction rights. This is because in 1963 all pre-existing water abstractors (who necessarily had either proprietary abstraction rights, or liberties as landowners to abstract groundwater under their land) were granted a licence to continue to do so as of right. And the current monopolistic private water supply companies are the successors of (and acquired the property, rights and powers of) the nationalised water companies which were formed in 1974, which were in turn the successors of, and acquired the property, rights and powers of, their myriad private and municipal water supply company predecessors.[70] So, in England we have a system in which historic proprietary use rights and liberties in water are entwined with regulation, and path dependence may make it unfeasible for us to change now to a regulatory no-property world for water governance.

Increasing role of new private property rights

The second feature is that, since privatisation in 1989, the significance of private property rights in water administration in England has been increasing, not diminishing. Current government policy is to attract private investment in the water industry and to privatise the allocation of water resources, in the belief that markets (necessarily dependent on alienable private property rights) are better at allocating water resources than the state can ever be. Privatisation has involved water governance functions, and ownership and control of the relevant water resources, being transferred from the public to the private for-profit sector, and, most recently, to the 'third sector' of private charitable bodies. So, water-related assets are increasingly privately owned. Most recently, in the for-profit private sector, water supply companies in England are, under pressure from the government, in the process of propertising and commodifying two of the water-related assets they hold: appropriated or 'bulk' water and water abstraction licences.[71] Whether these current government proposals are achievable is contestable. However, the point for present purposes is that the driving force behind both is marketisation, which necessitates an increased role for private property held for profit-generating purposes. So, we are not in a world where the role of property rights in water is diminishing. Rather,

[70] K. Bakker, *An Uncooperative Commodity: Privatising Water in England and Wales* (Oxford, Oxford University Press, 2003), pp. 45–73.

[71] Ofwat and Deloitte, *Water Trading – Scope, Benefits and Options*, Final Report, December 2015; Environment Agency, *Managing Water Abstraction*, October 2016.

it is expanding, but towards a greater role for the kind of private property interests that are commodifiable and obstruct water's functionality as a common treasury.

Integral role of communal property

The third feature of our system that rules out a no-property world for water is that, because of the physical and normative nature of water as a common treasury, water use and water administration are heavily dependent on the communal, the consensual and the cooperative. By necessity we all share water, and shared resource use continues to demand routine negotiation within and between ad hoc and formalised communities of various kinds holding communal property interests in water. In practice these communal property regimes are an integral part of our water management and regulation systems and, since they are inherently self-generating, they tend to develop in the interstices of regulatory frameworks: there is ample evidence that water-sharing communities will evolve their own rules to complement or fill any gaps left by top-down regulatory rules. For this reason alone a regulatory no-property world for water is probably not feasible, even if anyone thought it desirable.

The absolute ownership model

We have already noted that historically absolute ownership has been almost irrelevant to water in English law but it is now assuming greater importance because of marketisation of bulk water and water abstraction licences. For this reason it is worth saying more about why the kind of absolute exclusionary private ownership that Winstanley abhorred is inappropriate for interests in water if water is to function as a common treasury, and why the same applies to absolute ownership by the state.

Absolute state ownership

If a state is absolute owner of a resource, the government is free to choose from time to time how to use it, provided it keeps within the parameters set by its duty to act in the interests of the state and in accordance with principles of good governance. So, for example, it could be legitimate for the government to use the resource as a commodity in some circumstances so as to raise revenue for some unconnected purpose it considered more important, even if that meant disadvantaging those dependent on the commodified resource. This kind of freedom of use is not appropriate for a common treasury resource such as water. Water must be managed so as to fulfil the needs that people and the environment have for it. This involves a difficult and complex balancing of conflicting common treasury claims (what to do when, for example, there is insufficient water for both humans and animals in a severe drought, or environmental and human needs clash). However, it should never allow the subordination of common treasury claims to other claims, however worthy in their own right. This of itself rules out absolute ownership of water by the state.

As already noted, the freedom to commodify also rules out absolute private ownership of water and of water-related rights such as abstraction rights, but there are additional reasons why absolute private ownership is inappropriate for a common treasury, some relating to water's physical characteristics and others to its social and environmental functions.

Freedom of use

In the classic common law model posited by Honoré,[72] the incidents of full private ownership include the right to use and manage as well as transmissibility and absence of term.[73] None of these can appropriately be given to private individuals if water is to function as a common treasury.

Water cannot function as a common treasury if it is controlled by private individuals who are free to use it for any purpose they want, or for no purpose at all. Water rights holders of all descriptions, even private and state owners, must inevitably, because of the physical nature and social and environmental importance of water, hold their rights subject to multiple restrictions and regulations. Some will be enforceable by others who share use of the same resource or are affected by its use – a significant source of restriction and regulation because of the externalities of interactions with water already noted.[74] Other restrictions and regulations will be enforceable by the state and other public bodies who are in turn obliged to keep tight control over use and management of water because of its strategic importance and obligations owed to transnational and international bodies. The combined effect of all these restrictions and regulations is that private water rights holders can only have strictly limited specific rights, exercisable only for strictly limited purposes, and in many cases they will have to be put under a positive duty to carry out those purposes. They cannot even come close to enjoying the freedom to use and manage envisaged by Honoré.

Perpetual duration, transmissibility and commodification

Perpetual duration (what Honoré calls absence of term) and transmissibility are equally problematic. In this jurisdiction perpetual use rights in water historically have been the norm, but they are increasingly undesirable in modern states facing mounting pressure on water resources and unpredictable dramatic climate

[72] A. Honoré, 'Ownership', in A. Guest (ed.), *Oxford Essays in Jurisprudence* (Oxford, Clarendon Press, 1961), pp. 107–147.
[73] Honoré, 'Ownership', pp. 116–122.
[74] See 'The unique physical qualities of water' in Part II above.

fluctuations. These circumstances put states under intense political pressure to maintain tight control over water allocation at all times. Even states, such as ours, which have enthusiastically embraced privatisation of water abstraction and water supply services, recognise that effective state control demands control over the duration of private water rights and over the extent of the rights they confer. The state and relevant public agencies have to have the discretion to review, re-allocate, curtail, or limit the exercise of private property rights in water both routinely and in an emergency, and, where necessary, they have to be able to do so without incurring vast costs in litigation and compensation payments. On this basis, private property rights in water of perpetual length are arguably unsustainable, whether the rights are to abstract water, hold it or supply it.

As far as transmissibility is concerned, the essence of a transmissible property interest is that it can be passed freely from one person to another, by voluntary transfer or on death, bankruptcy or enforcement of security, without changing form, regardless of the identity of the recipient. This has never been thought appropriate for common law proprietary use rights in water such as rights to abstract it or use it to generate power, at least as far as surface water is concerned. These rights have never been commodifiable because they were (and are still) not freely alienable: they are either appurtenant to the ownership of land contiguous with, containing or benefited by the relevant water source[75] or vested in statutory corporations licensed (and required) to carry out water functions such as public supply. But even apart from the question of commodification, transmissibility is not appropriate for property rights in water. It has to be a prerequisite for property rights holders that they can demonstrate that they will exercise their rights for mandated purposes and that they will do so competently and efficiently. The problem with water markets is that there are formidable (perhaps insuperable) difficulties in making them operate so as to vest the traded water rights in the person best able to ensure that the optimal efficient use is made of the water traded, never mind the optimal common treasury use of it. As Freyfogle points out, water markets ignore externalities such as the actual impact of transferring water flows from areas where water is embedded in communities to other areas where the environment has been moulded by a specific level of water scarcity.[76] Water trading is blind to impacts of changes in water flows, just as it is to common treasury imperatives such as the need to implement the human right to water.

Perpetual duration and transmissibility are inappropriate for property rights in a common treasury for another reason. The stable, easily realisable capital value they give to the relevant property right not only enables marketisation. It also entitles the rights holder to protection from requisition by the state except in the public interest and on payment of full compensation. This is a serious inroad into

[75] Howarth, 'History of Water Law', pp. 76–77.

[76] E. T. Freyfogle, 'Water Rights and the Common Wealth', *Environmental Law*, 26 (1996), 27–51 at 32.

the freedom of the state to reallocate water whenever necessary to ensure that it best fulfils its common treasury role.

Incompatibility with human rights

Finally, there is the problem of incompatibility between absolute private property and the human right to property we noted in Part II, where we pointed out the inherent incongruity of commodification of a resource and fulfilment of a human right to it. The aim of the human right to water is to give all people the right *to* water. This distinguishes the right from many other human rights such as the right to the enjoyment of property, which aims to protect what a person already has. The right *to* water gives a right to all people to have something which they may not already have. But if the water needed to satisfy their needs is subject to private property claims of others, there is obvious potential for a clash.[77] The human right to water is compatible with the notion of a common treasury, which reflects the needs of human beings for drinking water and effectively subsumes the human right, but if the human right is to mean anything at all it cannot be required to compete with the rights of private owners to exclude others from resources they control for their own benefit.

Alternative conceptions of private property and state ownership

We argue above that the determination of water as a common treasury dictates that water is a right and responsibility of us all, giving us all a right to use it in common with all others and putting us all under a duty to ensure that it is used for the common good and the preservation of the environment – both anthropocentric and ecocentric aims. As we see in the following paragraphs, others have argued that more or less the same objectives can be achieved by utilising a modified version of either private property or state ownership. One set of the arguments we outline below involves grafting notions such as public trust and stewardship on to private property or state ownership. Another involves conferring rights to manage water resources on third sector private charitable bodies, limited by their constitutions to exercising their rights and purposes for mandated public purposes. Yet another involves conferring the equivalent of private property rights on the environment itself (or on certain aspects of it), giving the environment standing in the resolution of conflicts between competing private claims on water.

[77] A. Clarke, 'Property, Human Rights and Communities', in T. Xu and J. Allain (eds), *Property and Human Rights in a Global Context* (Oxford, Hart Publishing, 2012), pp. 19–39 at pp. 25–27.

Public trust and stewardship

Public trust and stewardship are presented as resource-holding institutions which are parasitic on notions of private and state ownership – that is, they accept the neoliberal premise that natural resources (or at least rights to make use of them) must inevitably be 'owned' by private individuals or by the state, but they argue that the notion of 'ownership' must be tweaked so as to require the owners to use water or exercise the relevant water right not for their own benefit, but for the common and environmental good.

There is a fundamental theoretical incompatibility, which we do not explore here, between this acceptance of the primacy of private or state ownership, even in these modified forms, and Winstanley's conception of water as given in common to humankind, and indeed our own conception of water as a common treasury to meet social and environmental needs. Here we concentrate instead on the practical shortcomings of these institutions grafted on to private/state ownership.

The public trust doctrine is said to be Anglo-American in origin, but although it is widely accepted in the USA and elsewhere,[78] it has never developed in this jurisdiction. It requires the state to hold natural resources on trust for the public, but the problem is that the precise scope of the obligations this imposes is unclear. Some states have articulated the content and scope of the public trust explicitly and comprehensively, and in terms which come close to requiring the state to treat water as a common treasury.[79] In others the state's obligations are left open, or narrowly focused on, for example, local community interests.[80] In England, however, water has never been regarded as within the ownership of the state, and in any event at present there seems very little likelihood that a general doctrine of public trust would ever be introduced, either by legislation or by judicial activism.[81]

Stewardship is a more diffuse doctrine. It has been advocated as a means by which all private owners can be required to take into account the interests of the environment, and/or of local stakeholders, either generally or in specific ways, and either instead of acting for their own benefit, or in priority to their own interests, or just as factors to be taken into account.[82] Various legal provisions in this

[78] C. F. Wilkinson 'The Headwaters of the Public Trust: Some Thoughts on the Source and Scope of the Traditional Doctrine', *Environment Law*, 19 (1988–1989), 425–472; J. L. Sax, 'The Public Trust Doctrine in Natural Resource Law: Effective Judicial Intervention', *Michigan Law Review*, 68 (1970), 471–566; M. C. Wood, *Nature's Trust: Environmental Law for a New Ecological Age* (New York, Cambridge University Press, 2014).

[79] See for example South Africa's National Water Act 1998, preamble and section 3.

[80] Craig demonstrates the range in 'A Comparative Guide to the Western States' Public Trust Doctrines' and 'A Comparative Guide to the Eastern States' Public Trust Doctrines'.

[81] See contra B. Freeman and E. Shirley, 'England and the Public Trust Doctrine', *Journal of Planning and Environment Law*, 8 (2014), 839–848.

[82] W. Lucy and C. Mitchell, 'Replacing Private Property: The Case for Stewardship', *Cambridge Law*

jurisdiction do have the effect of imposing elements of stewardship on some holders of property interests in water in some circumstances.[83] However, the obligations imposed tend to be fairly narrow and specific, and we are a long way from recognising a comprehensive stewardship that would require all holders of private property rights in water to take into account social needs and environmental concerns, let alone to give common treasury requirements priority over their own interests. Indeed, one of the greatest obstacles to the development of a concept of stewardship in this jurisdiction is the decision in *Bradford v Pickles* which we considered earlier.[84] In *Bradford v Pickles* the House of Lords decided that if (as the court found) it was lawful for Pickles to carry out the works and drain the water from his land, then it could not be made unlawful by his motive in doing so. Pickles' ostensible purpose in carrying out the works was to quarry for flagstones which he claimed were under his land but swamped by the water feeding the spring, but the water company insisted that his sole objective was to force the water company to buy his land or pay him not to carry out the works. It seems likely that the water company was right,[85] but the House of Lords took the view that it was simply irrelevant, thus halting the development in this country of the abuse of rights doctrine which has emerged in so many other jurisdictions.[86] This rejection by the House of Lords of an abuse of rights limitation gives private property rights and liberties in water an absolute quality in this jurisdiction which is wholly at odds with the notion that holders of those rights and liberties might be constrained by stewardship.

Third sector ownership

Private ownership can also be modified so as to require water to be used for public benefit in various forms by creating a special-purpose private charitable company to take over the management and control of a water resource, binding it by its constitution to use the resource for a specified public purpose. Public water bodies have been privatised in this way using the powers conferred by the Public Bodies Act 2011, and in 2012 these powers were used to transfer the property and functions of the British Waterways Board (responsible for the running of most canals

Journal, 55 (1996), 566–600; B. Lange and M. Shepheard, 'Changing Conceptions of Rights to Water? An Eco-Socio-Legal Perspective', *Journal of Environmental Law*, 26 (2014), 215–242 at 217–218.

[83] Lange and Shepheard, 'Changing Conceptions of Rights to Water?', 217–218; D. McGillivray, 'Water Rights and Environmental Damage: An Enquiry into Stewardship in the Context of Abstraction Licensing Reform', *Environmental Law Review*, 15 (2013), 205–224.

[84] *Bradford v Pickles*, [1895] AC 587. See 'The no-property option' in Part II above.

[85] The House of Lords clearly thought so, and it is amply confirmed by the narrative in M. Taggart, *Private Property and Abuse of Rights in Victorian England: The Story of Edward Pickles and the Bradford Water Supply* (Oxford, Oxford University Press, 2002).

[86] See further E. Reid, 'The Doctrine of Abuse of Rights: Perspective from a Mixed Jurisdiction', *Electronic Journal of Comparative Law*, 8 (2004): www.ejcl.org/83/art83-2.html.

and some rivers) to the newly formed Canal & River Trust, a private charitable company limited by guarantee.[87] The objective of this kind of privatisation seems to be to attract private investment to supplement public funding, usually in the form of grants and donations from charitable institutions and individual sympathisers and enthusiasts, and also to increase participation by stakeholders and the public. The Canal & River Trust, like the other third sector successors of the public bodies eligible for privatisation under the 2011 Act, has a narrow primary focus to which it is required to give priority, although it must also take into account specific related social and environmental concerns.[88] So, these third sector bodies do not have full common treasury objectives and in any event their primary focus must take precedence. Even if this were not the case, it is questionable whether directors of private charities are best placed (or best qualified) to balance competing common treasury objectives, especially if driven by fundraising imperatives.

Environmental rights

An alternative approach is environmental rights, which also accepts the private property model but aims to give the environment a voice in conflicts with and between competing private interests. They are a tool to allow environmental concerns to compete on equal terms with private interests: they do not ensure that social and environmental needs will take absolute priority over private interests, as required by the common treasury model. The argument for a right for nature from an ecocentric perspective is a developing argument adopting a different approach also on a rights basis.[89] But again, neither of these approaches challenges the neoliberal approach to private property: they merely seek to overlay private property rights with other rights. Inevitably, the contest between such rights (property versus nature) means that battle lines are drawn and there will be winners and losers – or weak compromises.[90] Likewise, the argument that water should be treated as a common concern of humankind in international terms is another example of the approach which accepts the traditional private property model but seeks to add limitations – a moral boundary to a legal right.[91]

[87] The British Waterways Board (Transfer of Functions) Order 2012/1659.
[88] Canal & River Trust, *Governance Handbook*, November 2016: https://canalrivertrust.org.uk/media/original/26919-governance-handbook.pdf.
[89] S. Borras, 'New Transitions from Human Rights to the Environment to the Rights of Nature', *Transnational Environmental Law*, 5 (2016), 113–143.
[90] C. T. Reid, 'Pitfalls in Promoting Environmental Rights', in S. Bogojevic and R. Rayfuse (eds), *Environmental Rights in Europe and Beyond* (Oxford, Hart Publishing, forthcoming).
[91] E. Brown Weiss, 'The Coming Water Crisis: A Common Concern of Humankind', *Transnational Environmental Law*, 1 (2012), 153–168.

Communal property

However the crucial point about these alternative private/state property conceptions is that they are top-down. They envisage a paternalistic benevolent dictator who can be directed by legislation to formulate and implement policies to ensure that water fulfils its common treasury role, and to create and monitor appropriate institutions.[92] They ignore the empirical evidence demonstrating that water governance, if it is to work at all, needs to build on the self-generated cooperation and collaboration in water management that exists in any system,[93] represented on the property spectrum by communal property institutions in various forms. These different types of communal property institution demonstrate the actuality, and the potentiality, of communal property institutions to manage and regulate water as a common treasury. Because of the physical nature of water, those who share its use and the effects of its use have every incentive to collaborate for their mutual benefit, so it is not surprising that, in England as elsewhere, they form communities, sometimes of users, sometimes of stakeholders with diverse interests in the same water resource. So, we find farmers abstracting water from source who form water abstractor groups to manage their abstraction rights collectively, and negotiate with outsiders;[94] irrigation communities who build and manage communal reservoirs and other irrigation systems for their collective benefit;[95] surface and groundwater users who form or participate in bottom-up associations to preserve the quality of their water resources;[96] local riparian owners who generate and enforce their own rules regulating the use of their stretch of river by each other and by outsiders; and communities of stakeholders, usually individuals or organisations with diverse

[92] For difficulties in implementing top-down trust/stewardship water policies even when common-treasury-type objectives are clearly defined, see H. Mostert and C. Young, 'Natural Resources as "Regulated Property": The Challenges of Resource Stewardship in South Africa', in Godt, *Regulatory Property Rights*, pp. 141–168.

[93] A. Agrawal and C. C. Gibson, 'Enchantment and Disenchantment: The Role of Community in Natural Resource Conservation', *World Development*, 27 (1999), 629–649.

[94] B. Leathes et al., 'The Emergence and Evolution of Water Abstractors Groups in Eastern England', *UK Irrigation*, 35 (2007), 7–10.

[95] Ö. K. Uysal and E. Atis, 'Assessing the Performance of Participatory Irrigation Management over Time: A Case Study from Turkey', *Agricultural Water Management*, 97 (2010), 1017–1025; Environment Agency and Cranfield University, 'Thinking about an Irrigation Reservoir?', p 13: www.ukia.org/pdfs/Reservoirs.pdf.

[96] L. Whaley and E. K. Weatherhead, 'Power-Sharing in the English Lowlands? The Political Economy of Farmer Participation and Cooperation in Water Governance', *Water Alternatives*, 8(1) (2014), 820–843; E. Schlager, 'Community Management of Groundwater', in M. Giordano and K. J. Villholth (eds), *The Agricultural Groundwater Revolution: Opportunities and Threats to Development* (Oxfordshire, CAB International, 2007), pp. 131–152; P. Figueiredo and P. E. Perkins, 'Women and Water Management in Times of Climate Change: Participatory and Inclusive Processes', *Journal of Cleaner Production*, 60 (2013), 188–194.

interests in a water resource such as a river basin or catchment area, who form their own boards to coordinate and implement policy.[97]

All these water communities are primarily self-interested, in that their immediate objectives are to manage their water resource in their own best interests, which do not necessarily coincide with common treasury objectives. Nevertheless, there are good reasons for thinking that the broader common treasury objectives of water governance are at least as likely to be achieved by communal property regimes as by other property rights regimes. In general, they are not geared towards making profits out of their water resource to use for non-water-related purposes, nor to fundraising. Instead, their commitment is to long-term sustainability of their resource, and it is arguable that their local knowledge and expertise make them best qualified to decide what action is most likely to achieve the environmental sustainability of their part of the ecosystem. Connected with this is the fact that communities are by their nature intergenerational, in that there is a constant process of retiring and exiting members being replaced by successors to their interests. They are therefore well placed to take into account the interests of future as well as present generations. We also have considerable empirical evidence that self-generating and self-regulating communities of the kind we describe thrive best when they do not operate in isolation, but are nested within what Elinor Ostrom describes as polycentric governance institutions which take into account wider strategic objectives.[98] These can be, and to some extent already are, provided by our complex regulatory frameworks. It is no part of our argument that communal property institutions make national and international water regulation unnecessary: our argument is rather that they are more likely than other property rights holdings to make regulatory systems work effectively.

Part IV: Conclusion

We have argued that the normative approach to water should be as a common treasury because of its special and unique status as one of the earth's resources. And, what works best to realise its use and management as a common treasury is not the paternalistic, benevolent-dictatorship private property models provided

[97] K. Grecksch, 'Adaptive Capacity and Regional Water Governance in North-Western Germany', *Water Policy*, 15 (2013), 794–815; R. C. de Loë, D. Murray and H. C. Simpson, 'Farmer Perspectives on Collaborative Approaches to Governance for Water', *Journal of Rural Studies*, 42 (2015), 191–205; V. I. Grover and G. Krantzberg (eds), *Water Co-Management* (Boca Raton, FL, CRC Press, 2013).

[98] E. Ostrom, 'Beyond Markets and States: Polycentric Governance of Complex Economic Systems', *American Economic Review*, 100 (2010), 641–672; D. Huitema et al., 'Adaptive Water Governance: Assessing the Institutional Prescriptions of Adaptive (Co-)Management from a Governance Perspective and Defining a Research Agenda', *Ecology and Society*, 14 (2009), 26: www.ecologyandsociety.org/vol14/iss1/art26/.

by public trusts, stewardship or the third sector, still less the market mechanism model facilitated by untrammelled private property. Rather, it is the collaborative, cooperative and communal resource management/governance models which can be provided by communal property operating within regulatory frameworks.

Index